# OneStream Security Essentials

Teresa Catron Kress

OneStream Press

**Disclaimer**

# About the Author

I have spent over 29 years in a variety of roles in corporate accounting, financial analysis, system administration and consulting. My career has been split equally between financial system administration at companies and consulting for companies. And so, I write this book with both audiences in mind, as both are equally important. The consultant lays the framework of security that the OneStream administrator will maintain. Both audiences need to have an in-depth understanding of OneStream security to make the best decisions for their company or project.

Some days I feel like that person walking into a glass castle in Pittsburgh, in a freshly pressed suit and pantyhose (yes, pantyhose), ready to start my first post-college job. And other days I feel like the seasoned veteran that nearly 30 years working can give you. Today I have traded in pantyhose and a glass castle for yoga pants and a home office. But I am still that same person, still passionate about learning and sharing as much as I can with others.

I want to thank my life mentors along the way, from my first boss out of college who taught me everything I needed to hit the ground running, to the CFO who trusted me to lead a financial systems team, to my girlfriends (old and new) with whom I share my work tribulations and triumphs, and my husband who always encourages me to reach higher. And most importantly, my parents. They have always championed and believed in me, taught me humility, encouraged me to get an education, showed me that hard work does pay off, and unconditionally loved me. Look mom and dad, I am an author! Could you have ever imagined? I am sure you did.

# Technical Reviewers

**Chul Smith.** Chul has over 25 years of accounting, finance and IT experience using, maintaining, implementing and supporting consolidation and finance systems as both client and consultant. In 2006, he moved from corporate consolidations in Minneapolis, MN, to HFM consulting in Paris, France. In 2007, he relocated to London, England where he spent the next four years consulting with a small Swedish IBM Cognos Controller consultancy. The use of Controller across Europe expanded his work experience to nine countries in multiple industries.

His 2012 United States homecoming triggered his return to HFM & FDM as a freelance consultant with projects in New York City, Montreal, and Sherbrooke, Quebec. He began working with OneStream in 2013 and a year later, was hired to join their services team. Today, he's a Distinguished Architect within OneStream's Strategic Customer Advisory team.

Chul holds a Bachelor of Science in Accounting from the University of Minnesota – Carlson School of Management and a non-practicing CPA license in the state of Minnesota.

**Tony Dimitrie.** Tony joined OneStream Software in January 2012 as employee #10. Tony dedicated his first year to OneStream's first customer and did whatever was needed in order to make the partnership a success. This soon transitioned into being a Subject Matter Expert for customer implementations led by partners. Tony started the Implementation Support department, which can be identified as Remote Consulting Support (RCS) today. Tony has a wealth of OneStream product and organizational knowledge, which helps serve Tony in his current role as Vice President of Training & RCS.

# Errata

Despite best efforts, mistakes can sometimes creep into books. If you spot a mistake, please feel free to email us at **errata@OneStreamPress.com** (with the book title in the subject line).

The errata page for this book is hosted at **www.OneStreamPress.com/Security**

# Version Updates

The OneStream platform is constantly evolving, with each release bringing new features and capabilities. The majority of the material in this book covers the OneStream Platform Version of at least 8.4.

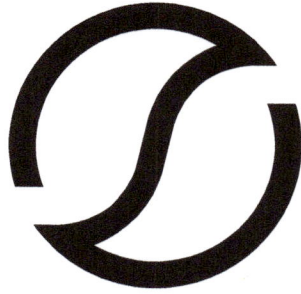

# 25% OFF VOUCHER

# Certification

Validate your technical competence and gain industry recognition with OneStream Software.

In purchasing this book, you are eligible to claim a 25% discount on any OneStream Certification Exam.

To request your voucher, open a case with Credentialing via the ServiceNow Support Portal (https://onestreamsoftware.service-now.com/).
Include proof of purchase that contains your name and address, the book title, date of purchase, and proof of payment.

Terms & Conditions:
One (1) certification exam voucher per book. All vouchers per receipt must be claimed at one time; if a receipt is for the purchase of 10 books, all 10 vouchers must be claimed at the same time. Vouchers are valid for post-beta production exams only. This offer is only valid for one year from the purchase date on the invoice or receipt.

onestream

# Contents

# 1
# Introduction

Someone once said to me, "Teresa, you are passionate about OneStream security." I had to think about that for a moment. I mean, I am passionate about a lot of things – travel, speaking foreign languages, certain sports and sporting teams, family, and being the best aunt I can be – but OneStream security? The thought had not crossed my mind, but *that moment* became the inspiration for this book.

I am passionate about sharing what I understand to help others in their learning journey, whether it be as a consultant on their first or tenth OneStream project, a new system administrator, or a seasoned finance professional. I enjoy sharing my knowledge and the best practices learned in my career, and hopefully picking up new knowledge myself along the way. Any wisdom I can impart to make someone else's work life easier, or a company's OneStream system more secure, I am happy to do so. So, yes, by that definition, I am passionate about OneStream security!

## Overview

Like death and taxes, system security is unavoidable. No matter how simple (or complex) an organization may be or how few (or many) users a company has, granting everyone or nobody access, while possible, is not practical. So, where does that leave you?

How you design, implement, and maintain your OneStream security is a balancing act between data governance and ease of use, between adequately controlling and easily maintaining. OneStream does not dictate how simple or complex your security model will be. You, as an administrator or consultant, will have to determine the best overall approach to meet your company's needs. This book will give you not only an in-depth understanding of how security works, but will also cover common approaches, best practices, and everything you want to know as you tackle the design, implementation, and maintenance of your OneStream security.

Metaphor time. Think of system security in the same way as securing a new house. In the beginning (the design phase), when you are just starting construction, there is not much to secure, and the building site is open. As construction on your home progresses (the build phase), you may add fencing and put in a temporary lock to secure building materials. Finally, when the construction is complete and you are ready to move in (go-live), you will have to decide how you want to secure your new home from that point forward (maintain).

Sure, you could leave all your doors and windows unlocked (i.e., 'Everyone' has access), but that is not realistic. You could lock everything down (i.e., 'Nobody' has access), but that is also not an option. Therefore, you will likely choose some intermediate level of security by using deadbolts, fencing, cameras, motion detectors, and other alarm systems. How much effort and cost you put into securing your home will depend on how many members are in your family, the ages of family members, if you have a lot of valuables, how large your house is, and your tolerance for feeling safe.

OneStream security is similar. Early in a project life cycle, there is no need to secure many items. But as a project progresses, you have to start considering *what* and *how* you want to secure, and what layers or checkpoints you want to add to your security framework. You will have to consider things like your user base, your CFO, your IT department, and your auditors, as well as what data is stored in OneStream, any audit or governance requirements, and your company's risk tolerance versus its need for control. All these things will need to be taken into consideration as you walk the line between data governance, ease of use, control, and maintenance.

Keep in mind that while you may have an initial security strategy, it can change over time, even after go-live. Just like with home security, you may not install cameras at first, but then – after living in your home for a couple of years – decide to install those security cameras after all.

OneStream security is similarly flexible in that, while you want to have an upfront methodology and approach, it can change over time to meet your changing business or company needs.

As we progress through this book, we will talk about the different layers to OneStream security...

- Framework and Environment
- Users and Groups
- Application Objects
- System Objects
- Metadata
- Workflows

... and how these layers work together to form your overall security model and user experience within OneStream. OneStream allows for flexibility in how every company secures its data, allowing companies to tailor each of the layers to meet their company needs.

So that brings us to the three native security groups that exist in every customer environment: **Everyone, Nobody,** and **Administrators.** Additionally, there is one native user that exists in every customer environment, the **Administrator.**

These three groups and one user are set up from day one in any OneStream environment, and exist across every company using OneStream. As we will learn later, they serve different purposes within your application and environment, and can be leveraged in different ways to achieve your security model.

Where you go from these three groups and one user will depend on your company's needs. You, along with your implementation team, will decide a methodology or framework for how you want your security to work and be maintained.

Security is used within OneStream not only to control access to data and sensitive information, but also to drive the end-user experience. You can use your OneStream security to limit what people can and cannot see, not only to secure access within an application, but also to create a simplified user experience (e.g., why does someone in Europe need to see something related to a workflow process in Mexico?).

As you read this book, keep these data security and user experience goals in mind. And, as mentioned before, also keep in mind the balance between data governance, ease of use, control, and maintenance as they will all play a role in how you shape your security.

# 2
# Framework

## Environment

The first layer in your security model is the ability to access a OneStream environment, and a company may have one or multiple environments to meet its business needs. OneStream security is *organized* by environment.

If you have one environment for OneStream (e.g., PRD1), then you have one security **Framework** that supports all application(s) that exist in *that* environment. If you have multiple environments (e.g., PRD1 & DEV1), your OneStream security is specific to *each* environment as shown in Figure 2.1 below:

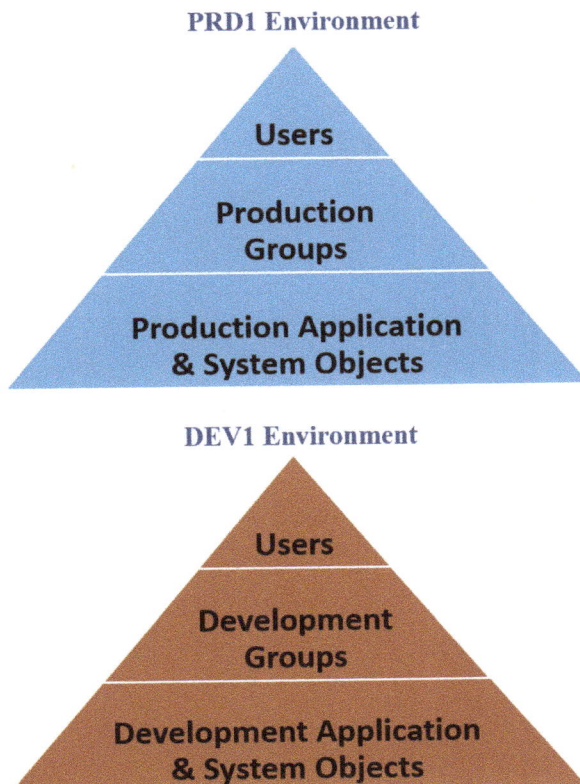

**PRD1 Environment**

Users

Production Groups

Production Application & System Objects

**DEV1 Environment**

Users

Development Groups

Development Application & System Objects

Figure 2.1

Within each environment, there is a SQL database referred to as the **Framework Database**, which is where OneStream's security resides to support all application(s) within that environment. In Chapters 5 and 6, we will go into more detail about the tables that exist within the framework database to support a customer's system and application security.

Using the house analogy, think of an environment like a gated community. Within a gated community (e.g., PRD1), there can be multiple houses (e.g., application(s)). The first layer of defense to your home (e.g., application) is, therefore, the entrance gate to the community (e.g., PRD1 versus DEV1). Someone may have an access card to get into the community, but they may only have an entrance key to a specific house(s) within that community. Your framework security is the same. It is the first layer to your overall OneStream security and determines who can get in through the first gate.

A system administrator can see this by logging into the OneStream environment and going to the System tab. They will notice that it remains the same no matter which application they are logged into within that environment. The security framework is specific to all application(s) within *that* environment.

If the system administrator logs into a different environment, the security framework and thus its System tab are separate for that environment, and all application(s) that exist in that additional environment. It is important to note that you can migrate security from one environment to another, which will be covered in Chapter 8.

# Types of Authentication

OneStream provides several flexible security authentication methods to meet customers' needs, including, but not limited to, MSAD, LDAP, Azure AD, Okta, SAML 2.0, PingFederate, and Native authentication. OneStream supports Native authentication, authentication with one external identity provider, or both Native and external provider authentication methods.

What method is chosen is not dictated by OneStream but is dependent upon a company's preference. This is normally addressed at the time of the initial environment setup, but can also be adjusted later.

This book is not intended to be a reference guide for the authentication process, but is merely to make you aware of the different options available, as this is the first layer of security. You will need to work with OneStream's Cloud Team and reference the **Installation and Configuration Guide** for more information on how to set up authentication methods.

## SSO

OneStream supports external single sign-on (SSO) user authentication. SSO can be via an external authentication process – where user names and passwords are not stored within OneStream – or where a native user name and password are stored within OneStream.

If an external SSO is used, the user experience at initial logon to OneStream will be dependent upon the company's chosen authentication provider. For example, a company may require multi-factor authentication, prompting a user to provide a unique code or approve authentication on their mobile device before being allowed to pass into OneStream's environment.

## Native

If a company chooses to allow the Native authentication logon method to OneStream, a user name and password will be stored within OneStream's framework database. There is a toggle setting of True/False in the Application Server Configuration Settings that controls whether a company permits native authentication to OneStream. These configuration settings can only be accessed by OneStream Support for cloud customers and are typically determined at the time of the initial environment setup, but can be later changed. If a company has selected True to Enable Native Authentication, then native users can be set up and work within their OneStream environment.

Using a Native authentication method means that all OneStream user names and passwords are maintained *inside* your OneStream framework database. This means that SSO, in accordance with your company's authentication methods, is not being used, and instead, you rely upon user setup and password maintenance within your OneStream framework database.

There are a handful of properties, as shown in Figure 2.2, that can be set by OneStream Support to control the password security of your native users. You will want to work with OneStream Support if any of these requirements need to be changed to satisfy your auditor's or company's IT policies.

| Native Authentication | □ × |
|---|---|
| ⊟ General | |
| Enable Native Authentication | True ▼ |
| OK to Use Same Password after Reset | False |
| Password Expiration (days) | 0 |
| Password Minimum Length | 10 |
| Password Maximum Length | 100 |
| Password Requires Letters | True |
| Password Requires Numbers | True |
| Password Requires Mixed Case | True |
| Maximum Invalid Logon Attempts | 5 |

Figure 2.2

## OIS

**OneStream Identity Server** (OIS) is an SSO service available for customers hosted in the OneStream Azure Cloud environment. The OneStream Cloud Team will manage the initial configuration to use OIS at the time a customer's environment is set up; for existing customers, the Cloud Team can assist with the conversion to OIS.

OIS can support many different forms of external identity providers (including native, OIDC, or SAML 2.0), depending on the customer's preference. If OIS with SSO is selected, external provider user accounts are passed through to OneStream for authentication and access. The benefits of using OIS include flexible authentication to multiple identity providers, the management of identity providers and personal access tokens by the customer, the ability for native users to reset their own passwords, and a streamlined login process. OIS governs logon for the Windows app, Browser UX, Excel Add-In, and API access. For more information on OIS, refer to OneStream's **Identity and Access Management Guide**.

# Application Server Configuration

There are specific Application Server Configuration Settings that control what users can and cannot do within their OneStream environment. We have already mentioned one of these options, which is the True/False toggle switch to allow Native Authentication, but there are many other options that are set at the environment level and control what is allowed within OneStream.

In this book, I will touch upon those (Figure 2.3) that are relevant to security, meaning those settings that will or will not allow an administrator to take certain actions within a OneStream environment. The settings described in detail to follow are typically limited to a company's OneStream administrator and are not often changed once the initial environment setup is complete. But we will still cover them, so a system administrator can understand their implications on OneStream security.

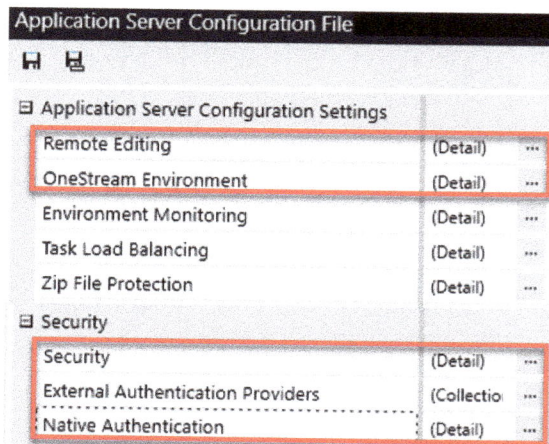

Figure 2.3

# Remote Editing

Within the Remote Editing section, shown in Figure 2.4, you can find True/False toggle switches for the following:

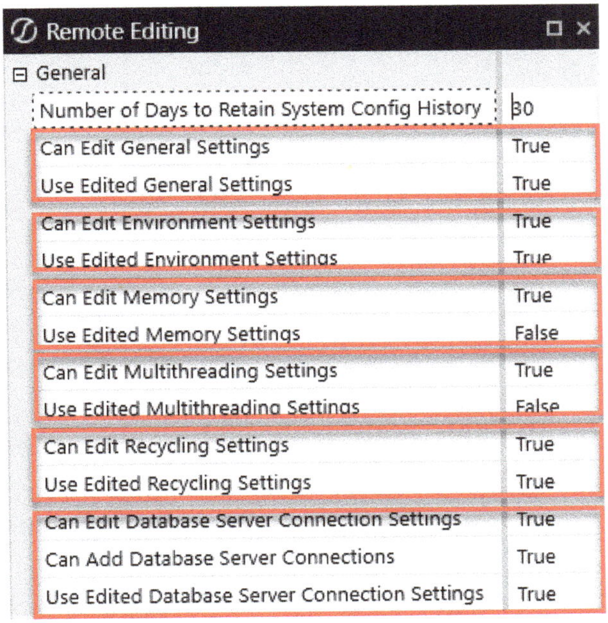

| Remote Editing | |
|---|---|
| □ General | |
| Number of Days to Retain System Config History | 30 |
| Can Edit General Settings | True |
| Use Edited General Settings | True |
| Can Edit Environment Settings | True |
| Use Edited Environment Settings | True |
| Can Edit Memory Settings | True |
| Use Edited Memory Settings | False |
| Can Edit Multithreading Settings | True |
| Use Edited Multithreading Settings | False |
| Can Edit Recycling Settings | True |
| Use Edited Recycling Settings | True |
| Can Edit Database Server Connection Settings | True |
| Can Add Database Server Connections | True |
| Use Edited Database Server Connection Settings | True |

Figure 2.4

These settings will determine whether an administrator can perform these actions from *within* your OneStream application. If any of these are set to False, the customer will need to reach out to OneStream Support to make a change.

If any of these are set to True, those options will be editable by a customer's OneStream administrator from within the System tab of their OneStream environment. A new page is exposed on the System > System Configuration tab, which will show additional pages for any options set to True:

Chapter 2

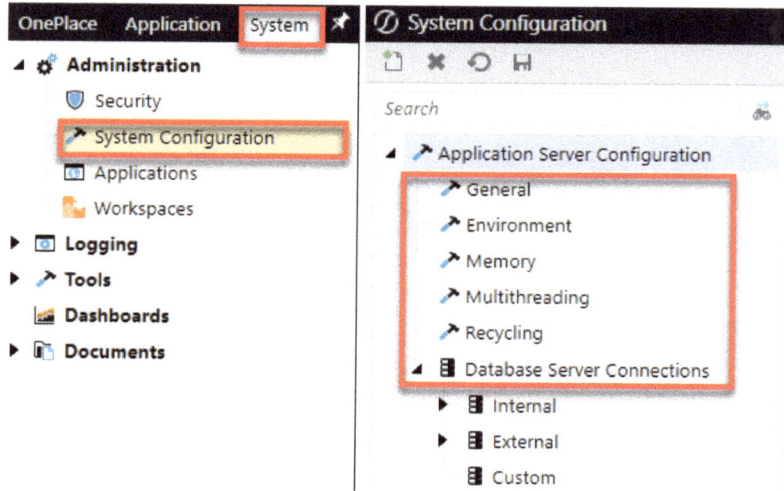

Figure 2.5

## General

When True is enabled in Figure 2.4 for General Settings and a security group has been assigned on the Security > System Security Roles page for the Manage System Configuration, the following page is exposed within your OneStream environment:

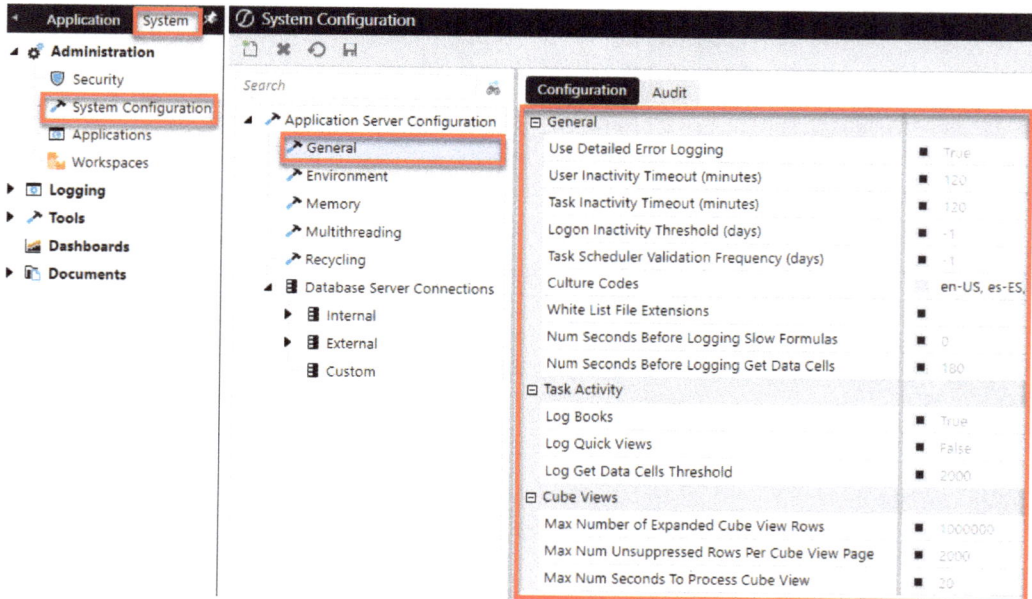

Figure 2.6

An administrator can choose to edit the settings above (by unchecking the box in front of the setting and making changes), some of which directly impact the environment's security.

For example, User Inactivity Timeout (minutes) can be viewed as a security risk. By default, this is set to 120 minutes of inactivity before OneStream will require a user to log back in. However, once the General settings are set to True, a system administrator can edit this setting, as well as the others listed in Figure 2.6. It is important to remember that these settings apply to the *entire* environment and are not specific to any one application. They are considered system-level environmental settings.

## Environment

When OneStream Environment settings are enabled as True (Figure 2.4) and a security group has been assigned on the Security > System Security Roles page for the Manage System Configuration, the following page is exposed within your OneStream environment:

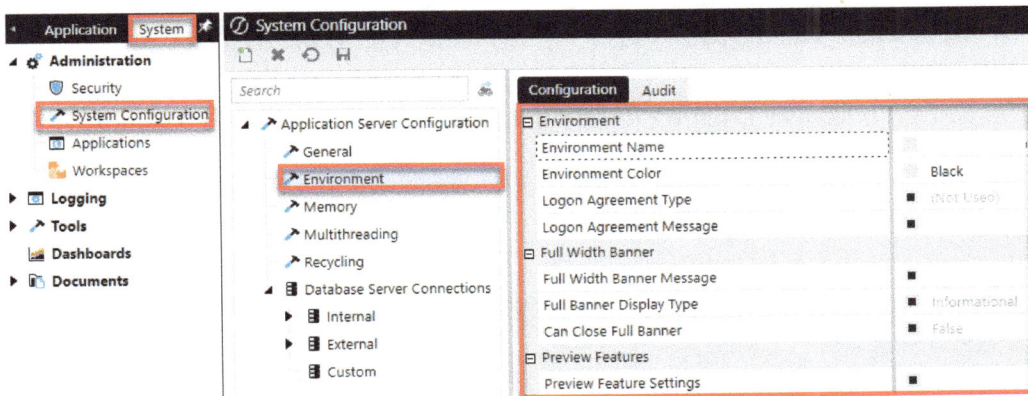

Figure 2.7

Again, these settings will determine whether an administrator can perform these tasks from *within* your OneStream application System tab. If any of these are set to False, the customer will need to reach out to OneStream Support to make a change. If any of these are set to True, those options will be editable by a OneStream administrator from within the System tab of their OneStream environment.

The ones relevant to environment security are the Logon Agreement Type, Logon Agreement Message, and Full Width Banner Message. These items can be displayed to a user when they log into the environment and require interaction, such as the agreement or acknowledgment of a message.

## Memory

By default, the memory settings are typically set to False when a new environment is set up and relate to system performance. Because these settings directly impact an environment's performance, they should only be edited by someone familiar with their implications. There are no settings within this section that directly impact environment security; therefore, I will not cover them. Should they need to be edited, you will want to work with OneStream Support to make changes.

## Multi-Threading

Likewise, and by default, multi-threading settings are typically set to False when a new environment is set up and relate to system performance, not system security. Because they directly impact an environment's performance, these settings should only be edited by someone familiar with their implications.

## Recycling

Over time, server memory may become fragmented, which can affect performance and stability. The default configuration of a daily recycling process is standard, and thus the recycle settings are typically set to True by default when an environment is set up, and thus editable by a system administrator from within the OneStream application.

When True is enabled (Figure 2.4 once again) for Recycle editing and a security group has been assigned on the Security > System Security Roles page for the Manage System Configuration, the following page is exposed within your OneStream environment:

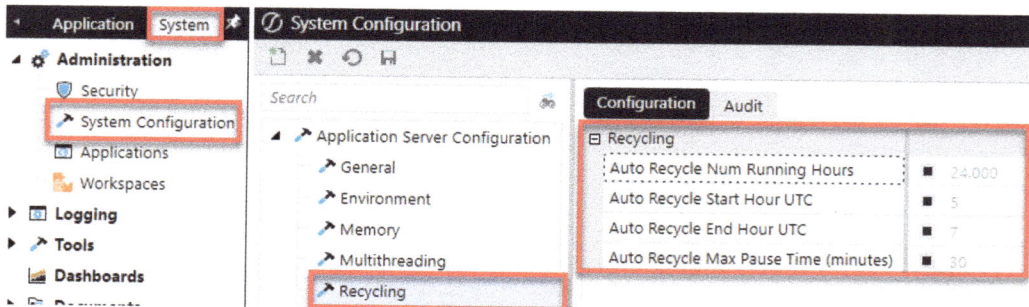

Figure 2.8

These settings again relate to the environment's performance and stability, and do not impact the environment's overall security. For more information regarding all these settings, please see the **OneStream Design and Reference Guide**.

# Database Server Connections

The Database Server Connection settings are typically set to True by default when an environment is set up, and thus editable by a system administrator from *within* the OneStream application. When the Database Server Connection Settings are True and a security group has been assigned on the Security > System Security Roles page for the Manage System Configuration, the following page is exposed within your OneStream environment:

Figure 2.9

The three most important security settings on this page pertain to the Ancillary Tables. We will review these settings more in Chapter 7 when we cover Solution Exchange security for tools requiring additional table access. What is important to note here is that you can edit the security groups assigned to access, maintain, or create ancillary tables within your environment from this Database Server Connection page.

# Environment

Within the OneStream Environment section of your Application Server Configuration Settings options, you can find True/False toggle switches for the following:

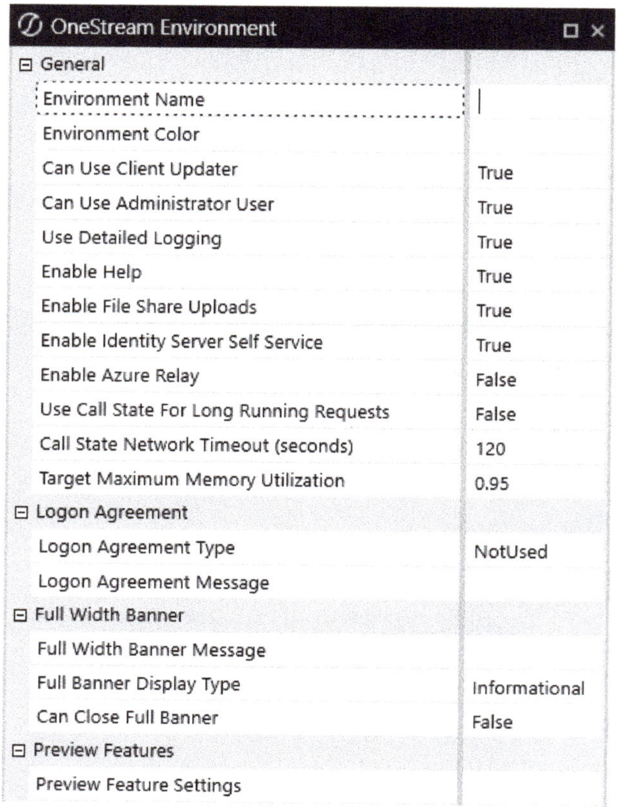

Figure 2.10

An administrator can work with OneStream Support to edit the settings above, some of which directly impact the environment's security. For example, Can Use Client Updater or Can Use Administrator User or Enable File Share Uploads are security-related items under your OneStream Environment section. But these are not exposed from within the OneStream application (with the exception of Environment Name and Environment Color), and a system administrator must open a case and work with OneStream Support to make modifications to these.

## Security

The Security setting of your Application Server Configuration Setting options is where you can set a Logon Inactivity Threshold (days). If set to -1, no logon inactivity threshold is enforced. If set to 90, in contrast, any user who has not logged in during the past 90 days will be unable to access OneStream without an administrator's intervention.

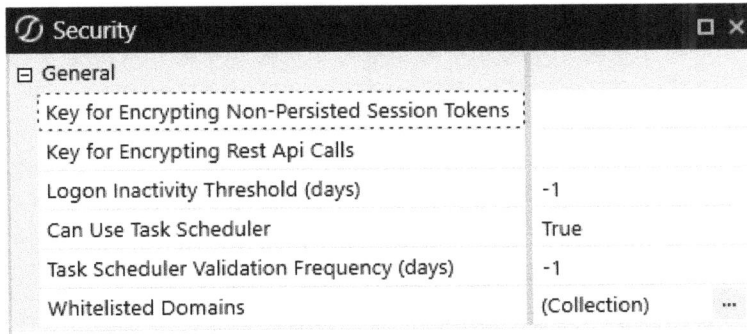

Figure 2.11

Now that we have covered the framework database and some high-level environmental security options and settings that pertain to an entire OneStream environment, let's move on to the process of setting up users and groups and granting access to application(s) within an environment.

# Users

After establishing the first layer of security for an environment (the authentication method), the next step is to set up users. At the heart of your OneStream security model are **Users** and **Groups**. Users are placed into one or more security groups. Security groups are assigned to application and system objects *or* nested inside other security groups. Security groups, and how they are nested and assigned to application and system objects, determine what a user can or cannot do in OneStream. The security pyramid for an environment is shown in Figure 2.12 and starts with users, placing users in group(s), and then assigning groups to application and system objects, or embedding groups in other groups:

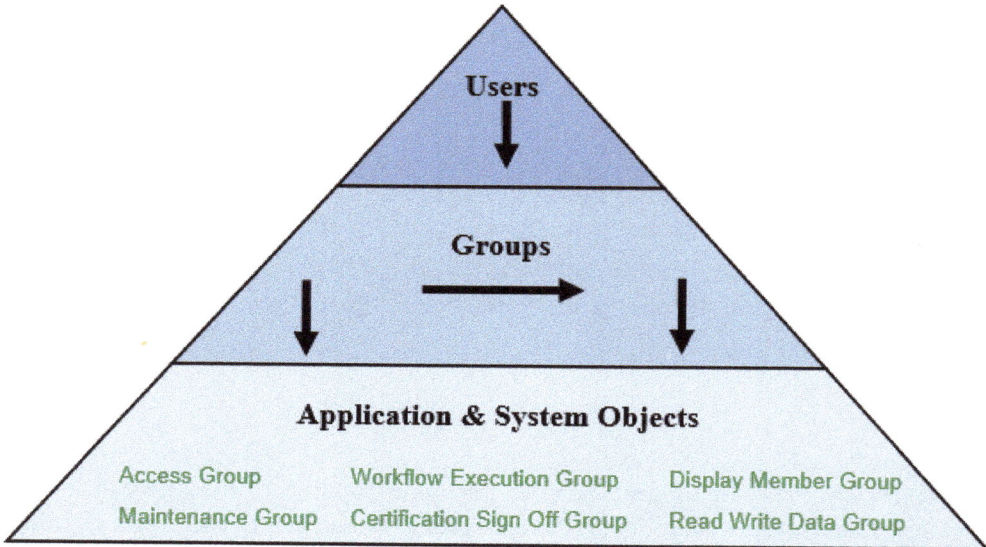

Figure 2.12

What is important to understand with users is that they cannot be individually provisioned to application or system objects, meaning you cannot go from the top of the pyramid to the bottom level of application and system objects. Users must be placed into security groups in order to inherit rights to application and system objects.

The starting point for setting up users (and groups discussed later) can be found on the System > Security page within your OneStream environment:

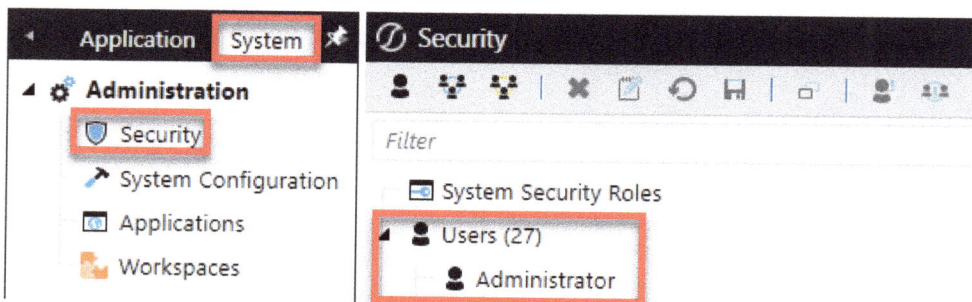

Figure 2.13

Every OneStream environment contains a default native user called **Administrator**, which is the only user that exists at the initial installation and creation of your OneStream environment. This default user name will always appear as the first user in your list of users within OneStream, regardless of alphabetical sort order (as in Figure 2.13).

A random password generator is used to generate a long, complex password for this user, which is then stored in OneStream's encrypted key vault in Azure. OneStream Support uses this ID when you open a support case and grant them permission for troubleshooting or upgrades.

You can change the password or disable this user, but it is not recommended, as it could cause delays in receiving support should you open a case for an issue or upgrade. If you need to change the password, you will want to coordinate with OneStream Support. You will need to schedule a time when your environment will be offline for approximately two hours, to get this password changed and restored in the encrypted key vault.

What is the purpose of this default Administrator user, apart from allowing OneStream to support your environment as needed? This user name is unaffected by inactivity thresholds and password expiration requirements that prevent users from logging in after a specific period elapses or being forced to change their password. Also, it cannot be deleted. This is the one user who can always manage artifacts, data, and tools within an environment. If you look at this default user name, you *cannot* add or remove any groups from this user (Figure 2.14). It is the one user name that has complete access to your OneStream environment. Think of it as a non-expiring system user.

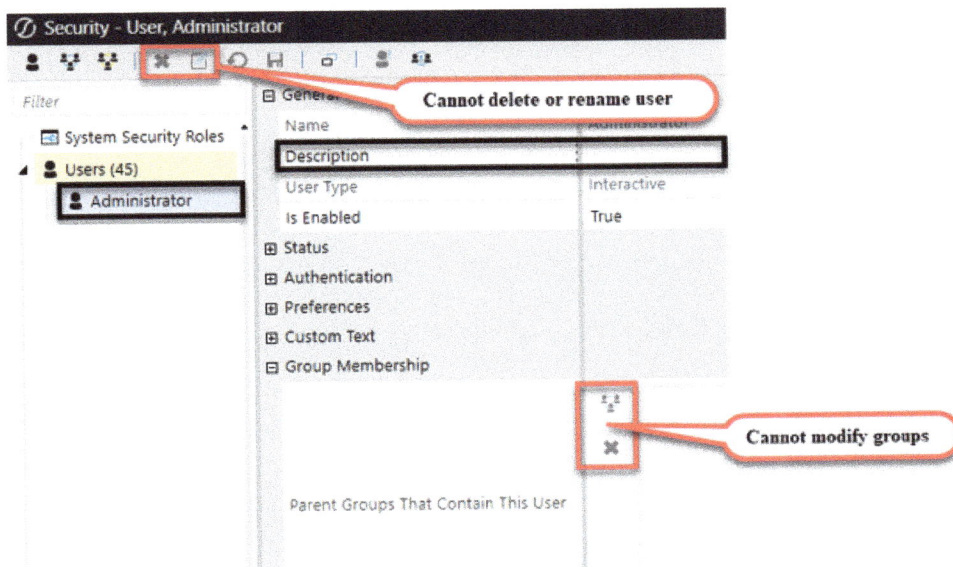

Figure 2.14

For cloud customers, in addition to this one administrator user name, OneStream Support will set up one or more company contacts as initial users who can validate your environment setup and authentication. These initial users are individuals who will act as a company's OneStream administrator(s) going forward.

Once your authentication is established and a company contact has verified a successful login, you are ready to create additional users. At this point, OneStream Support is no longer involved in the process of setting up additional users, as that responsibility falls on a company or partner resource. Should further support be required, a case will need to be opened with OneStream Support and support access enabled, allowing OneStream Support to log in to your environment using the Administrator user.

There are three ways you can set up users.

You can set up users manually, using the Create User icon: 👤 in the ribbon along the top of the System > Security page. You can set up one user by copying from another user with the Copy Selected Item icon ⊡

Lastly, users can also be set up en masse, using a **security template** found in the Productivity section on the OneStream Solution Exchange:

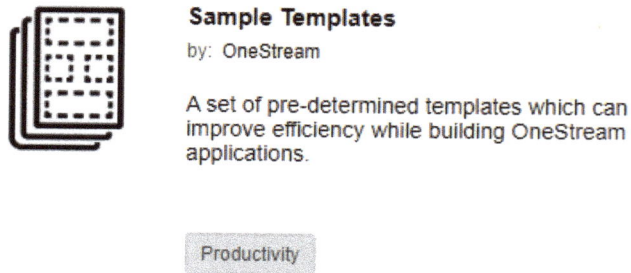

**Sample Templates**
by: OneStream

A set of pre-determined templates which can improve efficiency while building OneStream applications.

Productivity

Figure 2.15

Whether you choose to set up users one-by-one, via a copy method, or using the security template, you will be required to fill out certain properties. The following section describes the user properties, which ones are required, and how they impact an individual user.

# User Properties

When setting up users, below is a list of user properties, some of which are **required** and others which are *optional*:

| General | |
|---|---|
| **Name** | **nvchar100**<br><br>Name that will appear in all OneStream logs, and be available in business rules, Cube Views, and dashboards via the substitution variable (\|UserName\|)<br><br>Tied to a unique ID *behind* the scenes.<br><br>This is *not* the name used for external authentication.<br><br>OneStream stores and references a UniqueID behind the scenes, which will not change when you rename or delete a user. |
| *Description* | *nvchar200*<br><br>*A non-unique identifier that can be included on security reports.* |
| **User Type** | Classification that controls the license type that governs the user's access to artifacts and OneStream offerings. It does not control the user's security, but classifies them according to a dropdown list that includes:<br><br>• **Interactive**: Can use all features and tools.<br><br>• **View**: Can access data, reports, dashboards, and associated database, but cannot load, calculate, consolidate, certify, or change data.<br><br>• **Restricted**: Cannot use *some* Solution Exchange solutions due to contractual limitations.<br><br>• **Third-Party Access**: Can access applications with a third-party application by logging in using a named account. Cannot change data, modify artifacts, or access the Windows application or a browser-based application.<br><br>• **Financial Close**: Can use Account Reconciliation and Transaction Matching Solution Exchange solutions. |
| **Is Enabled** | A True/False toggle switch. Setting to False will prevent a user from logging in (e.g., if a user has been terminated). |

Chapter 2

| Authentication | |
|---|---|
| **External Authentication Provider** | **nvchar500**<br><br>If using external authentication, there will be a dropdown list of providers set up in your OneStream server configuration:<br><br> |
| **External Provider User Name** | **nvcharMAX**<br><br>If using external authentication, this is required to be the user name that is recognized by your external provider.<br><br>*If external authentication is **not used**, this should be left **blank**.* |
| *Internal Provider Password* | ***Only** used if (Not Used) is selected under External Provider User Name, meaning you are using a native user name to log in to OneStream.*<br><br>*You will set a password in OneStream that will be required to be changed the first time this native user logs in. Native password expiration and other requirements can be set in the OneStream Application Server Configuration settings:*<br><br> |

| Preferences | |
|---|---|
| *Email* | *nvchar2000*<br><br>*Email address that can be leveraged if you set up certain notifications within OneStream; for example, due date notifications in Task Manager or notifications via a BR.* |
| **Culture** | A dropdown list of language(s) set up in your server configuration. It will default to the primary language if there is only one setup.<br><br>If a user is set to a culture other than the default culture, this will allow them to see alternate language descriptions for any dimension members in Cube Views, dashboards, etc., where secondary descriptions have been added.<br><br>This culture setting does not change menu navigation. |
| **Grid Rows Per Page** | A dropdown list between 10 and 1,000, with a default value of 50.<br><br>Controls the number of rows that are displayed on the screen in a Cube View or grid component before a page break. The preference is to set it to a maximum of 1,000 unless connectivity or screen resolution is slow. This number can be reduced to improve the performance rendering of Cube Views and grids, if needed. |
| **Custom Text** | |
| *Text 1 – 4* | *Fields that can be used to categorize users on reports or drive certain behaviors within OneStream.* |
| **Group Membership** | |
| **Parent Groups That Contain This User** | *While not required, as all users are a part of the 'Everyone' security group by default, this is the security group(s) that will control user access in OneStream.* |

Figure 2.16

What is most important from Figure 2.16, apart from establishing a user's ability to login, will be a user's **Group Membership** properties. By adding security groups to a user, you are determining what that user will be able to do within that environment and any application(s) in that environment. The user will inherit the privileges of the Parent Groups That Contain This User by adding those groups to this user.

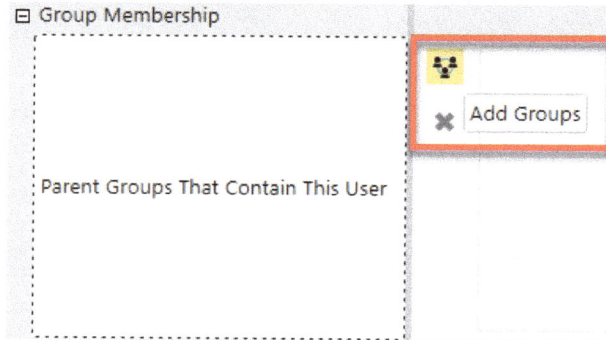

Figure 2.17

It is important to understand that a user can be in more than one group. If a user is in only one group, they will be able to do what that particular group is allowed to do. If they are in multiple groups, they will inherit the privileges of both groups if the groups are mutually exclusive. If the added security groups have overlapping privileges, the user will inherit the rights of the *least* restrictive group.

For example, if a user is in a view group for all data and a modify group for specific data, they will inherit modify rights to the specific data while retaining view rights to all data. This means that the least restrictive group (modify for specific data) will supersede the more restrictive view rights for all data, in the case of that specific data.

One additional item of note is that if the native administrators group is added to a user, no additional group membership is necessary. As we will discuss more in the Security Groups section, the native administrators group has full access to everything. Native administrators bypass all security (except Nobody); therefore, it is redundant for that user to be added to any other groups, with two exceptions that we will discuss in Chapters 5 and 6.

Lastly, if no groups have been added to a user, then – at most – that user will be able to authenticate to an environment and is considered part of the **Everyone** security group. Typically, as you build your application security, as discussed later, very few doors will be left open to everyone.

Using the home security analogy, once you move into your new home, you are not likely to leave your exterior doors unlocked. The same is true for your OneStream security, so if a user has no group membership, other than initially authenticating to the environment, they will not be able to log into an application or access anything additional within that environment.

## Deleting vs Disabling

Now that we have discussed how to create users, you may be wondering how to remove or deactivate users. There are two ways you can remove a user's ability to log into a OneStream environment; you can disable a user by setting the Is Enabled property to False (see Figure 2.16), or you can delete the user with the Delete Selected Item icon: ✖ at the top of the System > Security page.

Deleting a user from a OneStream environment will not directly impact that user's audit history. Any task activity and error log history for that user will be retained (in accordance with your retention periods) as those items are maintained in the database tables using a Unique ID behind the scenes. There is no risk of losing an audit trail of that specific user if deleted. However, deleting a user does mean that user name will no longer appear on the System > Security tab from within OneStream. The security audit reports discussed in Chapter 8 show a list of deleted users, so – from an audit perspective – you still have an audit trail of deleted users.

Disabling a user means that user will still appear in the user list on the System > Security tab from within OneStream. If needed, the user could be re-enabled at a future point in time. Disabled users also appear in a list on the security audit reports discussed in Chapter 8, so there is still visibility as to which users were disabled, and when. And all task activity and error log history are also retained for disabled users. Both methods, whether disabling or deleting, free up the user license.

So, which is recommended? Disabling users is the safest and most conservative approach to maintaining your OneStream security.

Why? The one gotcha with deleting a user is that it frees up that user name (not the external authentication name, but the user name inside OneStream), and it will not appear on the System > Security page in your OneStream environment. Therefore, you could set up a new user (or rename an existing user) with the same name as someone who *previously* existed.

Using our house analogy, this is a front yard versus back yard problem! All audit logs and task activity performed previously under the deleted user will show up under that *recycled* user name on the front-end. That can be misleading as those actions were taken by a different user under a different, unique user ID behind the scenes. However, in the application, the unique user ID is not displayed on audit reports, task activity logs, etc. Therefore, it would give the impression that the new user or renamed user performed those actions.

If you instead chose the safer option of disabling the user, that user still appears on the System > Security tab on the front-end. As such, that user name is not available when you set up new users or rename existing users. This keeps your front and back yard tidy as it enforces the uniqueness of user names (which are always unique in the back-end tables with their unique ID) and prevents you from recycling user names (on the front-end).

If your company has a retention policy around audit logs such that – after a certain period of time – audit logs are purged, then at that same time, you could go through disabled users and purge (delete) them periodically as well, since the consequence of misrepresenting which user did what within the logs would no longer be a relevant argument for keeping all user names.

Of course, the safest option is to disable and not delete users, but the consequence of this may be an ever-growing list of user names on the front-end in your System > Security tab. It is up to you to decide if your company is of the mindset "When in doubt, throw it out" (aka delete); or if your company prefers the "I may have use for that again someday, so I will keep it just in case" (aka disable).

## Support vs Application Users

It is important to distinguish between support users and application users. Support users are those set up for a customer or partner that allow them to access OneStream's Customer Support Portal for items like knowledge base articles, One Community, Navigator, the Solution Exchange, and support cases:

Figure 2.18

That user access is gained via a OneStream OKTA account sign-on and is maintained outside the OneStream environment by an account maintenance team within OneStream. It is the access for a customer or partner that will allow them to use OneStream-related content, per their license agreements.

For example, an IT resource or a OneStream project manager may have access to the OneStream Customer Support Portal to track enhancements and open cases for their customer. However, that IT resource or project manager may not actually be a OneStream application user.

Application users are users who are set up inside a customer environment with access to authenticate to an environment and potentially access applications within that environment. While there are overlaps in these user groups, their security and authentication are maintained independently, with one maintained by a OneStream account maintenance team and the other within a customer environment. This book focuses on the latter security or application user security.

Should you require changes to your support users, you will need to open a case with OneStream's account maintenance team.

# Groups

As mentioned in the introduction, every OneStream environment has three native security groups: Everyone, Nobody, and Administrators. The properties of these three groups *cannot* be changed (as shown in Figure 2.19), except for having the ability to add users to the Administrators group. And these three groups will always appear as the first groups in your list of security groups, regardless of alphabetical sort order.

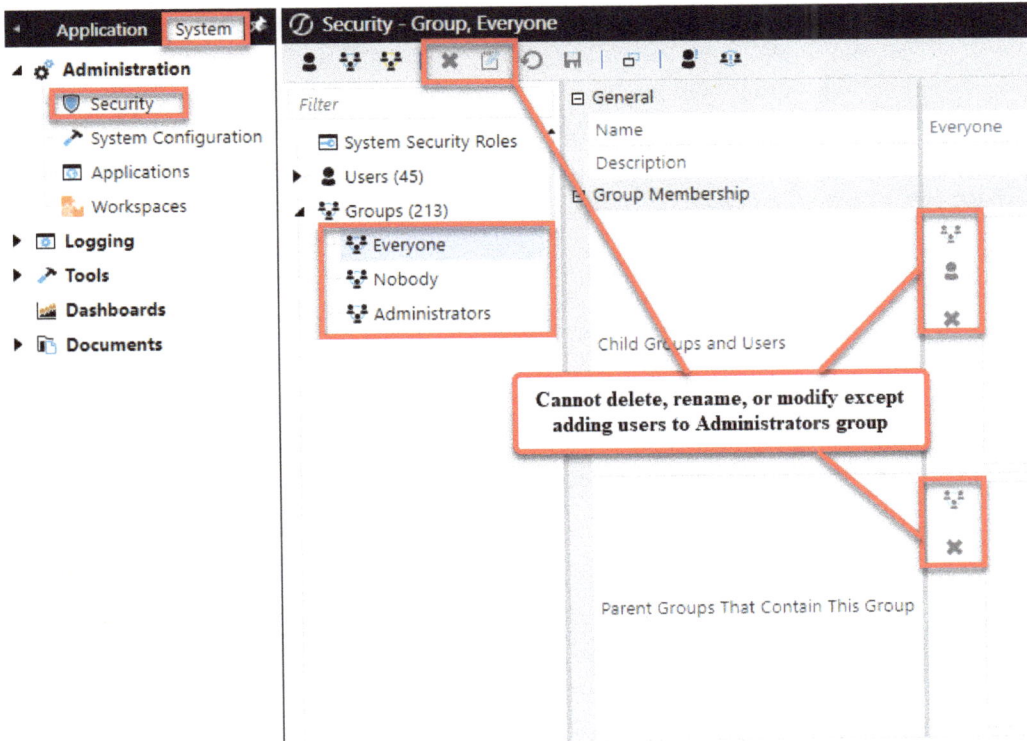

Figure 2.19

The Everyone group refers to everyone who has passed the first layer of security and authenticated to your OneStream environment. Once a user has passed the first layer, even if they have not been placed into any other security groups, they will still be able to do anything assigned to Everyone within your environment.

So, what is typically assigned to Everyone? By default, most application security roles and application user interface roles are all initially set to Administrators. This means even if a person passes the first layer of authentication to an environment, unless they have been granted *additional* security groups, they will not be able to log in or perform any actions within the environment.

While it is true that application security and user interface roles are initially set to Administrators, it is also important to understand that as you create new artifacts or objects *within* an application (e.g., new Cube Views, data management sequences, or dimension members), those objects default to Everyone. This may sound counterintuitive, but it does make sense in the overall context of your security layers. Because Everyone cannot log into an application by default, as new objects in that application are created it does not matter, therefore, that those objects default to Everyone.

Reflect again upon the home security analogy. If a person does not have a key to the front door of your home (e.g., an application security role), it is of no consequence that you have left the interior doors unlocked (e.g., new artifacts). Just to reiterate here, OneStream is the same in that as new objects are created, they default to the Everyone security group; application security and user interface roles default to Administrators, so this is of little consequence.

Next, the Nobody group means *even* those individuals who have passed the first layer of security and authenticated to your OneStream environment, regardless of whether you have placed them into any additional security groups, *cannot* access artifacts set to Nobody. This includes the native Administrators group; it truly does mean nobody! This security group is used sparingly throughout your OneStream environment, but there are a handful of situations where this group is assigned to objects, and we will get into those in later chapters.

By assigning the Nobody security group, if someone needs to have access to this object, it requires deliberate action. You must first change the security group from Nobody to another group before someone is able to access that object. So, think of it as protecting Administrators from themselves.

For example, say there is an old well on your home site that you do not want anyone accessing because it is dangerous. Therefore, you put a tight cover over it with a padlock. Closing up that old well makes it a deliberate action if someone needs to gain access. They will have to remove the padlock first and then pry off the cover before they can gain access. This defines the Nobody group.

Lastly, the Administrators group is the most important one in your environment. This is the native OneStream group that gives an individual(s) the keys to the whole kingdom. Again, this may sound counterintuitive, but it does serve an important purpose. This group will typically consist of just a few (depending on your organization's size) individuals who are well-trained in OneStream. Do not forget that also included in this Administrators group is the Administrator native user we discussed earlier. In Chapter 4, we will delve more into how to segregate administrative users by application or function, but understand that you will want at least one user in this group.

When OneStream Support initially stands up your environment and sets up the original company users, it will place those first users into the Administrators security group. This is done before the baton is passed to the customer or partner so that the customer or partner has full access to their own environment.

So, now that we have discussed the three native security groups, let's move on to groups that you will create yourself.

## Group Properties

When setting up security groups, you will use the Create Group icon: on the System > Security page. When you create a group, there is a list of properties, some of which are **required** and others that are *optional*:

| General | |
|---|---|
| **Name** | **nvchar100** |
| | Name that will be assigned on system and application objects and/or nested in other security groups. |
| | Tied to a unique ID *behind* the scenes. |
| *Description* | *nvchar200* |
| | *A non-unique identifier that can be included on security reports.* |
| **Group Membership** | |
| *Child Groups and Users* | *While not required to be filled out, this box typically has users and groups assigned.* |
| | *Groups and Users added here inherit the rights of the group into which they are placed.* |
| *Parent Groups that Contain This Group* | *Adding Groups here means that the selected group has rights over these groups.* |
| | *If this box does not contain any groups, this typically means the selected security group is attached to objects in the system or application.* |

Figure 2.20

What is most important from Figure 2.20 is Group Membership, and how to add users to groups and nest groups within other groups.

If you are like me, you have probably stared at the Child Groups and Users and Parent Groups That Contain This Group a million times and cannot remember into which box to add users, groups, or both to accomplish your goals!

I will lay out a systemic approach to these two items. Generally, there will *always* be something in the Child Groups and Users property, but there will *not always* necessarily be something in the Parent Groups that Contain This Group property. This may seem backward, as *not* everyone has children, but every child has a parent. So, let's take a closer look at how we assign group membership to users and groups with a simple use case.

Take a read security group for German entities. We will call this group 004_ENT_DE_READ (Chapter 3 will discuss naming conventions). Assume that you have assigned this German read security group to the Read Data Group property for all your German entities.

Now you are ready to assign Group membership. Assume a couple of things:

- You have one user (Heidi Klum) who has read rights to German entities.

- You have one EMEA read group (004_ENT_EMEA_READ) that will also have read rights to German entities (in addition to other European countries).

To achieve both of these things, you put the user Heidi Klum and group 004_ENT_EMEA_READ into the Child Groups and Users box one (as per Figure 2.21).

Any user or group you add to box one *inherits* rights to that security group. Think of this as nesting users and groups into box one, as children of the Germany read group.

Here is how this appears from the perspective of the German Read Security Group:

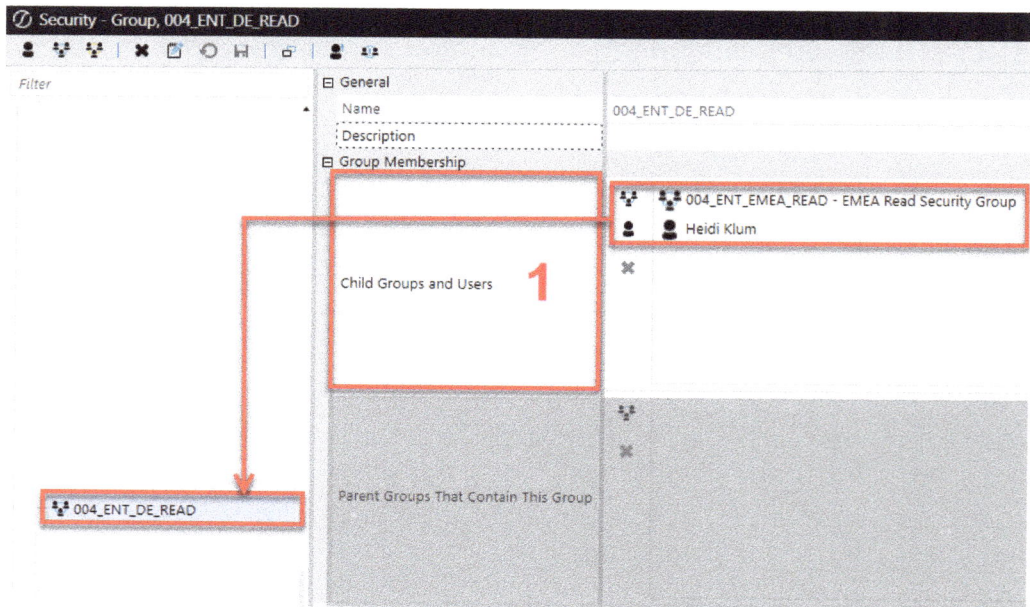

Figure 2.21

In the case of the German read group, the Parent Groups That Contain This Group box was not used. This is because, in our use case, Germany is the lowest entity level to which we need to apply entity security. The German read group, therefore, does not have rights over any other groups as it is the lowest level attached to the German entities in OneStream.

Now, let's consider what this looks like from the perspective of the EMEA read group. Let's assume a couple of additional things:

- We have three users (Brenda Matheus, Katia Schneider, and William Smith) who have the rights to read EMEA entities.

- We want to give the EMEA group rights to German (004_ENT_DE_READ), Spanish (004_ENT_ES_READ), French (004_ENT_FR_READ), and United Kingdom (004_ENT_UK_READ) entities.

First, we will start again with box one, the Child Groups and Users box. We add the three EMEA users into box one so that they inherit the rights of the EMEA read group (004_ENT_EMEA_READ). This is similar to adding Heidi Klum to the Germany read group, as we saw above. Users in box one are children and *inherit* the rights of the security group into which they are placed.

Next, we can move on to box two (Parent Groups That Contain This Group). Groups in box two are the reverse logic. Any groups nested in box two are groups over which the current parent group has rights.

Figure 2.22 shows how this looks from the perspective of the EMEA Read Security Group. Again, the users with rights to EMEA are placed into box one. The groups over which EMEA has control are placed into box two.

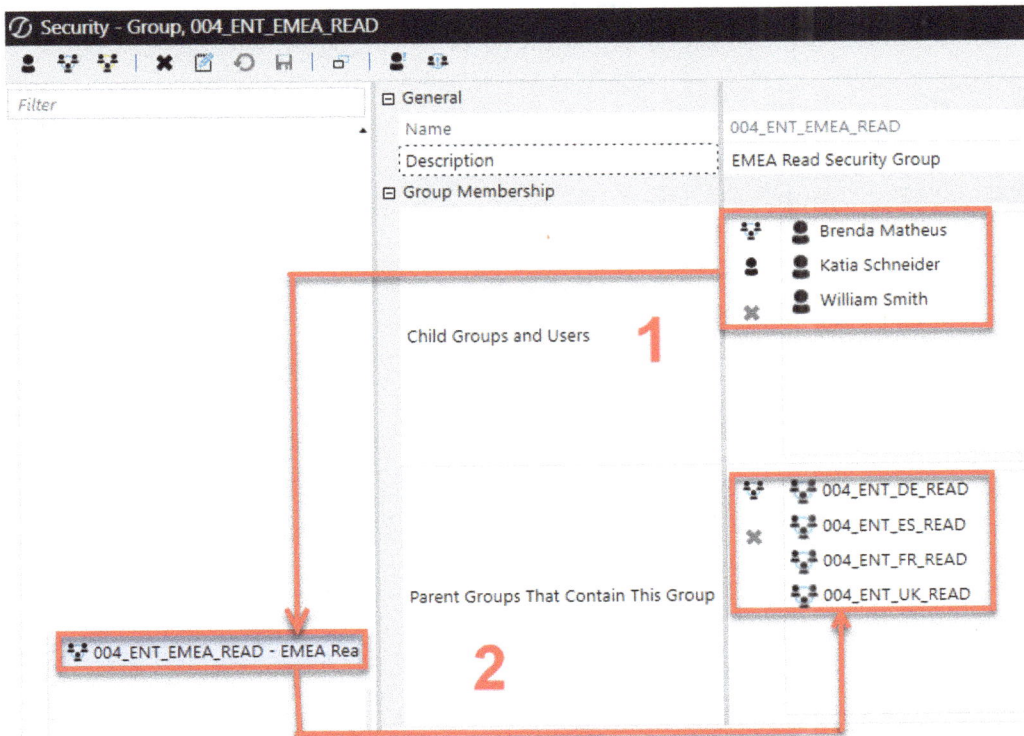

Figure 2.22

In the case of the German read group, box two was not used; however, because we wanted to create access control rights for the EMEA group over the German, French, Spanish, and UK entities, we did fill the Parent Groups That Contain This Group box for the EMEA read group.

Another way to think about the child groups versus parent groups is as shown in Figure 2.23. Child Groups and Users *inherit* the rights of the example security group.

And the example security group, in turn, is the Parent Groups and *controls* the rights of the other groups. Again, it may seem counterintuitive, but think of it as children inherit from their parents (box one), and parents control their children (box two).

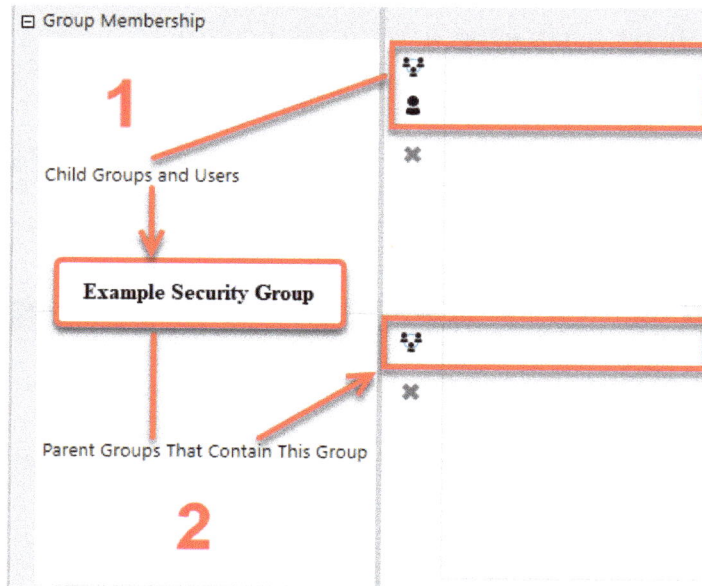

Figure 2.23

In subsequent chapters, we will delve into naming conventions around setting up security groups, how to assign security groups to application and system objects, and how to achieve your security model by nesting users and groups. But, for now, understanding the basic principles around setting up users and groups is key.

Once again, let us review the ways in which users and groups are placed into security groups.

Option 1: Navigate to each group into which the user or other groups need to be placed, and add the child user or group to each group individually:

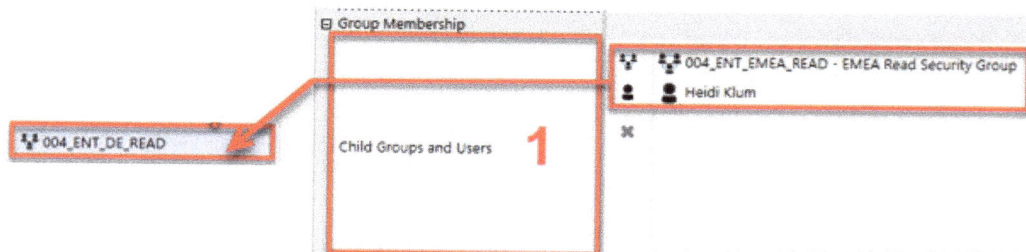

Figure 2.24

Option 2: Navigate to the parent group, and add all necessary users and groups to it:

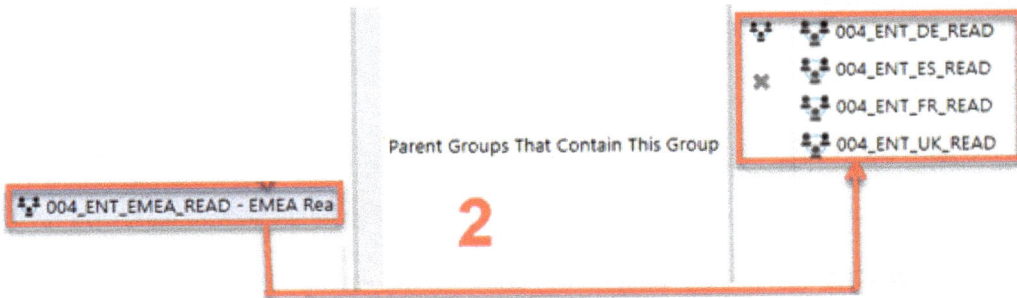

Figure 2.25

Both methods will yield the same result; users will inherit the rights of the groups into which they are placed, and groups will have access rights over other groups into which they are placed.

I prefer the second approach (parent groups) as that is a more all-encompassing approach. Typically, you will know into what groups a user should be added, so it is fewer clicks to navigate to that user and add all the groups to that user at once. The same applies to nesting groups. Once again, you generally know which groups a parent group should have access to, so if you navigate to the parent group, you can add all groups over which it should have control in one step.

However, as with many things in OneStream, there is more than one way to achieve the desired result, and nesting groups and users are no exception. A third way to grant users access to security groups is to copy the user's access from another user, as shown in Figure 2.26.

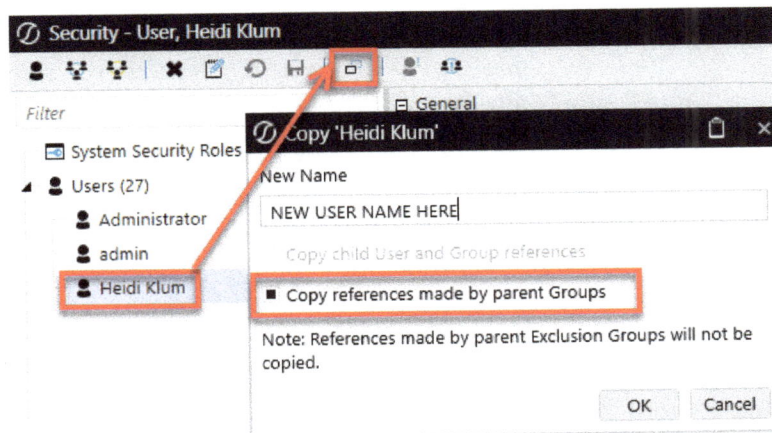

Figure 2.26

By using the copy icon: ▢ on the user toolbar and checking the box for Copy references made by parent Groups, the new user will inherit the same security as the user being copied. This third option is a way to shortcut a user's setup, when you already have other users working and know that your new user needs to be identical to an existing user. Just know that there are many ways to achieve the same result in OneStream!

## Exclusion Groups

The last type of group that can be set up in OneStream is called an Exclusion Group. These groups are not common but are utilized within your environment when you want to grant privileges by exception to already established groups. For example, you may have a security group with 100 users, and you may want to grant all 100 users, with the exception of two users, access to a particular object. Rather than having to create a group with 98 users that can access the object and another group with the remaining two users, you can use an exclusion group to grant access by exception.

To create one of these, you use the Create Exclusion Group icon: 🐾 on the System > Security page. When you create a group, there is a list of properties, some of which are **required** and others which are *optional*:

| General | |
|---|---|
| **Name** | **nvchar100**<br><br>Name that will be assigned as security group on system and application objects and/or nested in other security groups.<br><br>Tied to a unique ID *behind* the scenes. |
| *Description* | *nvchar200*<br><br>*A non-unique identifier that can be included on security reports.* |
| **Group Membership** | |
| *Child Groups and Users* | *While not required to be filled out, this is where you will permit and deny access for other security groups.*<br><br>*Access is granted or denied based on the order in which the groups or users appear in this property.* |

Figure 2.27

In keeping with our previous example, let's set up an exclusion group for EMEA that includes all users except for one user:

- We have three users (Brenda Matheus, Katia Schneider, and William Smith) who have the rights to read EMEA entities.

- We want to give the EMEA group rights to German (004_ENT_DE_READ), Spanish (004_ENT_ES_READ), French (004_ENT_FR_READ), and United Kingdom (004_ENT_UK_READ) entities.

- We want to have an exception where William Smith cannot view Spain's entities (004_ENT_ES_READ).

To achieve this, we will set up an Exclusion Group (999_ENT_ES_ExceptWilliam) which appears as follows:

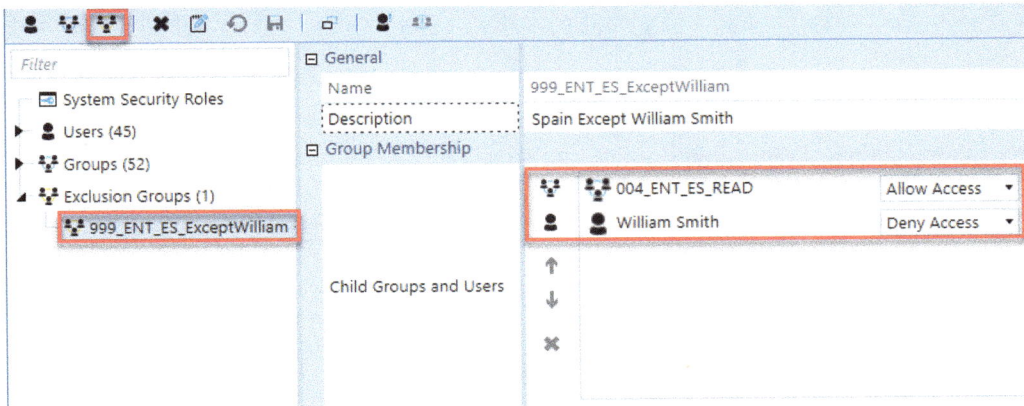

Figure 2.28

We first grant the Spain read group (004_ENT_ES_READ) access (appears first in Figure 2.28), and then we restrict William Smith's access to Spain (second in Figure 2.28). So, in this case, William Smith can be in the EMEA read group, which will give him access to all countries in Europe except Spain (004_ENT_ES_READ).

By attaching this exception security group (999_ENT_ES_ExceptWilliam) on all Spanish entities, everyone else in the EMEA Read group will retain their rights to Spanish entities, and William Smith will be denied.

While Exclusion Groups are rare, they can be used in an efficient manner to grant or deny rights to large groups of users and other security groups on an exception basis.

# Key Takeaways

There are several key takeaways thus far:

- The need to balance data governance, ease of use, control, and maintenance will impact the complexity of your security model.

- OneStream security is flexible and can change over time.

- Security resides in one framework SQL database per environment.

- Security includes several layers: environment, users and groups, system and application objects, metadata, and workflows, which work together to control access.

- There are three native groups: Everyone, Nobody, and Administrators, and one native user, Administrator, in every customer environment.

- The native administrators group has full environment access.

- Users cannot be provisioned to objects; users inherit rights to objects via group membership(s).

- Users can be in one or many groups.

- Users inherit all rights of the least restrictive group if groups overlap.

- Groups are assigned to objects.

- Groups can also be nested into other groups.

Now that we have an overview of some security basics in OneStream, in the next chapter, we are going to take a deeper dive into the questions a partner or customer may want to ask to understand how complex (or simple) their security model should be. We will get into details around naming conventions, best practices, and common types of users and security groups that may be utilized in a security model.

# 3
# Design

## Security Methodology

As you may know by now, there are many ways to tackle things in OneStream, and security is no different. Your approach to handling security can be simple to complex and will depend on many factors, such as the number and sophistication of your users, your company policies, any data governance requirements, the data you are storing in OneStream, etc.

As discussed in the prior chapter, OneStream can flexibly satisfy the simplest to the most complex security models. For some organizations, the best approach is often to start with minimal security and layer in additional security as needs arise. Companies with a small user base or that do not have many data governance requirements can start small and add complexity only if needed. It is easier to add security later than it is to scale back or unwind complex security.

However, large organizations or those that are more tightly controlled may know – from the get-go – that securing their OneStream data granularly is a high priority. In those organizations, it will be important to understand requirements early on in a project life cycle so that the right security can be applied and tested as the build progresses.

Whether you start simple or know you need complexity upfront, there are some general approaches that, when followed, can make setup and maintenance easier.

In this chapter, we will cover what questions you need to ask (to determine the best approach) and common naming conventions to use as you build and maintain your security. We will also take a deeper dive into the layers and checkpoints a user must pass through to access OneStream cube data and objects.

In Chapter 2, we learned about the first checkpoint to your OneStream security, the framework (aka environment) layer. Once you are past this first layer, the next layer of security can be thought of in two parts: application objects and system objects.

The **application security** layer will cover all the security you can apply *inside* specific OneStream application(s). It is the security that most closely controls your end-user experience. In this chapter, we will start to peel back this layer by going over the *types* of objects that you can secure within an application, and the *ways* in which you can secure those objects. In Chapter 5, we will dig even more into the application security layer and go through all options related to it.

Chapter 3

**System security** is a layer of security that pertains to *who can do what* across an *environment*, and it is not application-specific. We touched lightly upon system security in Chapter 2 when we discussed users and groups. The system security layer will be covered in detail in Chapter 6.

In this chapter, we will focus primarily on the application security layer, as that is the one that is most relevant to end-user security, and the one where overall design and methodology are important to understand as you build your security.

When we speak about application security, the logical question is: what *can we* secure in OneStream? The answer to that is almost anything!

This list of elements includes the following, and all these pieces ultimately make up the end-user security experience in an application:

1. Application(s)
2. Cube(s)
3. Scenario(s)
4. Entity(s)
5. Workflow(s)
6. Data slice(s)

These elements are shown in Figure 3.1, with users and groups being a part of the framework (discussed in Chapter 2) and application elements residing within individual application databases.

**Framework**                    **Application(s)**

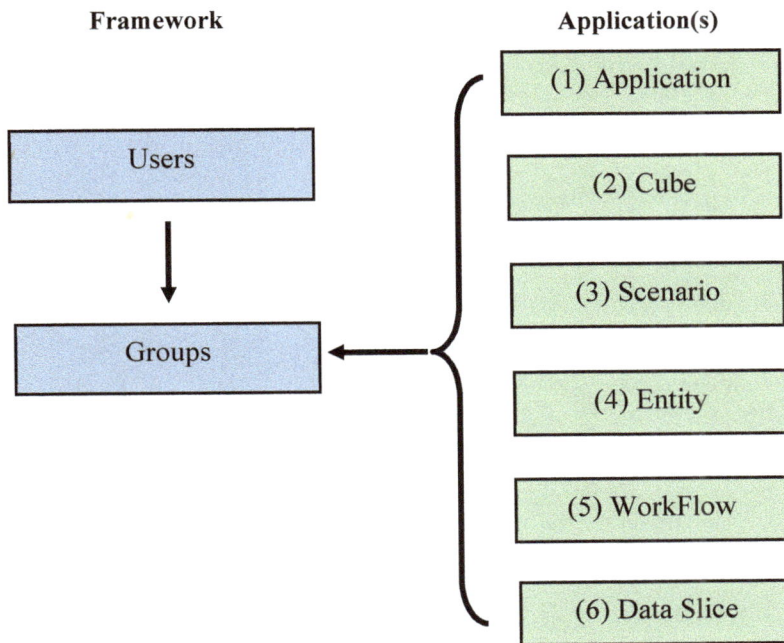

Figure 3.1

It is a combination of the first five application elements (six if securing User Defined Dimensions) that will grant the user the ability to do certain things or see certain cube data within an application.

For example, if you grant a user the ability to open or login to a particular application (e.g., the Open Application security role) but do not grant that user the remaining four application elements (cube, scenario, entity, and workflow), the user will be able to do nothing more than log in to the application.

If you grant that same user the ability to open the application *and* see certain application pages (e.g., the Spreadsheet page) but you have not granted that user any access to cubes, entities, or scenarios, the user will be able to log in and navigate to the Spreadsheet page, but see no data.

In almost all use cases when securing cube data, it is a combination of those five security elements that will control what a user can see and do within a single application. How you design these application elements will also control the look and feel of the end-user experience.

It is important to understand that, within those five key application elements, there is both *object* security and *data* security. It is the intersection of both a user's object *and* cube data security that will determine their access within an application, as shown in Figure 3.2.

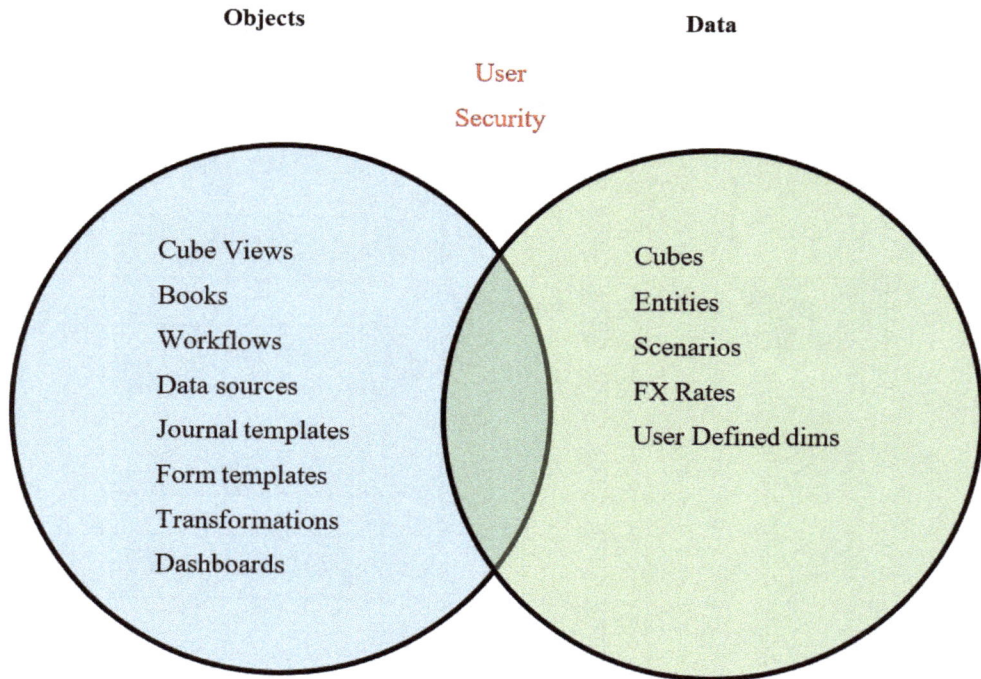

Figure 3.2

For example, you may have a report that everyone can access. That report (e.g., Cube View) is considered an application object.

When a user runs that report (the *object*), the data displayed to the user will be controlled by their cube, scenario, and entity (their *data*) security rights. You may have one report for an income statement by cost center (entity) as an example. When users run that report, they will only have the ability to see the cost center (entities) data to which they have been granted access.

So, one object (an income statement Cube View) can satisfy the reporting needs of an entire organization (cost centers) because users' *data* security will control what information is displayed on that Cube View.

Relating this back to our home security analogy we started in Chapter 1, think about object security as the doors, fences, and windows to a home. You may have access to open certain doors, fences, and windows (*objects*), but you may not have further access, like keys to a safe or passwords to a computer (*data*).

OneStream *object* security includes the following:

- Application roles and pages
- Workflows
- Cube Views
- Business rules
- Dashboards
- Data management jobs
- Data sources
- Transformations

All of these elements are objects within a OneStream application and can be secured on their own. They are separate from the security that you apply to your *data* elements. Chapter 5 will go into all application security elements in more detail.

When we talk about OneStream *data* security, we are referring to:

- Cubes
- Entities
- Scenarios
- Data Slices

Why is it important to understand the difference between object security and cube data security?

Understanding the two different types of element security – and how they intersect – will help inform how simple or complex you make your data model.

You may choose to leave certain objects unlocked to Everyone, and rely upon your data security (cube, entity, scenario) to control what people can and cannot see. This is a simplified approach to your overall security: the 'Less is More" approach.

Or you may choose to take a conservative approach where you not only limit a user's cube *data* security but also limit their *object* security as well, leading to more complexity in setup and maintenance, but lower risk.

Think again about your home security. While you lock your exterior doors and windows, once inside your home you may take a more modest approach where not every door, drawer, or computer is individually locked. This makes moving around and living in your house easier, but it does come with some added risk. If someone were to break in and you have not locked all the drawers, safes, and laptops, you run the risk that those may be compromised.

But balancing that risk with ease of living is something each person decides for themselves, much in the same way your company will decide the right balance of control and maintenance. Which security approach you take will depend on your company's risk tolerance, the sophistication of your user base, how you want their user experience to be within OneStream, your auditors, and so on.

Now that we understand that application security is comprised of both object-level security and data security, let's take a look at the upfront questions you will want to ask as you design your security.

## Design Questions

As we mentioned previously, OneStream security is flexible and does not limit or constrain your security approach. When faced with so much flexibility – the proverbial blank slate – how do you know where to begin your security design?

There are several important questions that need to be understood, either upfront or, if you are changing your security approach, during a later phase. Here is a list of potential (not exhaustive) questions that should be asked and understood to choose the right approach:

- Who will be loading what data?
- Is your load process centralized or distributed?
- Will you load data via imports, or will you need manual inputs as well?
- Who will be viewing what data?
- Who will maintain data mappings?
- Who will maintain what metadata?
- Who will maintain reports?
- Should certain reports only be available to certain users?
- Will distinct groups be creating, approving, or posting JEs?
- Will you have different review, confirmation, or certification levels?
- Who can lock and unlock data?
- Who can consolidate and calculate data?
- Do you split responsibilities by process? (e.g., Actuals versus Budget)
- Do you need to enforce segregation of duties among tasks?
- Will you have various levels of administrators?
- Do you want to secure data by entity and, if so, to what level (e.g., base entities, groups of entities, regional, etc.)?
- Do you want to secure data by scenario?
- Do you need security on any specific User Defined dimensions?

As you ask the above questions, the answers will start to form the basis for your security approach. A lot of times, companies think they can take a simple or modest approach to security, but in asking the above questions, it becomes clear they need more layers and checkpoints than they originally envisioned.

Keeping the full picture and *all* the answers above in mind, you can adopt a methodology to meet your company's needs with the right balance of control and ease of maintenance.

Once you have gathered answers to key design questions and understand your company's needs, you can move from design concepts to build. You are now ready to apply naming conventions and standards as you begin to build out your security. We will cover some best practice naming conventions in the next section.

## Naming Conventions

If you have worked in an accounting or financial system, you will know that a common approach to naming conventions can make understanding, organizing, auditing, transferring knowledge, and maintaining everything infinitely easier.

I will lay out one approach to security group naming conventions in this section that I find easy to follow, but you can choose your own path. What is most important with any naming convention is not so much *what* you choose, but *adhering* to those rules. Be consistent!

Commonly, since a user needs access to a minimum of the first five application elements, it follows that our security group naming convention can also follow a five-tiered structure (as per Figure 3.3).

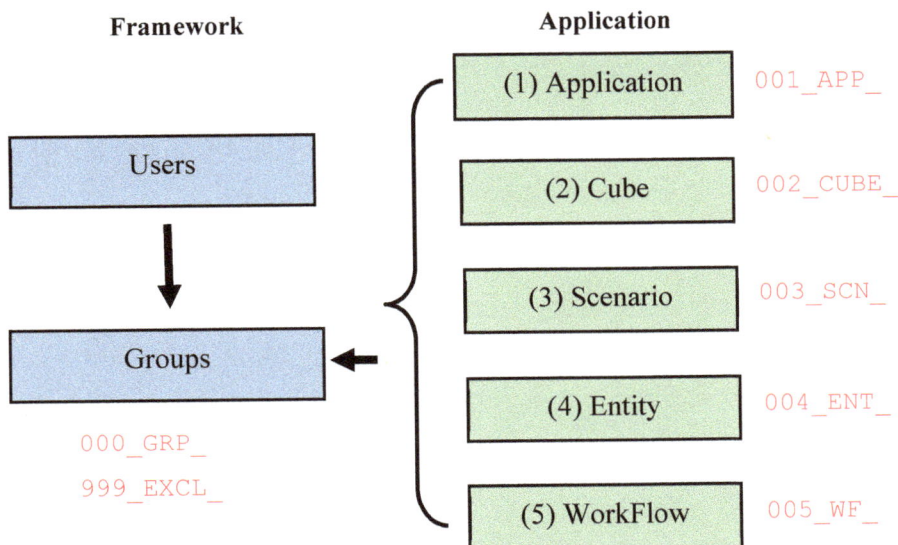

Figure 3.3

## User Group Names

As we learned in Chapter 2, users cannot be granted individual privileges. Users *only* obtain access by being placed into security groups. The reason to start *user* security groups with 000_GRP (and exclusion groups with 999_EXCL) is so that all user groups sort to the top of the screen on the System > Security tab.

Why is this important? By starting all user groups with 000 they will appear first, after the three native security groups of Everyone, Nobody, and Administrators. And because exclusion groups are rare, I like to start them with 999 so they sort to the bottom of the security group screen.

This makes it easier to add or remove users from security groups, as they will be arranged for easy access. This is shown in Figure 3.4:

Figure 3.4

## Object Group Names

Next, we can start the remaining security groups that pertain to both objects and cube data within an application with 001 to 005. These groups will then be nested in our 000 user groups. Because we know it takes a combination of at least one of each of those five security groups to achieve a complete security picture for a user group (000), you can easily scan a particular user group and notice if one of the five elements is missing.

For example, when we focus on a given 000_GRP_POWERUSER group, we should see at least one of each of the 001 to 005 groups in the Parent Groups box, as shown in Figure 3.5:

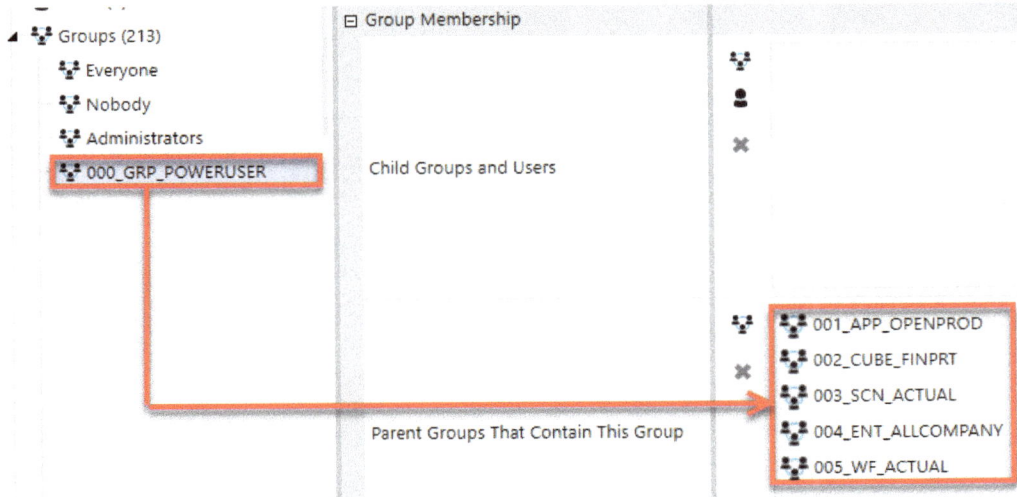

Figure 3.5

If this group had any element missing, for example if `000_GRP_POWERUSER` did *not* have any `003_SCN` security groups embedded, this user group would be missing a piece of access to complete rights to access a particular scenario of data. This assumes that you have not left the scenario group set to `Everyone`.

While a user in this group could log in (`001_APP_OPENPROD`), access a cube (`002_CUBE_FINPRT`), access all entities (`004_ENT_ALLCOMPANY`), and even navigate to an appropriate workflow (`005_WF_ACTUAL`) *because* the group is missing access to a particular scenario of data (`003_SCN_ACTUAL`) users in the group will still not be able to access data.

> This brings us to our first *rule of thumb*, in that it takes at least one of each of the first five security groups (`001` to `005` groups) to complete a user's access (`000`).

The only time this is not the case is if you have `Everyone` assigned to certain objects or data. Say you are taking a modest or simple approach to your security, and you leave all cubes open to `Everyone`. In that case, then *no* `002_CUBE` group is required to be nested in your user group (`000`).

If it is the case that you leave an object – such as cube(s) – open to `Everyone`, then you can simply remove that from your numeric naming convention, as shown in Figure 3.6. Again, this can be the case if you are taking a simple approach to security.

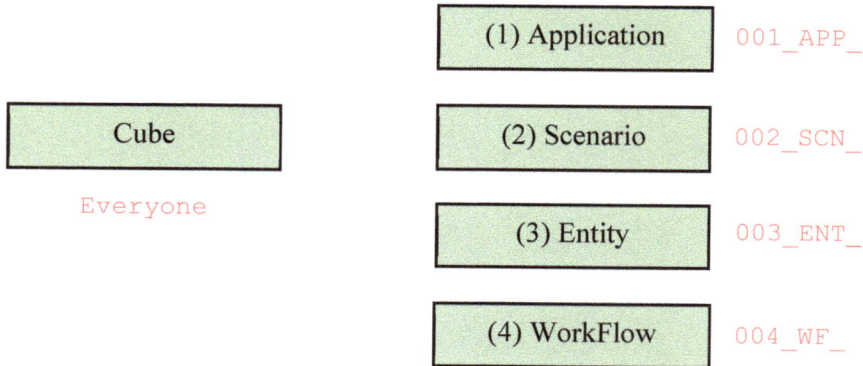

| | |
|---|---|
| (1) Application | 001_APP_ |

| | | | |
|---|---|---|---|
| Cube | | (2) Scenario | 002_SCN_ |
| Everyone | | | |
| | | (3) Entity | 003_ENT_ |
| | | (4) WorkFlow | 004_WF_ |

Figure 3.6

Another example is if your company decides not to have scenario-specific security, and relies *only* upon entity and workflow security. For example, if you allow your users to see all data – whether that is Actual, Forecast, or Budget data for whatever entities to which they have access – you may assign the Everyone security group to all your scenarios. In that case, once again, you would not need any scenario-specific security groups (003_SCN) and thus could eliminate that 003 group from your numeric naming convention, as in Figure 3.7.

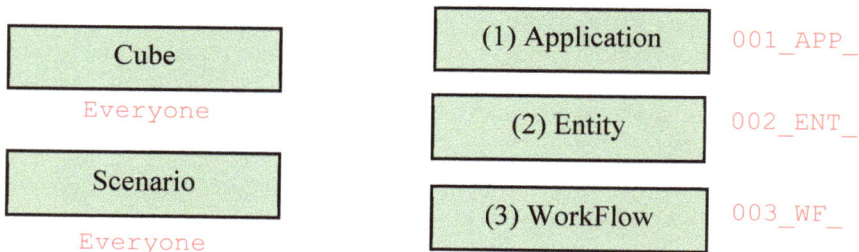

| | | | |
|---|---|---|---|
| Cube | | (1) Application | 001_APP_ |
| Everyone | | | |
| | | (2) Entity | 002_ENT_ |
| Scenario | | | |
| Everyone | | (3) WorkFlow | 003_WF_ |

Figure 3.7

You can see that, once again, this is a simple approach where you are leaving cubes and scenarios open to Everyone and relying upon a user's entity and workflow security to control what they can and cannot see or do in OneStream.

So, what happens if your organization decides it wants to secure scenarios and cubes after go-live or years later? As we mentioned, security is flexible and can be changed as an organization's needs change. In that case, I would simply create 004_CUBE and 005_SCN security groups, assign them to appropriate objects, and nest them in your 000 user groups (and, of course, test the changes along the way). Remember, it is not so much that you follow the *exact* naming convention I have laid out above, but that you adhere to whatever naming convention you do establish!

For smaller organizations or those with less IT or regulatory oversight, leaving some objects open to Everyone may provide the right balance between ease of maintenance (e.g., you do not have to maintain cube or scenario-specific security groups) and risk (relying solely on entity and workflow security groups).

For more complex organizations or those companies with demanding IT or regulatory needs, leaving cubes and scenarios open to Everyone may prove too risky, and thus, they may want all five elements (001 to 005 security groups) as a part of their overall user security (000 groups).

The nice thing is that this numeric naming convention can suit both approaches. It is a flexible guide that can be applied and modified to meet each company's individual security needs. It provides rules to follow that can be tailored to fit a simple or complex security model, as you can see in the above examples.

## Nesting Groups

As we reviewed in Chapter 2, security groups can be embedded, aka nested, into other groups to create inherited rights *between* groups. Nesting security is a common OneStream practice to limit the number of security groups that get assigned to users, making it easier to audit, troubleshoot, and assign end-user security.

As we mentioned in the previous section, user groups should start with 000 and contain 001 to 005 nested groups (as desired) to achieve the goals of that user group. Then, users are placed into the 000 security groups.

> That brings us to our second rule of thumb with security groups. When nesting groups into each other, the data security groups for cube (002), scenario (003), and entity (004) should only contain other 002 cube groups, 003 scenario groups, and 004 entity groups, respectively. And you want to *avoid* embedding 001 groups into other 001 groups and 005 groups into other 005 groups.

Why is this rule of thumb true for the data security groups? Because cube groups (002) should only be attached to cubes, scenario groups (003) should only be attached to scenario properties, and entity groups (004) to entity properties, it follows that when you nest data groups into each other, you only want to do so *within* the same family of data. This is to prevent mixing apples and broccoli (different families) and then trying to understand why users can or cannot do something in an application.

Plain and simple, it makes it challenging to validate and audit your security if you *cross*-embed the data groups (003 in 004, 002 in 003, 002 in 004).

And why does this rule of thumb apply to the object security groups for application roles (001) and workflows (005)? Because the 001 groups pertain to *specific* individual application roles and pages, and the 005 groups pertain to *specific* individual workflows. If you commingle these object security groups, you lose transparency and flexibility in how each of these individual objects is secured.

The only exception to this rule is with your 000 user groups. The 000 groups themselves, by nature, are the final user groups into which you will place individuals. As such, your 000 groups *should contain* 001 to 005 groups.

Using the house analogy once again, you may have a single key that opens all exterior doors to your house, but you likely want different keys when it comes to opening bedroom doors *inside* your house. Using the same key on exterior doors as interior doors makes it hard to lock off certain parts inside your home.

Assume you have an entity group to grant full access to all entities called 004_ENT_ALLCOMPANY. One approach can be to embed all other 004 entity security groups in this group to create the correct inheritance for this parent. As I say, this is but one approach because, alternatively, you can use the Read Data Group and Read Data Group 2 to achieve this same thing without nesting. Remember, in OneStream, there are always multiple ways to achieve the same task!

In Figure 3.8, you can see we also *inadvertently* have an Actual scenario security group (003_SCN_ACTUAL) embedded in the 004_ENT_ALLCOMPANY entity security group. That will have unintended consequences as we have just created rights over the Actual scenario of data (apples) from an entity (broccoli) security group. If you have a user who should have access to all entities (004_ENT_ALLCOMPANY), but only for Budget data, by embedding a 003_SCN_ACTUAL into a 004_ENT group, you have broken your security model and granted unintended rights. Just remember that apples (003) and broccoli (004) just do not mix!

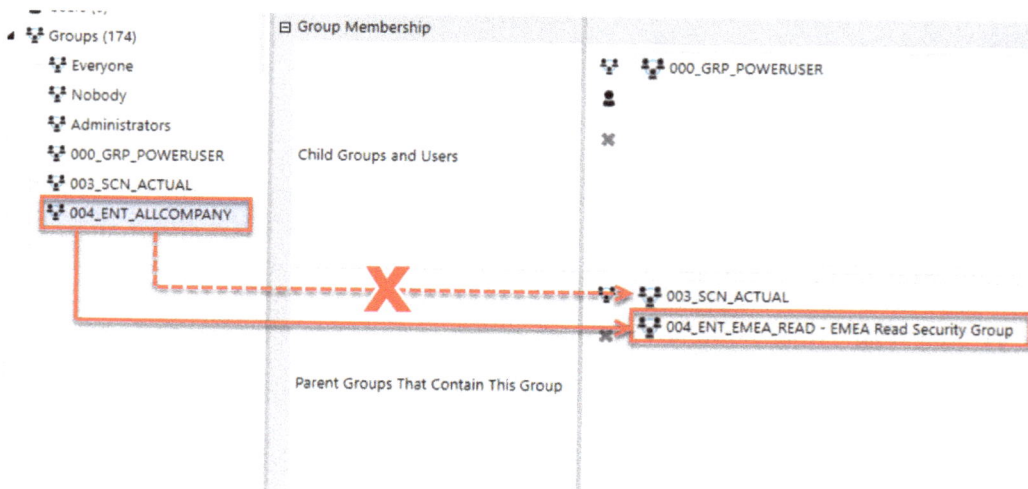

Figure 3.8

Using a number standard for security groups will make it easier to spot if data groups have been embedded into other dissimilar groups (as shown in Figure 3.8).

While we may want to grant permission to everyone to view all company data and also enable access to view Actuals, we do so by combining those two individual groups into a 000 user group, not by cross-embedding groups from different application data elements into each other.

The correct way to grant people access to all entities and the Actual scenario would be by combining those two data groups into a user security 000 group, as shown in Figure 3.9.

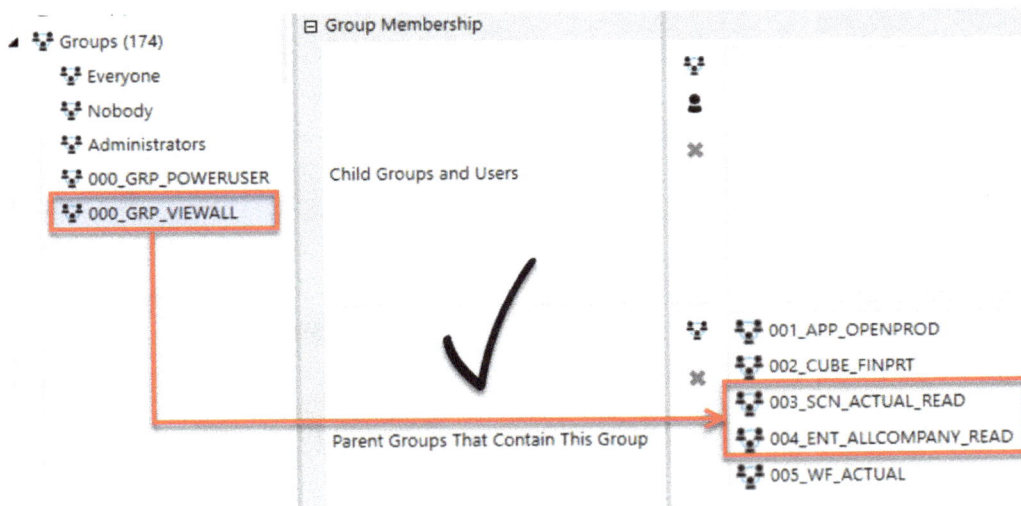

Figure 3.9

Next, let's walk through a couple of examples involving the object groups for application roles and pages (001) and workflows (005), to understand why we want to avoid embedding these groups into themselves.

Take, for example, the Manage Cube Views and Cube Views Page application elements (covered in more detail in Chapter 5). While you may want to grant certain users the ability to manage Cube Views, you may want to give *other* users the ability to see the Cube Views page but not modify Cube Views.

If you create one security group (001_APP_CUBEVIEWS) and attach it to *both* the Manage Cube Views and Cube Views Page application elements, you have lost the ability to segment those who can manage Cube Views from those who can merely access the Cube Views page.

Or if you create two security groups (001_APP_MANAGECUBEVIEWS and 001_APP_CUBEVIEWSPAGE) and nest one into the other, again you have commingled rights and made it hard to separate who can do what in relation to application roles and pages. Chapter 5 will go into more detail around application roles and application pages.

The same rule applies to workflow security groups. Say you have a workflow group for those who can access Actuals (005_WF_ACTUAL) and another group for those who can access Budget (005_WF_BUDGET). If you nest the Budget group in the Parent Groups of the Actual workflow group, you have now created unintended rights between two different Workflow Profiles. This is shown in Figure 3.10.

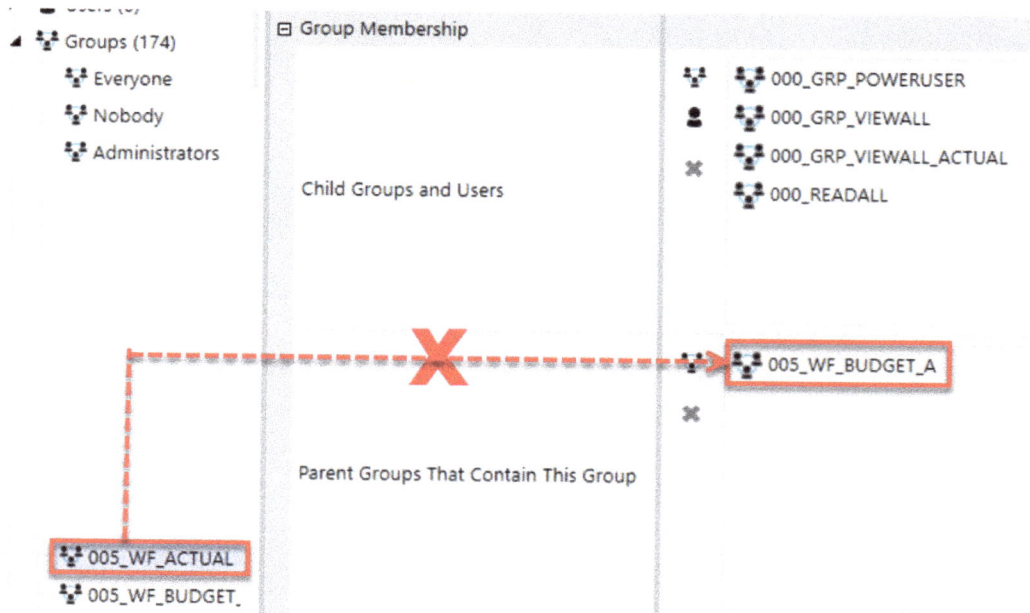

Figure 3.10

Now, any user who has access to Actual workflows assigned with 005_WF_ACTUAL will *also* have access rights to Budget workflows with 005_WF_BUDGET. The problem with embedding these two workflows into each other is that you may not want to grant *all* Actual workflow users access to Budget workflows. However, by nesting – as shown in Figure 3.10 – this is the unintended consequence.

If you have a person who needs access to both the Actual (005_WF_ACTUAL) and Budget (005_WF_BUDGET) workflows, you will do so again by combining those two groups in a user group as per Figure 3.11. In this way, you have flexibility, control, transparency, and auditability over which users can access which workflows, based upon the user group (000) and not due to inadvertent cross-nesting.

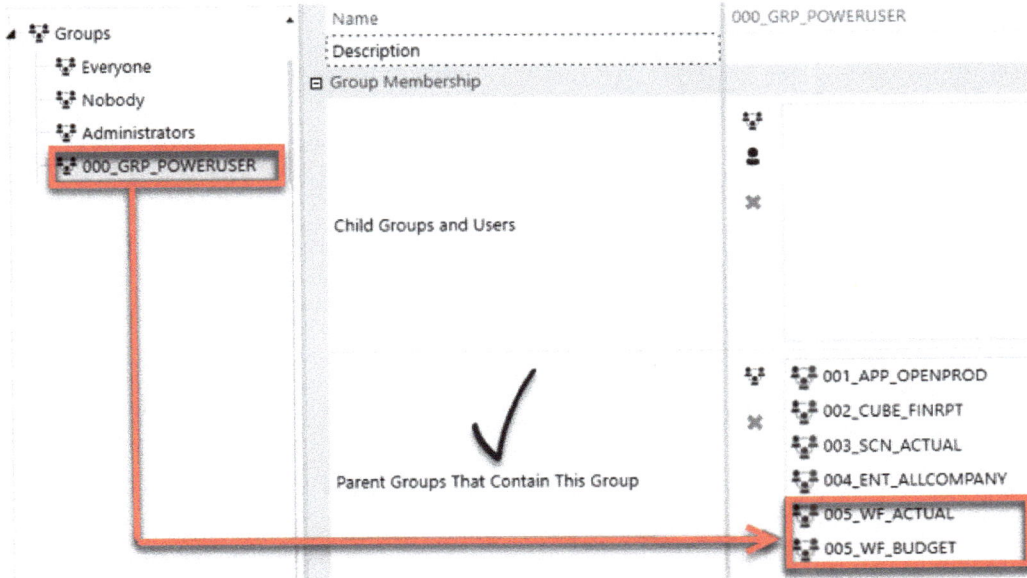

Figure 3.11

That is why the rule of thumb is not to nest 001 groups into other 001 groups and 005 groups into other 005 groups. Because application roles and pages (001) and workflows (005) are very specific to those objects, and to have flexibility in how you grant that access, you will not want to cross-embed them. Chapter 5 will go into more detail around the application roles and pages, as well as workflows. In this chapter, we are just laying the rules groundwork for how to embed (or not) various security groups.

## Group Name Recap

So, to recap our general rules, 000 security groups should contain at least one 001, 002, 003, 004, and 005 security group in their Parent Groups box to complete the security picture for a user (unless Everyone is being leveraged).

002 should only contain other 002, 003 only other 003, and 004 only other 004 groups to avoid complicating nested groups and granting rights across different sets of data.

And lastly, 001 application and 005 workflow groups should never be nested, as they pertain to specific objects.

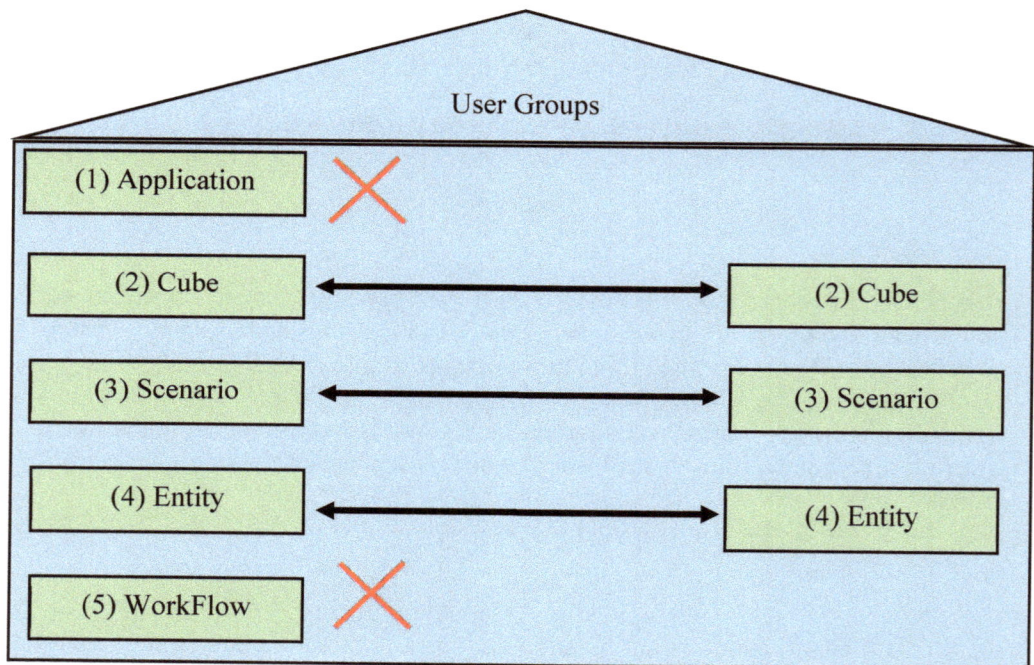

Figure 3.12

Remember that these are general rules or guidelines to be followed, but there can always be exceptions to these rules or modifications to them to meet each company's individual needs.

I have laid out one approach to naming conventions and rules of thumb that I think are easy to follow, audit, test, and maintain. Whatever method you choose, following it and documenting exceptions will be key!

## Optional Group Names

In addition to the first five groups that we have already discussed, you may *optionally* have security groups for data slice security (006), as well as Solution Exchange tools (007) and other (008) tools or needs. These optional security groups should also follow a numeric naming convention so they can be easily applied.

Slice security (006) is a very granular level of security that can be applied – most commonly – to UDs but also accounts, if needed. And Solution Exchange security groups (007) are groups that you will place around the dashboards that come with those solutions. We will cover both in more detail in Chapter 7.

Finally, 008 security groups are intended to capture any other miscellaneous items that you may want to secure in your application.

The number is not as important for any remaining elements, so long as you follow a convention. By establishing a standard naming convention (as in Figure 3.13) and following it, it will once again make implementation, testing, and ongoing maintenance more efficient.

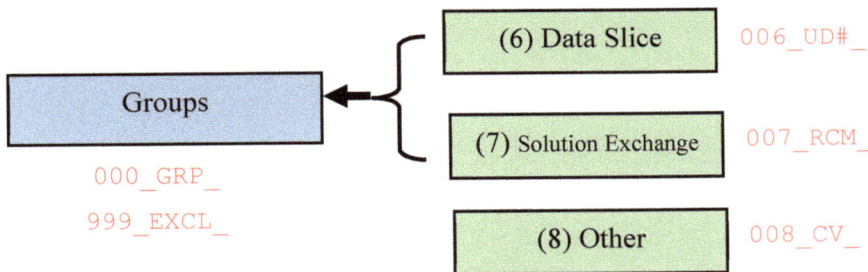

Figure 3.13

## Types of Access

Now that we have covered naming conventions for the key elements within an application, let's dive deeper and talk about the different ways in which you can secure those elements.

All elements in OneStream (whether an object or a data element) have one or more of the following security accesses associated with them:

- **Access**: Allows view access

- **Calculate**: Allows running scenario calculations

- **Certify**: Allows workflow certification

- **Display**: Allows an object to be seen *without* data

- **Execute**: Allows workflow execution of steps

- **Journal Create (Process)**: Allows creation of journals

- **Journal Approve**: Allows approval of journals

- **Journal Post**: Allows posting of journals

- **Maintain**: Allows maintenance

- **Manage**: Allows scenario data management jobs

- **Read**: Allows view access to entities or scenarios

- **Write**: Allows write access to entities or scenarios

## Access Naming Conventions

Depending upon which element you are securing, different security access options apply. Figure 3.14 shows the list along with related suffix naming conventions:

| Element | Type of Access | Examples |
|---|---|---|
| 001_APP_ <br><br> 001_SYS_ | Access | Application Roles and Pages <br><br> System Roles and Pages |
| 002_CUBE_ | _Access <br><br> _Maintain | Cube <br><br> ⊟ Security <br>     Access Group <br>     Maintenance Group |
| 003_SCN_ | _Read <br><br> _Write <br><br> _Calculate <br><br> _Manage | Scenarios <br><br> ⊟ Security <br>     Read Data Group <br>     Read and Write Data Group <br>     Calculate From Grids Group <br>     Manage Data Group |
| 004_ENT_ | _Display <br><br> _Read <br><br> _Write | Entities <br><br> ⊟ Security <br>     Display Member Group <br>     Read Data Group <br>     Read Data Group 2 <br>     Read and Write Data Group <br>     Read and Write Data Group 2 |
| 005_WF_ | _Access <br><br> _Maintain <br><br> _Execute <br><br> _Certify <br><br> _Journal Create (Process) <br><br> _Journal Approve <br><br> _Journal Post | Workflows <br><br> ⊟ Security <br>     Access Group <br>     Maintenance Group <br>     Workflow Execution Group <br>     Certification SignOff Group <br>     Journal Process Group <br>     Journal Approval Group <br>     Journal Post Group |
| 008_ACC_ <br><br> 008_FLW_ <br><br> 008_UD#_ | _Display | Accounts, Flow, UDs <br><br> ⊟ Security <br>     Display Member Group |

Figure 3.14

This type of access is the final piece of information needed to complete the security group naming conventions we started in the prior section. I prefer to add this access type as a suffix to the security group names.

For example, assume you want to create a security group for Germany Read (e.g., can view Germany data) users and then an additional group for Germany Write (e.g., can load Actuals, prepare Budget, or Forecast) users. When doing so, you would set up the following two security groups:

- 004_ENT_DE_READ

- 004_ENT_DE_WRITE

You would then assign the 004_ENT_DE_READ security group to all Germany entities as the Read Data Group entity property. Likewise, you would assign the 004_ENT_DE_WRITE security group as the Read and Write Data Group for those same entities. Notice that the ending suffix determines the type of access to an object; again, the final piece to complete security group naming conventions.

To demonstrate another example of using these suffixes to define the type of access, let's take the case of a corporate Workflow Profile. That Workflow Profile has an access, maintenance, execution, and certification security group assignment.

As such, there are security groups created for each of those types of access that all start with 005_WF_CORP and then – depending upon the type of access they are suffixed with – A, _M, _E, and _C to differentiate the workflow access. This is shown in Figure 3.15 below.

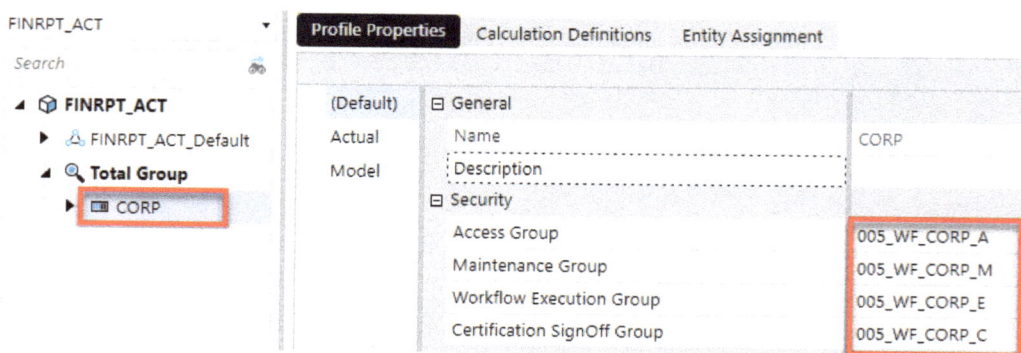

Figure 3.15

Now that we have a solid foundation in naming security groups using prefixes to denote the element and suffixes to denote the type of access, we will go over some common examples of types of security roles in the next chapter, and how their related security group access is established accordingly.

# 4

# Common Roles

## User Roles

Many companies will have common sets of users, including users who can view all data, users who may oversee the data load process, and other users who are not full administrators but are considered power users. Below, we will go through some common approaches to setting up these roles, knowing that specifics can be determined by each company's needs. The following are just some common examples.

In addition to some common types of user roles, and equally as important, determining who and how many people will be responsible for administering your OneStream environment and application(s) is key. In this chapter, we will also touch upon some ways to deliver different admin levels.

Lastly, we will cover some common user names you may want to set up to handle task automation.

## View Users

First, let's start with a common set of users: those who can view data that exists in a OneStream application. If you are a typical company, you will have a set of users upon whom you want to place no *data* restrictions, meaning this group of users should have the ability to view *all* cube data (cubes, scenarios, and entities).

You may have another set of users to whom you wish to grant view access, but with various restrictions as to *which* cube data, meaning they do not necessarily get to view all cubes, all scenarios, or all entities.

Both of these types of users can be accommodated. Let's start by setting up a basic user group that can view *all* data. There is an out-of-the-box application security role, View All Data, that will allow us to achieve this with minimal other setup required. This application security role negates the need for any specific cube, scenario, or entity data access.

By creating a security group (001_APP_VIEWALLDATA) and attaching this group to the application role object View All Data (as shown in Figure 4.1)…

Figure 4.1

…we can then set up our user security group (000_GRP_VIEWALL) and place this 001_APP_VIEWALLDATA group in our security group.

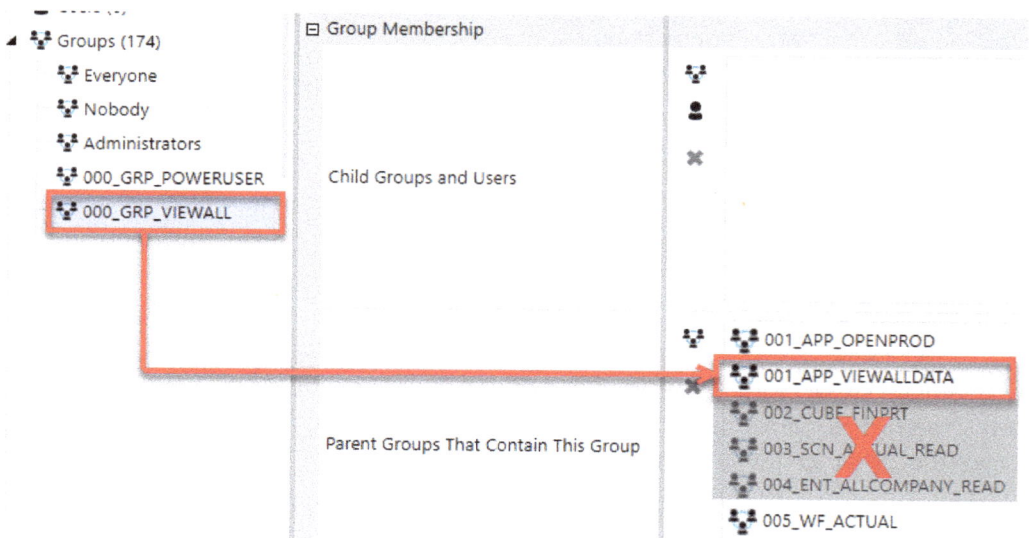

Figure 4.2

This out-of-the-box View All Data application security role negates the need for any 002 (cube), 003 (scenario), or 004 (entity)-specific data access as it inherently includes all cubes, all scenarios, and all entities within the application. Put another way, the View All Data application role supersedes the need for any other *data*-specific security.

So, this breaks our first rule of thumb from the prior chapter – that every 000 user security group should contain the first five elements. No sooner have we laid out basic rules in our naming convention than we break them! But this is a rare exception where an application security role (001) negates the need for specific data (002, 003, and 004) security groups.

As you can see in Figure 4.2, we embedded a workflow group (005) as well as an additional application security role group (001_APP_OPENPROD) as we still want to control which *objects* this user group can access. But, for the cube data security groups (002 to 004), this is a rare exception where the application security group (001_APP_VIEWALLDATA) supersedes them.

Now, let's consider the second type of view users that most companies have. These are users who will have access to view data; however, not necessarily *all* data. The approach for these types of users will be slightly different and a little more complex, and will follow the general rule of thumb that their security group will need 001 to 005 access.

Let's take the use case where you have a set of users that can view all Actual data but not any Budget or Forecast data. We start by setting up our user security group (000_GRP_VIEWALL_ACTUAL), but instead of utilizing the View All Data out-of-the-box application security role, which is too broad, we must embed specific data groups for 002 (cubes), 003 (Actual scenario), and 004 (entities) to achieve this, as shown in Figure 4.3:

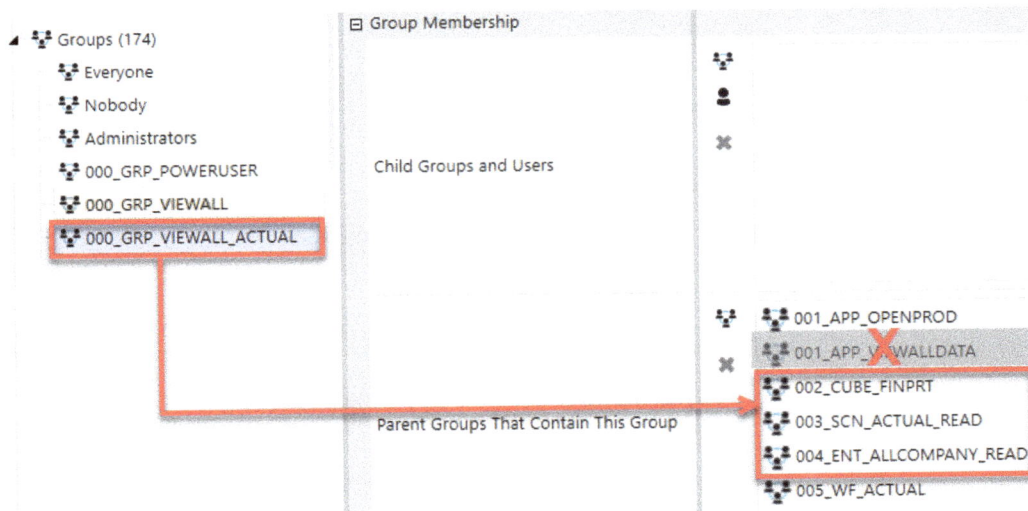

Figure 4.3

You can see that we have included only one scenario group (003_SCN_ACTUAL_READ) as we only want these view users to have access to Actual data. We, therefore, cannot utilize our previously created 001_APP_VIEWALLDATA security group because that group supersedes all data access and would give these individuals more access than is desired.

Chapter 4

With regard to the entity security group (004_ENT_ALLCOMPANY_READ), there are two approaches that can be taken with this data group. You can either assign the 004_ENT_ALLCOMPANY_READ group to the Read Data Group 2 as shown in Figure 4.4…

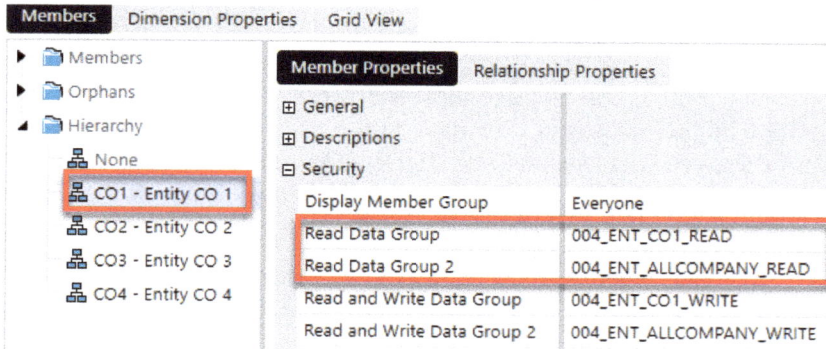

Figure 4.4

…or you can nest the 004_ENT_CO1_READ group into the Parent Groups That Contain This Group, as in Figure 4.5. Both will accomplish the same goal, that your users will obtain read data access to all entities.

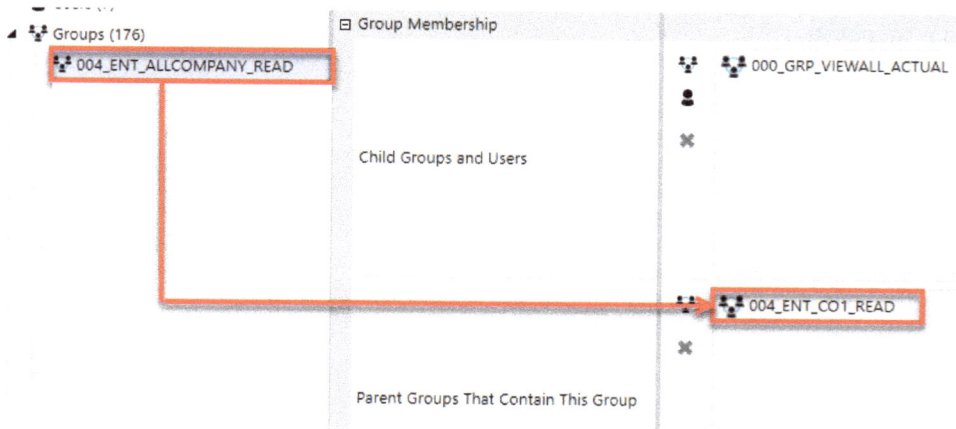

Figure 4.5

So, with view users, you have two common options: granting view access to *all* data or granting view access to specific subsets of data. The differences in setup can be seen in Figure 4.6.

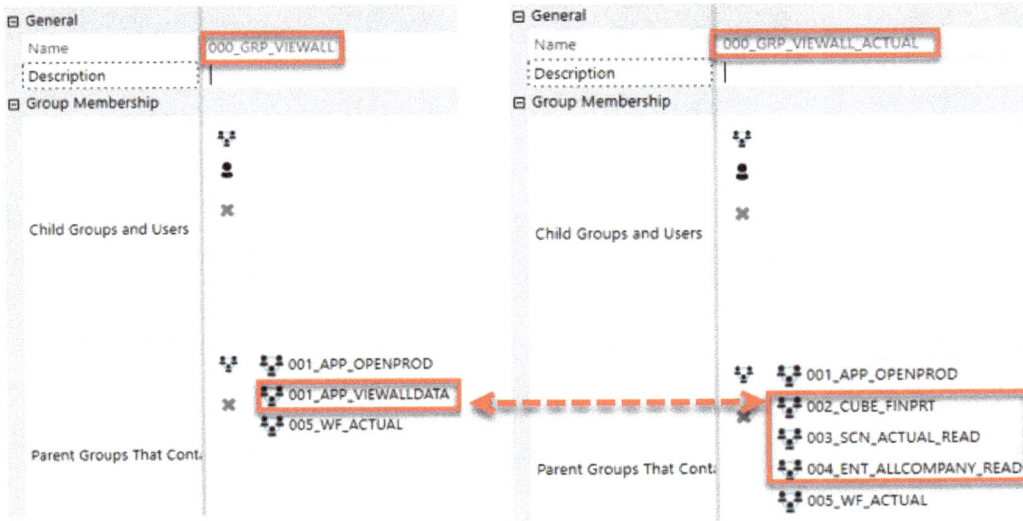

Figure 4.6

# Data Loaders

Another common type of user that a lot of companies have is a user who is responsible for the data load process. This data load process could be to load data from a source system (whether direct connect or via a flat file), such as an ERP or another financial system to OneStream, or even using data forms for manual input.

This group of users requires not only write access to the scenario (003) and the entity (004) to which data is being loaded, but will also require access to a specific Workflow Profile (005) where the data is being imported, as well as a specific application role (001).

Let's start with the Modify Data application role. Similar to what we saw in the prior section for viewing data, there is an out-of-the-box application object role to modify data. We will need to start by creating a security group (001_APP_MODIFYDATA) and attaching this group to the application role object Modify Data, as shown in Figure 4.7.

Figure 4.7

However, *unlike* the out-of-the-box View All Data application role, the Modify Data application role *does not* supersede the need for further data security around the cube (002), scenario (003), or entity (004). The Modify Data role, while required to allow a person to be able to edit or load OneStream data, is just the first piece needed to grant a user group the ability to load data.

To complete the data load user group, we will need to ensure we have write access to the scenario and entity to which we are loading, as well as the appropriate cube and workflow access. Let's look at how all these pieces come together in an example data load user group.

We can set up our user group for individuals that will load Actual data called 000_GRP_ACTUALDATALOAD. In that group, we will then nest the necessary pieces to complete this group's access.

As you can see in Figure 4.8, we have:

- a cube (002_CUBE_FINRPT) security group

- write access to the Actual scenario (003_SCN_ACTUAL_WRITE)

- write access to all entities, assuming this is a central load of data (004_ENT_ALLCOMPANY_WRITE)

- access to the import workflow where such data is loaded (005_WF_CORP_A)

- execute to the import workflow where such data is loaded (005_WF_CORP_E)

> **Note:** The workflow execution is what allows a data loader to execute the import, validate, and load steps for that Workflow Profile.

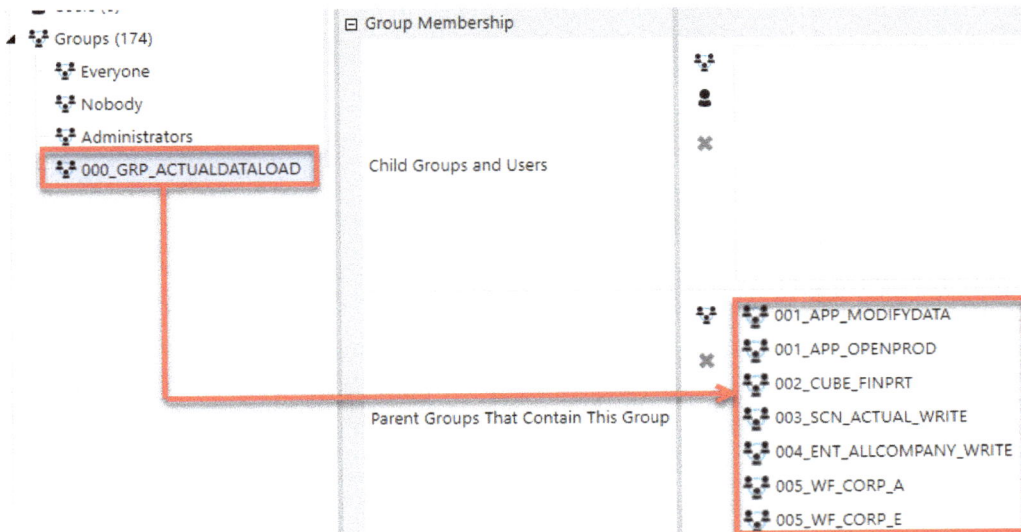

Figure 4.8

If any one of these elements is missing from a data load 000 user group, that user will not be able to import or manually adjust data. It is therefore important to understand that in addition to the out-of-the-box Modify Data role (001_APP_MODIFYDATA), the user will additionally need cube (002), scenario write (003), entity write (004), and appropriate workflow access and execution rights (005) to load data. This is again with the caveat that if any of those objects is set to Everyone, then it negates the need for that access (e.g., if cube access is set to Everyone, then no 002 group is required).

In this section, we covered a basic security group for data loaders and did not touch on the more in-depth data load topics of updating mappings or maintaining metadata. Those topics will be covered in Chapter 5, where we take a deeper dive into all application security elements.

The ability to update mappings and/or data sources is closely tied in with the data load process, but they can be a mutually exclusive sets of users. A company may have people responsible for the overall data load process, but that set of users may not have the ability to add new mappings, data sources, or update metadata. Chapter 5 will go into further detail about other data load considerations like maintaining mappings, data sources, and metadata.

## Power Users

The next user group we will touch upon is what might be considered power users. For each company, that could mean something slightly different. I think of power users as a group of individuals who fall somewhere between view users and your OneStream administrators – but that is a broad range and could still mean anything!

They are users who are perhaps savvy and responsible for *certain* aspects of your OneStream application, but are *not* full OneStream administrators.

By answering some of the design questions we laid out in Chapter 3, you will get a better understanding of what this group may be responsible for.

Let's imagine that the answers to the two questions below were as follows:

- Who will maintain what metadata? – power users, all metadata

- Who will maintain what reports? – power users, all reports

There is a lot to unpack with this user group in order to tackle these two items! First, let's start by creating this user group as 000_GRP_POWERUSER.

Okay, that part was easy.

Next, we will want to think through what out-of-the-box application pages and roles (001) this user group will need vis à vis the questions listed above, and then set up the corresponding 001_APP user groups that will allow the power user group to get to these elements.

Two out-of-the-box application roles facilitate metadata and Cube View maintenance: Manage Metadata and Manage Cube Views with related application pages (Dimension Library Page and Cube Views Page).

Similar to the View All Data application role, these two Manage roles supersede any other Cube View and metadata access. This means users in Manage Metadata will be able to modify all dimensions (entity, scenario, account, flow, and all UDs) regardless of their access to those specific dimensions. Similarly, users in Manage Cube Views will be able to maintain all Cube Views regardless of their rights to a particular Cube View. These application roles and pages are shown in Figure 4.9.

Figure 4.9

| Application Security Roles | | Application User Interface Roles | |
|---|---|---|---|
| AdministerApplication | | ApplicationLoadExtractPage | |
| AdministerDatabase | | ApplicationPropertiesPage | |
| AdministerApplicationWorkspac | | ApplicationSecurityRolesPage | |
| OpenApplication | 001_APP_OPENPROD | OnePlacePane | |
| ModifyData | 001_APP_MODIFYDATA | BookAdminPage | |
| ViewAllData | 001_APP_VIEWALLDATA | BusinessRulesPage | |
| CreateAuditAttachments | | CertificationQuestionsPage | |
| CreateFootnoteAttachments | | ClientUpdaterPage | |
| CertifyAndLockDescendants | | ConfirmationRulesPage | |
| UnlockAndUncertifyAncestors | | CubeAdminPage | |
| PreserveImportData | | CubeViewsPage | 001_APP_CVPAGE |
| RestoreImportData | | WorkspaceAdminPage | |
| UnlockWorkflowUnit | | DataManagementAdminPage | |
| ViewSourceDataAudit | | TaskSchedulerPage | |
| EncryptBusinessRules | | DataSourcesPage | |
| ManageApplicationProperties | | DimensionLibraryPage | 001_APP_DIMPAGE |
| ManageMetadata | 001_APP_MNG_METADATA | | |
| ManageFXRates | | | |
| LockFXRates | | | |
| UnlockFXRates | | | |
| ManageData | | | |
| ManageSmartIntegration | | | |
| ManageCubeViews | 001_APP_MNG_CUBEVIEWS | | |

If your company takes a simple approach and has a group of power users who maintain *all* metadata and *all* Cube Views, then adding these two manage groups to the 000_GRP_POWERUSER group – along with the related application pages – will be sufficient for this power user group to achieve those goals. Therefore, your power user group may appear as shown in Figure 4.10.

Chapter 4

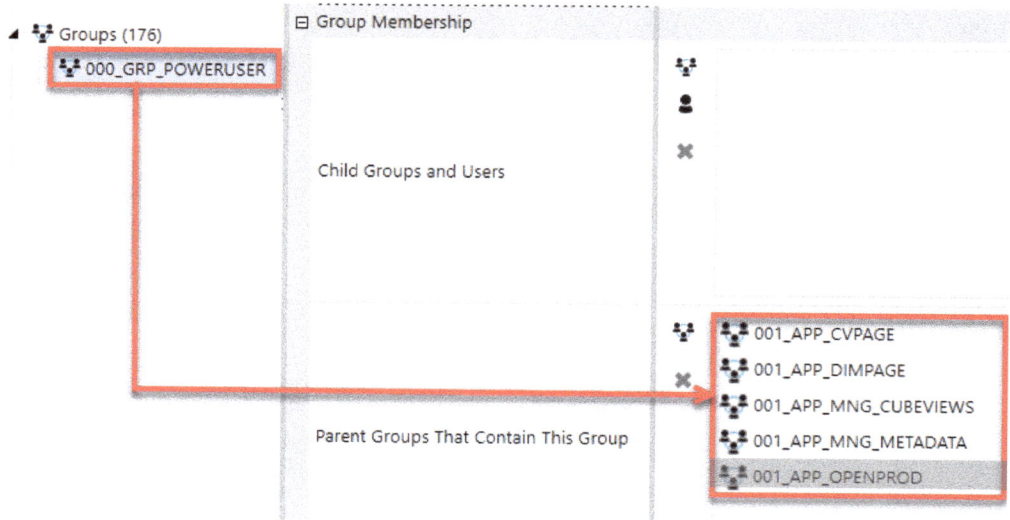

Figure 4.10

The end result for a user placed into this power user group (000_GRP_POWERUSER) will appear as shown in Figure 4.11. A power user with the security in Figure 4.10 will see both the Dimension page and the Cube View page and have full access to edit those pages.

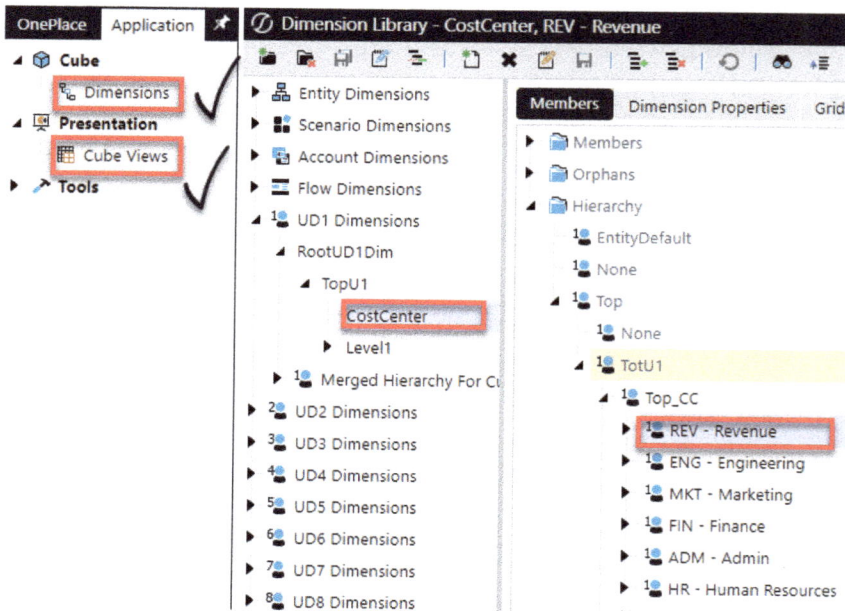

Figure 4.11

Instead, let's assume the simple approach for managing metadata and Cube Views will not work for your company. Say, for example, that your power users will maintain *certain* dimensions and Cube Views (e.g., the legal entity and reports for consolidations), but *not all* dimensions and Cube Views (e.g., the entity and reports used in an FP&A process are excluded).

Then, the simple approach in Figure 4.10 will not work for your company. Here, you do not want to grant your power users the two Manage application roles (Manage Metadata and Manage Cube Views) as they supersede all other security. Instead, you will need to grant your power user group the two pages (Cube Views Page and Dimension Library Page) and then individually layer on additional security groups that grant access to the specific dimensions.

Let's take the use case that you have power users who will maintain your financial reporting consolidation legal entities (004_ENT_FINPRT_M) and reports (008_CV_CONSOLCUBVIEWS_M), and another power user group that will maintain your management FP&A entities (004_ENT_MGMTRPT_M) and related Cube Views (008_CV_FPACUBEVIEWS_M).

In that case, we will set up two power user groups, and those groups will appear as shown on the right in Figure 4.12. Notice the difference between the simple power user group on the left, where we are able to leverage the two out-of-the-box application roles, versus the more complex setup, where we have to layer on individual access to particular metadata parts and Cube Views instead.

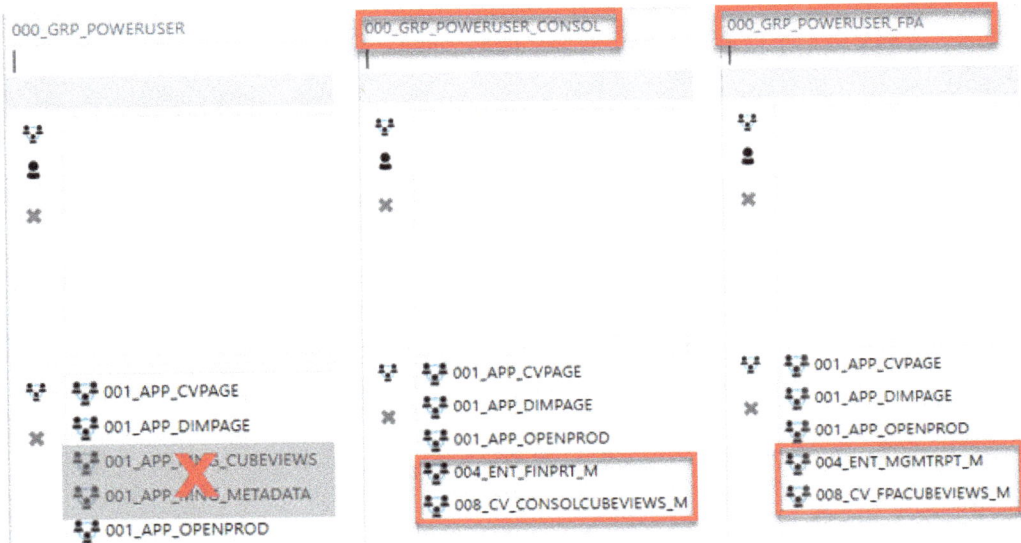

Figure 4.12

The takeaway is that OneStream can accommodate both the simple approach, where one group of users maintains all metadata and Cube Views, and the more complex approach, where such maintenance is limited to specific entities and specific Cube Views.

The important thing in all of these common user group examples is asking the right questions upfront to determine how simple or complex you need to go during the build process.

In general, and as mentioned previously, it is always easier to start simpler or more broadly with your security and layer on additional elements as needs arise. But conversely, if you know upfront that you will have different user groups responsible for different aspects of your application, and that you will need a more complex security model, the less reworking and turning back you will have down the road.

## Admin Users

The last group of users I want to touch upon in this chapter, but perhaps the most important, are a company's admin users. When we talk about administrators, these are the people who can sit across different groups of users with varying roles in an organization.

In the case of a simple company, administrators may be a small group of individuals who will have full access to everything OneStream-related within an environment. This group of individuals has full rights to set up users, assign security, and maintain all aspects of a company's OneStream environment. They are individuals who are trained and have a good understanding of administering OneStream. These folks are typically called your OneStream administrators.

Other companies, especially larger organizations or those more tightly controlled, may have other groups of administrators – such as finance admins – who are responsible for maintaining a single application but do not oversee security or other applications. Or, in the case of companies that have only one environment with both a development app and a production app, you may have groups of admins, some of whom have access to the production app and others who may only have access to the development app.

Another common group of admins is what could be called IT admins. These are the people who are responsible for overall security, adding users, and assigning groups to users, but are not knowledgeable in OneStream application administration itself.

So, the question becomes, how do you satisfy these various levels of OneStream administrators? The answer – as you might expect – starts back at the questions you ask during the design phase. Asking the right questions around what these various admins can or cannot do will help determine how simple or complex your approach will need to be.

As we learned in Chapter 1, there is a native OneStream `Administrators` security group in every customer environment. Anyone placed in this group will be able to see and do everything in the environment and administer all applications in that environment.

If your company has a small user base or favors simplicity over complexity, it may be enough to use the native Administrators security group and add a handful of individuals into this group whom you deem your OneStream admins. These are individuals who are trained in OneStream and know how to handle all aspects of your OneStream administration.

Adding users to this group is quick and easy. Any users who fall into this category will be added to the Child Groups and Users box of the native Administrators security group, as per Figure 4.13. Typically, no Parent Groups That Contain This Group are needed in the second box because, again, by nature, this group has full rights over all applications and elements within the environment.

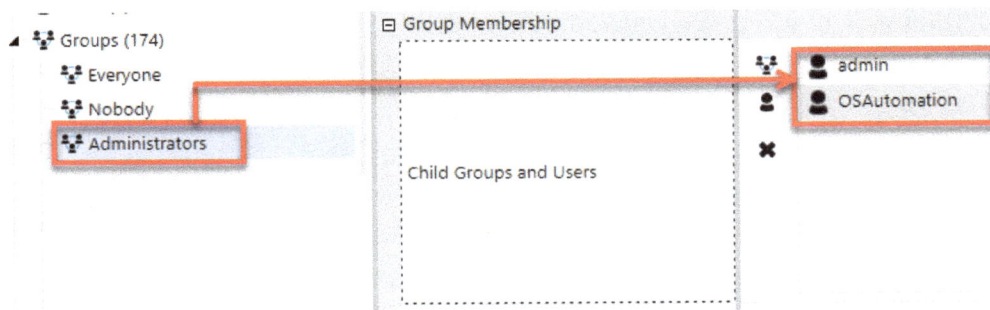

Figure 4.13

If you take this simple approach and use the native Administrators group, then you are assuming some level of risk – no matter how small – that individuals in this group have unlimited access to the environment and applications. Perhaps your organization is willing to assume that risk and will mitigate that risk by monitoring application audit and security reports (discussed in Chapter 8).

However, if your company desires different subsets of admins with varying levels of access, then the simple approach (i.e., only using the native Administrators group) will not work for you.

Fortunately, there are some out-of-the-box application and system security roles that can suit your company's needs. We will discuss these next.

Let's start with a group of users you may call finance admins or local admins. You want to grant them access to a particular application, but not necessarily *all* applications within an environment (e.g., access to a development app but not access to administer a production app). The Administer Application security role can satisfy this population of users.

How is this role different from the native Administrators group? Good question! The Administer Application role will grant users access to a *specific* application. These admins will be able to make updates and have admin rights over *that* application, but they will not automatically have access to other applications in that same environment or the System tab.

The Administer Application role is useful when you have multiple applications within one environment and you want to grant sets of user access to one application (e.g., development) but not access to administer other applications (e.g., production). This role does come with limitations, however.

Because this role does not include the System tab, these admins will not automatically have the rights to view things like the error log or set up new security groups that they wish to apply within the application. While there are limitations across the environment for this role, it is still a useful way to grant a set of users localized admin rights quickly.

You will want to set up an application role group (001_APP_ADMINISTER_DEV) and attach that role to this out-of-the-box application security role:

| Application Security Roles | |
|---|---|
| AdministerApplication | 001_APP_ADMINISTER_DEV |
| AdministerDatabase | Administrators |
| AdministerApplicationWorkspaceAssemblies | Administrators |
| OpenApplication | 001_APP_OPENPROD |
| ModifyData | 001_APP_MODIFYDATA |
| ViewAllData | 001_APP_VIEWALLDATA |

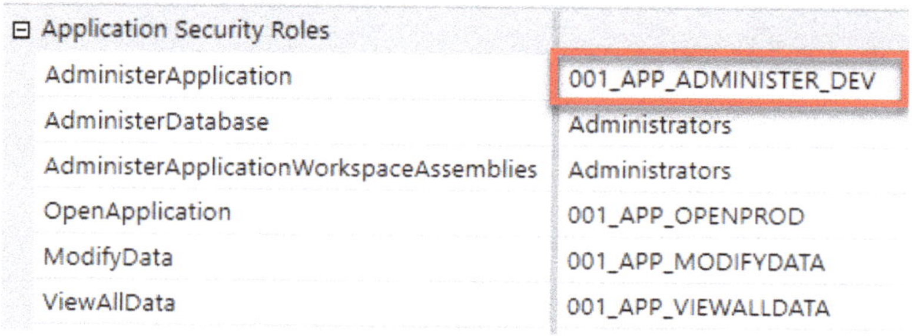

Figure 4.14

Then, set up a user group (000_GRP_ADMIN_DEV) with parent rights over this application role so you can place individuals in the Child Groups and Users box (see Figure 4.15) to leverage this out-of-the-box Administer Application role.

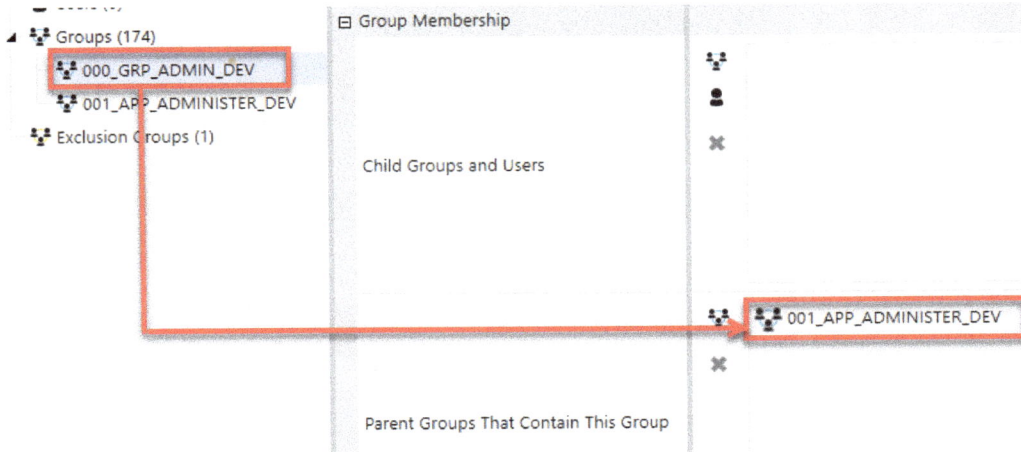

Figure 4.15

Next, let's assume you have a group of users who will be IT admins and whom you want to grant the ability to add users and assign groups to users, but *not* do anything else specific within individual applications. There are a couple of out-of-the-box system security roles intended for this purpose, as per Figure 4.16.

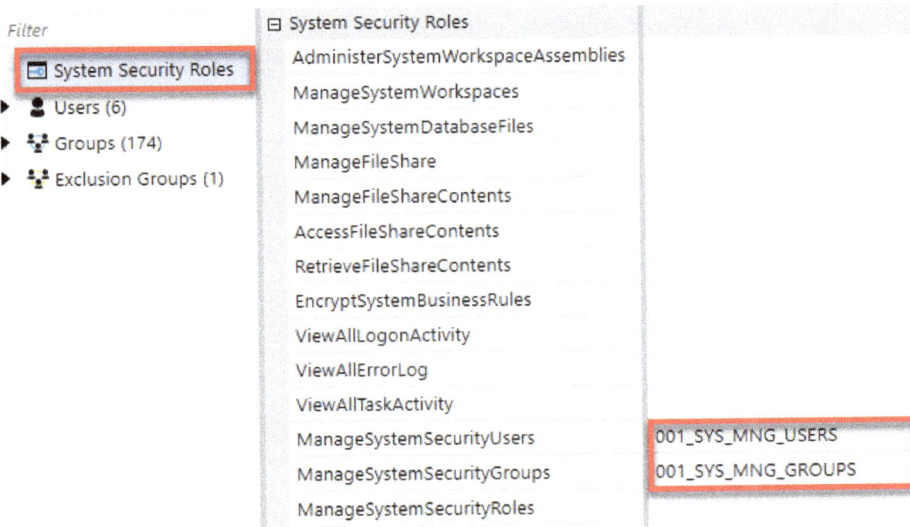

Figure 4.16

The Manage System Security Users and Manage System Security Groups roles can be found under the System Security Roles page on the System tab. By utilizing these two security roles and combining them in a user security group

(000_GRP_IT_ADMIN), you can place individuals in the Child Groups and Users box.

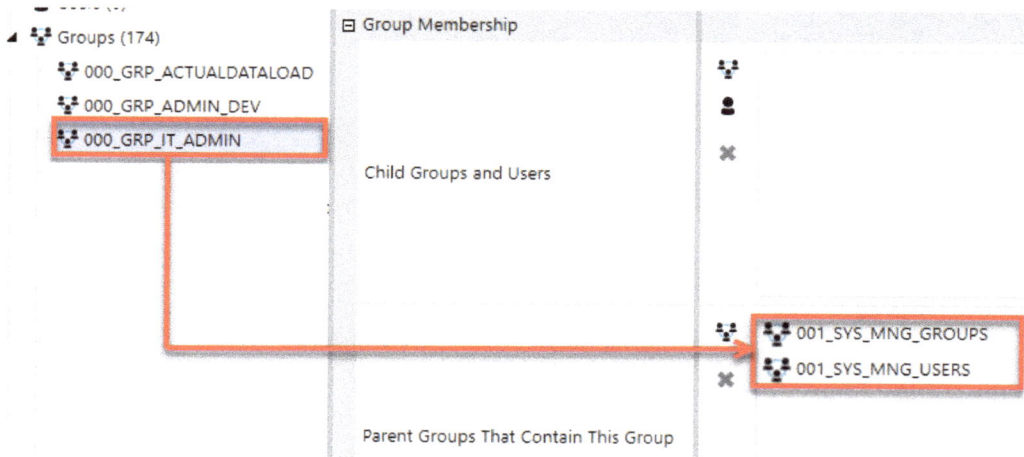

Figure 4.17

Where you go from these three examples, and how much access you grant beyond these examples, is ultimately up to your company's needs. Remember, OneStream security will not limit how much access you grant to various groups of users. The above are just three quick examples of ways to achieve different admin user groups.

It is important to remember – no matter how many varying levels of admin access you wish to grant to different sets of users – that you will always want at least one (in my opinion, at least two!) key user(s) who is part of the native Administrators group. After all, someone needs to have full access to your environment and applications to prevent you from locking yourself out.

And keep in mind that no matter how many individuals you place in the native Administrators group, the native Administrator user ID is *also* a part of this native user group.

## Native Users

Now that we have talked about some common user groups and how to set them up, I would be remiss if I did not also talk about some common users that you may want in your environment.

As discussed previously, every customer environment is set up with one Administrator native user from the get-go. This native user ID contains a random, complex password that is stored in OneStream's encrypted key value in Azure. OneStream Support uses this ID when you open a support case and grant them permission for troubleshooting or upgrades. This user ID cannot be edited and is inherently part of the Administrators native use group.

Many companies may have tasks they want to schedule to run overnight or in an automated fashion using OneStream's Task Scheduler. While you could do so using this native Administrator user ID, or even under the user ID of a specific named person, I prefer to set up a native system user ID to handle things like this.

The simple reason is that I do not like to mess with the Administrator ID set up in the beginning and used by support. But also, practically, if you set up tasks to run under a specific user, it will appear as if that individual is logged on at all hours of the night, running tasks in OneStream! While this may look good (or bad!?) for their work ethic, it does confuse matters when trying to ascertain what that person was really doing versus what was running on an automated schedule.

Therefore, I prefer to set up a native user ID to handle specific automated tasks. For example, you can create a native user ID called OS Automation. You can grant this specific user access to run various tasks overnight, such as data loads, consolidations, etc.

The benefit of setting up a native user for this purpose is that your OneStream administrators can control the password and access of this user. And anyone reviewing task activity logs will be able to easily spot tasks that individual users ran versus tasks that were scheduled to run automatically.

Another similar use case may be a native user ID that is used to run exports to another tool, such as Power BI. In this case, you may want to set up a native user ID called OS Export, for which your OneStream administrators can control the access and password. Again, it will be apparent in task activity logs what this user ID is running.

Another, although limited use case for setting up native IDs is during the build and testing phases. Security, even if simple, still needs to be tested before a UAT, parallel, or go-live. As a consultant or administrator, any time you set up new security or make changes to existing security, you will want to test that it has the intended access before placing users into that security group.

By setting up a native user ID such as Test_PowerUser or Test_ViewUser and putting that user into the new or changed security groups, you can then log in as that user and validate the security changes.

In Chapter 8, we will go into more detail about some easy ways to test security, but just know that the most efficient way to test security is to set up temporary native user IDs, place those users in 000 groups, and then log in as those users to confirm results. These native user IDs can be removed before a go-live, or temporarily added to test a security change and then removed.

It is important to understand that native IDs do count against your user license totals, so while they are useful to set up for various purposes, you will want to be mindful of how many of them you set up, and periodically review the list of native IDs to ensure compliance. And lastly, as we learned in Chapter 2, the ability to allow native authentication is a toggle setting of True/False in the Application Server Configuration Settings.

Chapter 4

Now that we have a solid foundation in design considerations, common use cases and roles, and example naming conventions, let's dive all the way into the application security layer in detail in Chapter 5, followed by the security layer in Chapter 6. The next two chapters will build upon this foundation and go through an exhaustive list of ways in which you can secure your OneStream applications and environments. Buckle up, as we are going to go deep!

# 5

# Application Security

In Chapter 2, we learned about the framework and environmental layer of your OneStream security. Then, in Chapters 3 and 4, we introduced the second layer of security within each environment, consisting of the application and system security layer.

In this chapter, we will take a deep dive into all security elements inside the application layer. As mentioned previously, the application layer of security is the one that most directly impacts your end-user's experience. It is the layer of security that will determine not only how secure your data is, but also drive overall end-user navigation and ease of use for your user population.

Many things contribute to the overall end-user experience within an application that go above and beyond a user's security. Things like your workflow design, report formatting, consolidation, and calculation performance, the level of data available, how frequently data is updated, and so on. But the one that typically leaves a first impression, and which puts guardrails around your end-users, is their application security.

Imagine entering a community with streets and homes in every direction but no street signs or house numbers posted anywhere. If you are looking for a particular home for which you have been provided the keys, but with no signs or house numbers, you may feel a bit overwhelmed.

Application security, if not applied correctly, can also leave a user feeling lost. You may be an end-user logging into OneStream regularly to perform tasks like running reports, entering key metrics, forecasting weekly sales, etc. But if you have access to everything upon entering OneStream, you will inevitably feel a bit lost. In addition to feeling lost, you may make wrong turns in OneStream and end up running reports for items to which you should not have access. Likewise, you could just end up clicking through various screens, trying to remember where you go to handle a task.

The right level of application security can help alleviate end-user confusion and protect application data. In this chapter, we will break down all the securable elements inside a OneStream application. It will be up to you to decide what the right level of security to apply within the application is, to suit your company and end-users' needs. This chapter outlines all the possibilities, but ultimately, you will need to make decisions on how to secure your application(s).

# Application Database

When talking about application security, it is important to note that there is one database per application within an environment. All application-specific tables reside in that database.

You can see this by going to the System > Tools > Database page within an application.

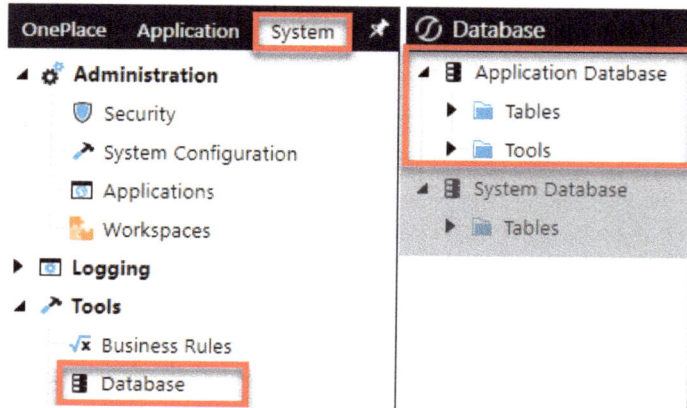

Figure 5.1

It may seem a bit counterintuitive that your *application* database can only be accessed from the System tab and not the Application tab, but this is because it is typically just your administrative users who will need access to view application tables. As such, access to application database tables is limited to being accessed from the System tab. Put a pin in that for now!

On the Database page (Figure 5.1), you will see that you have an Application Database. And, right below that, you have a System Database, which we will touch upon in detail in the next chapter.

These two databases contain all the tables necessary to support your application and system security. If you were to log out of a particular application, (e.g., OneStream Production application), and log into another application within the same environment, (e.g., OneStream Development), you will notice on this Database page that the Application Database tables pertain *only* to the application where you are logged in. In turn, the System Database tables remain constant.

This speaks to what we touched upon in Chapter 2; your framework database, aka the system database, applies to an entire environment. There is only one framework database per environment. However, application databases are one-for-one per application within an environment. Thus, to view application-specific tables, you must log into the application whose tables you want to view, even though you access them from the System tab.

Again, in this chapter, we are going to focus on the application security layer and thus be talking about all the elements that reside within the application database tables. In Chapter 6, we will go into the system database (aka framework) tables in detail.

# Application Roles & Pages

In the last chapter, we touched upon some out-of-the-box application security roles and application pages (application user interface roles) that exist in every customer environment. Let's review all of these in detail. These can be found on the Application > Tools > Security Roles page, as seen in Figure 5.2. There are 35 out-of-the-box application security roles and 25 application user interface roles.

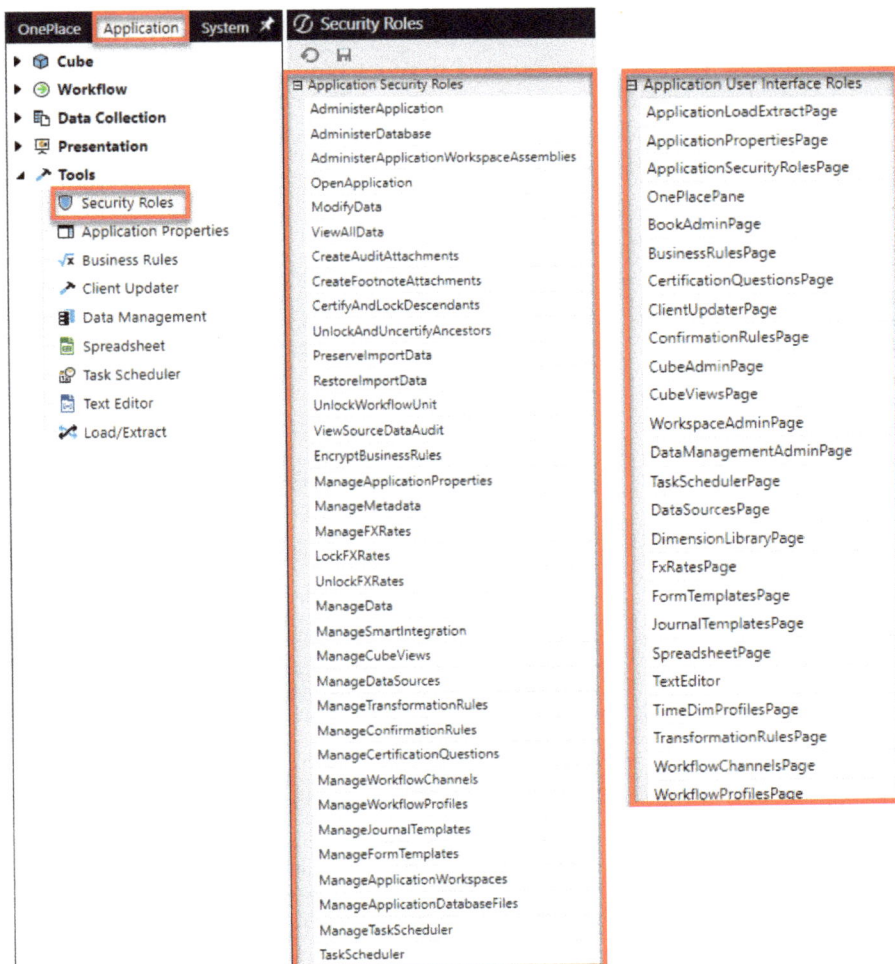

Figure 5.2

Chapter 5

# Application Security Roles

What are application security roles? They are standard (aka out-of-the-box) roles that exist in every customer application, and they allow you to manage different aspects of a OneStream application. The word "manage" can mean a lot of things. In terms of OneStream application security, it signifies the ability to do something within an application. It answers the question, "Can I do X?"

When granted, some of these roles will require additional security to do "X". Recall our example from Chapter 4, where we set up a security role to modify data (001_APP_MODIFYDATA). As we learned in Chapter 4, in addition to this role, a user will still need write access to an entity and scenario as well as cube and workflow access to be able to modify data.

However, there are some application roles that, when granted, supersede the need for additional security. Recall again the View All Data (001_APP_VIEWALLDATA) role covered in the previous chapter, which supersedes the need for specific entity scenario, cube, or workflow security.

The tables below go over the functionality of each of these 35 application security roles and point out which ones supersede the need for additional security versus which ones are prerequisites to do something but still require additional security to complete their functionality.

| Application Security Role | Description | Pre-requisites / + Additions |
|---|---|---|
| Administer Application<br>001_APP_ADMIN_DEV | Allows a user to administer a *particular* application. This is useful when multiple applications exist in one environment and different groups of users need to administer separate applications.<br><br>There are limitations to this local admin role. This role *cannot* change any application security roles or application user interface roles, nor get to the System tab.<br><br>📌 Your *application* database and error logs can only be accessed from the System tab. Therefore, if you do have local admins to whom you grant the Administer Application role, to allow them access to other admin functions, you may want to add the security shown to the right. | + 001_SYS_SYSPANE<br>+ 001_SYS_VIEWERRORLOG<br>+ 001_SYS_VIEWTASKLOG<br>+ 001_SYS_DBPAGE<br>+ 001_SYS_ERRORLOGPAGE<br>+ 001_SYS_TASKLOGPAGE |
| Administer Database<br>**Nobody** | This application-level role is intended for a few people who are allowed to mass-delete metadata and data, primarily using the database page.<br><br>This role type is unlike most other role types because administrators are not automatically given access to operations that require this role. | + 001_APP_ADMIN_DEV<br>+ 001_SYS_SYSPANE<br>+ 001_SYS_DBPAGE<br>Nobody **supersedes** Administrators |

| Application Security Role | Description | Pre-requisites / + Additions |
|---|---|---|
| **Administer Application Workspace Assemblies**<br>001_APP_WSADMIN | This allows the user to edit any assemblies. This applies to all dashboard groups within the generic default Workspace and all non-default Workspaces.<br><br>Maintenance Unit security determines access. | + 001_APP_WSPAGE<br><br>+ 008_DMU_X_M |
| **Analytics Api**<br>**Nobody** | Allows a user to access OneStream connectors to pull data into external systems. The role becomes available when access to Power BI is granted. | Access to Power BI connector |
| **Open Application**<br>001_APP_OPENPROD | Allows a user to see and open various applications. | N/A |
| **Modify Data**<br>001_APP_MODIFYDATA | Allows a user to modify data. The user is basically a read-only user throughout this application if he/she does not have this role.<br><br>However, users in this group will still need cube, entity, and scenario modify rights to edit data. | + 002_CUBE_<br><br>+ 003_SCN_X_WRITE<br><br>+ 004_ENT_X_WRITE<br><br>+ 005_WF_X_A/E |
| **View All Data**<br>001_APP_VIEWALLDATA | Allows a group of users to view all data in the application.<br><br>**Supersedes** all other metadata (cube, entity, and scenario) access. | N/A |
| **Create Audit Attachments**<br>001_APP_AUDITATTACH | Allows a user to create audit data attachments for supporting documentation.<br><br>Attachment Type<br>Annotation Detail<br>Annotation (Used With View Member)<br>Assumptions (Used With View Member)<br>Audit Comment (Used With View Member)<br>Footnote (Used With View Member)<br>Variance Explanation (Used With View Member)<br>Annotation Detail<br>Assumptions Detail<br>Audit Comment Detail | + 002_CUBE_<br><br>+ 003_SCN_X_READ/WRITE<br><br>+ 004_ENT_X_READ/WRITE<br><br>+ 008_CV_ |

| Application Security Role | Description | Pre-requisites / + Additions |
|---|---|---|
| **Create Footnote Attachments**<br>001_APP_FNATTACH | Allows a user to create a footnote attachment for supporting documentation.<br><br>Attachment Type<br>Annotation Detail<br>Audit Comment (Used With View Member)<br>Footnote (Used With View Member)<br>Variance Explanation (Used With View Member)<br>Annotation Detail<br>Assumptions Detail<br>Audit Comment Detail<br>Footnote Detail<br>Variance Explanation Detail | + 002_CUBE_<br><br>+ 003_SCN_X_READ/WRITE<br><br>+ 004_ENT_X_READ/WRITE<br><br>+ 008_CV_ |
| **Certify and Lock Descendants**<br>001_APP_CERTIFYLOCK | Allows a user to certify and lock descendants from the workflow. Users will need to execute and certify the appropriate workflow. | + 005_WF_X_A/E/C |
| **Unlock and UnCertify Ancestors**<br>001_APP_UNLOCKUNCERT | Allows a user to uncertify and unlock ancestors from the workflow. Users will need to execute and certify the appropriate workflow, as well as access to certify and lock. | + 005_WF_X_A/E/C<br><br>+ 001_APP_UNLOCKWF<br><br>+ 001_APP_CERTIFYLOCK |
| **Preserve Import Data**<br>001_APP_PRESERVEDATA | Allows a user to preserve data if changes need to be made. A user will lock the workflows and then preserve imported data when changes need to be made. The workflow can then be unlocked so changes can be made. | + 005_WF_X_A/E<br><br>+ 003_SCN_X_READ/WRITE |
| **Restore Import Data**<br>001_APP_RESTOREDATA | Allows a user to restore imported data to the original state. The workflow will need to be unlocked so data can be restored. | + 005_WF_X_A/E<br><br>+ 003_SCN_X_READ/WRITE |
| **Unlock Workflow Unit**<br>001_APP_UNLOCKWF | Allows a user to unlock or lock a *particular* Workflow Unit. | + 005_WF_X_A/E |
| **View Source Data Audit** | This is a legacy security role and is under review for relevance to future platform versions. | N/A |
| **Encrypt Business Rules**<br>**Nobody** | Allows a user to encrypt and decrypt a rule from the business rule screen on the Application tab, if the user is in the role. | Nobody **supersedes** Administrators |
| **Manage Application Properties**<br>001_APP_MNG_APPPROP | Allows a user to update this application's properties. | + 001_APP_APPPROPPAGE |
| **Manage Metadata**<br>001_APP_MNG_METADATA | Allows a user to edit ***all*** metadata under the dimension library for this application.<br><br>**Supersedes** all other dimension access. To restrict a person to only edit *specific* metadata dimensions, you cannot use this role and must individually provision dimensions. | + 001_APP_DIMPAGE |

| Application Security Role | Description | Pre-requisites / + Additions |
|---|---|---|
| **Manage FX Rates**<br>001_APP_MNG_FXRATES | Allows a user to *update* FX rates. | + 001_APP_FXPAGE |
| **Lock FX Rates**<br>001_APP_LOCKFX | Allows a user to *lock* FX rates. | + 001_APP_FXPAGE |
| **Unlock FX Rates**<br>001_APP_UNLOCKFX | Allows a user to *unlock* FX rates. | + 001_APP_FXPAGE |
| **Manage Data**<br>001_APP_MNG_DATA | Allows a user to manage data in all aspects, including but not limited to exporting data and clearing data completed through data management.<br><br>**Supersedes** all other data management access. To restrict a person to only edit *specific* data management units, you cannot use this role and must individually provision data management units. | + 001_APP_DMPAGE |
| **Manage Smart Integration** | This is a future security role and is under review for relevance to future platform versions. | N/A |
| **Manage Cube Views**<br>001_APP_MNG_CUBEVIEWS | Allows a user to create new Cube Views and manage Cube View groups and profiles.<br><br>**Supersedes** Cube View *group* access but does not supersede Cube View *Profile* access. To manage Cube View Profiles, a user will need maintenance rights to the profile(s). | + 001_APP_CVPAGE<br><br>+ 002_CUBE_<br><br>+ 008_CV_ |
| **Manage Data Sources**<br>001_APP_MNG_DATASOURCES | Allows a user to create new data sources, which can subsequently be used to import data via a workflow import profile. | + 001_APP_DSPAGE<br><br>+ 002_CUBE_ |
| **Manage Transformation Rules**<br>001_APP_MNG_MAPPING | Allows a user to create new transformation rules and manage transformation rules groups and profiles.<br><br>**Supersedes** transformation rule group and profile maintenance access. | + 001_APP_MAPPINGPAGE<br><br>+ 002_CUBE_ |
| **Manage Confirmation Rules**<br>001_APP_MNG_CONFIRM | Allows a user to create new confirmation rules and manage confirmation rules groups and profiles.<br><br>**Supersedes** confirmation rule group and profile maintenance access. | + 001_APP_CONFIRMPAGE<br><br>+ 002_CUBE_ |
| **Manage Certification Questions**<br>001_APP_MNG_CERT | Allows a user to create new certification questions and manage certification question groups and profiles.<br><br>**Supersedes** certification rule group and profile maintenance access. | + 001_APP_CERTPAGE<br><br>+ 002_CUBE_ |
| **Manage Workflow Channels**<br>001_APP_MNG_WFCHANNELS | Allows users to create new workflow channels. | + 001_APP_WFCHANPAGE |
| **Manage Workflow Profiles**<br>001_APP_MNG_WFPROFILES | Allows a user to create new Workflow Profiles.<br><br>**Supersedes** Workflow Profile maintenance access. | + 001_APP_WFPROFILEPAGE<br><br>+ 002_CUBE_ |

Chapter 5

| Application Security Role | Description | Pre-requisites / + Additions |
|---|---|---|
| Manage Journal Templates<br>001_APP_MNG_JOURNALS | Allows a user to create new journal templates and manage journal groups and profiles.<br><br>**Supersedes** journal template group and profile maintenance access. | + 001_APP_JOURNALPAGE<br>+ 002_CUBE_ |
| Manage Form Templates<br>001_APP_MNG_FORMS | Allows a user to create new form templates and manage forms groups and profiles.<br><br>**Supersedes** form template group and profile maintenance access. | + 001_APP_FORMPAGE<br>+ 002_CUBE_ |
| Manage Application Workspaces<br>001_APP_MNG_WSAPP | Allows a user to create new application dashboards and manage dashboard groups and profiles.<br><br>**Supersedes** Dashboard *profile* access but does not supersede dashboard *group* access. To manage dashboard groups, a user will need maintenance rights to the group(s). | + 001_APP_WSPAGE<br>+ 008_DMU_X_M |
| Manage Application Database Files<br>001_APP_MNG_FILES | By default, a user has full access to his/her user folders and files in the application file explorer.<br><br>This role **supersedes** all access, allowing users read and write access to *all* public folders and files. | N/A |
| Manage Task Scheduler<br>001_APP_MNG_TASKSCH | Allows a user to view, create, edit, delete, enable or disable **all** tasks. | + 001_APP_TASKSCHPAGE |
| Task Scheduler<br>001_APP_TASKSCHEDULER | Allows a user to view, create, edit, delete, enable or disable *their own* tasks. You can view all user tasks, but only edit your own. | + 001_APP_TASKSCHPAGE |

Figure 5.3

The above table demonstrates that you have a lot of flexibility with out-of-the-box security roles, allowing you to determine what your users can do within an application. These application security roles form a starting point to allow you to put guardrails around your users. Next, let's talk about the roles that will determine where a person can navigate in OneStream.

## Application User Interface Roles

I like to think of application user interface roles simply as application pages. While application security roles answer "Can I do X?", application user interface roles answer "Can I get to X?"

You may want to allow some users to view X, but you do not want to allow them to manage X. So while application roles and application pages *can* go hand-in-hand (meaning that if a person can do X, they will also need to get to X) they can also be separate in the case of allowing a user to view but not manage X.

Therefore, as mentioned in Chapter 3, when applying security to both application security roles and application pages (001_APP), you will want to use distinct groups for each so that you can separate the viewer from the doer.

Having said that, application user interface roles are very straightforward and literally mean exactly what they say. Simply put, they will allow certain users to reach that page within OneStream. They are starting to form the basis of what paths you illuminate with street signs (thinking back to our neighborhood analogy) to point your users in the right direction.

There is no need to overcomplicate application pages. You want to ask yourself, "Do I want certain users, everyone, or only administrators to get to these pages?" If the answer is everyone or only administrators, then you can use the native security groups of Everyone or Administrators on these pages.

Suppose you want to grant certain pages to subsets of users. In that case, you will set up corresponding security groups (001_APP_XPAGE), assign the groups to those pages, and then nest these group(s) into your various user groups (000_GRP).

*Not* granting users the ability to get to certain pages is the primary method of putting fences around items in OneStream, and limiting your end-user from feeling overwhelmed. Remember, security can be used to control the overall end-user experience in addition to protecting your application.

For example, if a user only needs to *view* Cube Views but will never need to *maintain* Cube Views, there is no need to grant the user access to the Cube Views page. Your user will access Cube View reports through OnePlace, workflows, dashboards, or perhaps even Excel. There is no need to grant that user access to the Cube Views page, as that will only serve to confuse your end-user. We will revisit this in the Reporting Security section of this chapter.

Once a user has access to reach a page, then additional layers of object security, introduced in Chapter 3 and discussed in more detail later in this chapter, will apply which will determine *what* the person can see or do once they get to that page. Figure 5.4 lists all application user interface roles and what access they will grant.

| Application User Interface Role | Description of Access |
|---|---|
| **Application Load Extract Page**<br>**Administrators** | Allows access to the application load/extract screen.<br><br>Load   Extract<br><br>File Name |
| **Application Properties Page**<br>001_APP_APPPROPPAGE | Allows access to the application properties screen where global time and scenario, currencies, standard formats, company logos, workflow channels, etc., can be edited.<br><br>**General**  Dimensions  Standard Reports<br><br>(Default) — Global Point Of View<br>Actual — Global Scenario — None<br>Administration — Global Time — 2024<br>Budget — Company Information<br>Control — Company Name<br>Flash — Logo File (png, height ~50 pixels)<br>Forecast — Workflow Channels<br>FXModel — UD Dimension Type For Workflow Channels — UD7<br>History — Formatting<br>LongTerm — Number Format — N2<br>Model — Currencies<br>Operational — Currency Filter — CAD, EUR, GBP, USD<br>Plan — Transformation (Default)<br>Sustainability — Enforce Global POV — False<br>Target — Allow Loads Before Workflow View Year — False<br>Tax — Allow Loads After Workflow View Year — False<br>Variance — Certification (Default)<br>Lock After Certify — False |
| **Application Security Roles Page**<br>**Administrators** | Allows access to the application security screen, where all security roles for an application can be edited.<br><br>⊞ Application Security Roles<br>⊞ Application User Interface Roles |

| | |
|---|---|
| **OnePlace Pane**<br>**Everyone** | This tab is the starting point for all users in OneStream. It allows users to navigate to the workflows, Cube Views, dashboards, and documents to which they have access.<br><br>OnePlace<br>Workflow<br>Cube Views<br>Dashboards<br>Documents |
| **Book Admin Page**<br>001_APP_BOOKPAGE | Allows access to the Book Designer screen.<br><br>Designer   Preview |
| **Business Rules Page**<br>001_APP_BRPAGE | Allows access to the business rules screen.<br><br>Finance<br>Parser<br>Connector<br>Conditional Rule<br>Derivative Rule<br>Cube View Extender<br>Dashboard Data Set<br>Dashboard Extender<br>Dashboard XFBR String<br>Extensibility Rules<br>Spreadsheet |
| **Certification Questions Page**<br>001_APP_CERTPAGE | Allows access to the certification questions.<br><br>Question Groups<br>Question Profiles |

| | |
|---|---|
| **Client Updater Page**<br>**Administrators** | Allows access to the screen that determines if a user's OneStream Excel Addin is up to date.<br><br>Current OneStream Version: **8.4.0.16413**<br><br>Client Module<br>OneStream Excel Addin ▾<br><br>Installation Folder: C:\Program Files (x86)\OneStream Software\OneStreamExcelAddIn<br>OneStream Excel AddIn OneStream Version: **8.4.0.16413**<br>**OneStream Excel AddIn is up to date.** |
| **Confirmation Rules Page**<br>001_APP_CONFIRMPAGE | Allows access to the confirmation rules screen.<br><br>▶ •• **Rule Groups**<br>▶ ⁂ **Rule Profiles** |
| **Cube Admin Page**<br>001_APP_CUBEPAGE | Allows access to the cube admin screen.<br><br>FINRPT<br>FINRPT_Base<br>Cube Properties  Cube Dimensions  Cube References  Data Access  Integration |
| **Cube Views Page**<br>001_APP_CVPAGE | Allows access to the Cube Views screen.<br><br>▶ **Cube View Groups**<br>▶ **Cube View Profiles** |
| **Workspace Admin Page**<br>001_APP_WSPAGE | Allows access to the dashboard Workspace admin screen.<br><br>▶ **Workspaces**<br>▶ **Dashboard Profiles**<br>▶ **Cube View Profiles** |
| **Data Management Admin Page**<br>001_APP_DMPAGE | Allows access to the data management admin screen.<br><br>▶ •• **Data Management Groups** |

| | |
|---|---|
| **Task Scheduler Page**<br>001_APP_TASKSCHPAGE | Allows access to the task scheduler screen.<br><br> |
| **Data Sources Page**<br>001_APP_DSPAGE | Allows access to the data sources screen.<br><br> |
| **Dimension Library Page**<br>001_APP_DIMPAGE | Allows access to the dimension library screen.<br><br> |
| **FX Rates Page**<br>001_APP_FXPAGE | Allows access to the FX rates screen.<br><br> |

| | |
|---|---|
| **Form Templates Page**<br>001_APP_FORMPAGE | Allows access to the form templates screen.<br><br> |
| **Journal Templates Page**<br>001_APP_JOURNALPAGE | Allows access to the journal templates screen.<br><br> |
| **Spreadsheet Page**<br>001_APP_SPREADSHEETPAGE | Allows access to the Spreadsheet screen inside a OneStream application.<br><br> |
| **Text Editor Page**<br>**Administrators** | Allows access to the text editor screen, which is used to create, edit, and view text documents like those created in Microsoft Word.<br><br> |

| Time Dim Profiles Page<br>001_APP_TIMEPROFILEPAGE | Allows access to the time profiles and calendars within an application. For example, this is where the short and long descriptions for a time period can be updated. 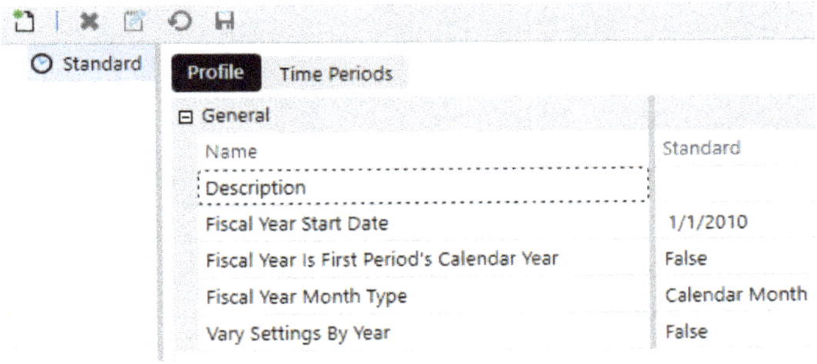<br> |
| --- | --- |
| Transformation Rules Page<br>001_APP_MAPPINGPAGE | Allows access to the transformation rules screen. <br> |
| Workflow Channels Page<br>001_APP_WFCHANPAGE | Allows access to the workflow channels screen. 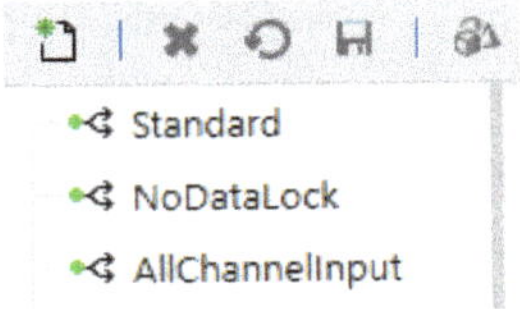<br> |
| Workflow Profiles Page<br>001_APP_WFPROFILEPAGE | Allows access to the Workflow Profiles screen. 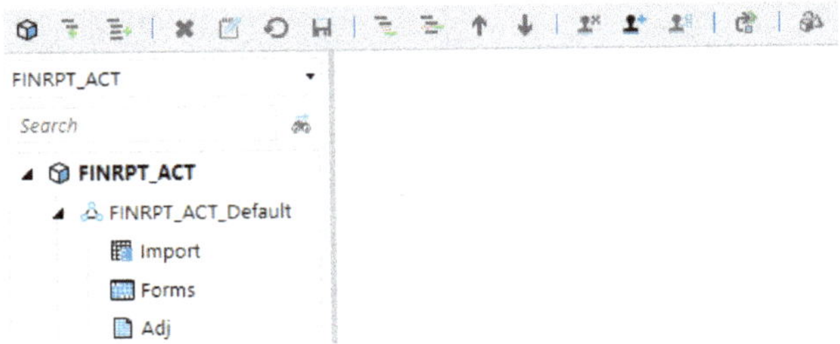<br> |

Figure 5.4

Chapter 5

A common theme with application user interface roles is that they allow a user to get to a specific application page; however, other security access will determine what that user can see and do once on that page. For example, a user may have access to the Cube Views page (001_APP_CVPAGE), but the user will only have view or modify access to Cube View groups and profiles on that page as determined by those additional security groups (e.g., 008_CV_A/M). This is shown in Figure 5.5.

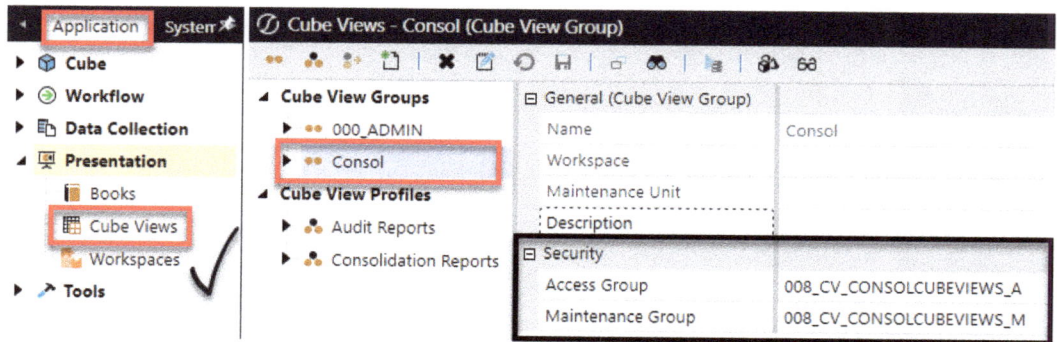

Figure 5.5

As mentioned previously, of the 35 application security roles, two-thirds (20) of them require additional page access via a corresponding application user interface role. This means if a person can do X, they will naturally also need to be able to navigate to X.

The last item worth noting is the naming convention we established in Chapter 3. All application roles start with 001_APP, as this is the *first* layer of security once you are logged into an application.

To bring all these out-of-the-box roles together, Figure 5.6 shows the correlation between application security roles (doer) and application user interface roles (viewer).

| Application Security Role | + | Application User Interface Role |
|---|---|---|
| Administer Database<br>001_APP_DBADMIN | + | Database Page<br>001_SYS_SYSPANE |
| Administer Application Workspace Assemblies<br>001_APP_WSADMIN | + | Workspace Admin Page<br>001_APP_WSPAGE |
| Manage Application Properties<br>001_APP_MNG_APPPROP | + | Application Properties Page<br>001_APP_APPPROPPAGE |
| Manage Metadata<br>001_APP_MNG_METADATA | + | Dimension Library Page<br>001_APP_DIMPAGE |
| Manage FX Rates<br>001_APP_MNG_FXRATES<br>Lock FX Rates<br>001_APP_LOCKFX<br>Unlock FX Rates<br>001_APP_UNLOCKFX | + | FX Rates Page<br>001_APP_FXPAGE |
| Manage Data<br>001_APP_MNG_DATA | + | Data Management Admin Page<br>001_APP_DMPAGE |
| Manage Cube Views<br>001_APP_MNG_CUBEVIEWS | + | Cube Views Page<br>001_APP_CVPAGE |
| Manage Data Sources<br>001_APP_MNG_DATASOURCES | + | Data Sources Page<br>001_APP_DSPAGE |
| Manage Transformation Rules<br>001_APP_MNG_MAPPING | + | Transformation Rules Page<br>001_APP_MAPPINGPAGE |
| Manage Confirmation Rules<br>001_APP_MNG_CONFIRM | + | Confirmation Rules Page<br>001_APP_CONFIRMPAGE |
| Manage Certification Questions<br>001_APP_MNG_CERT | + | Certification Questions Page<br>001_APP_CERTPAGE |
| Manage Workflow Channels<br>001_APP_MNG_WFCHANNELS | + | Workflow Channels Page<br>001_APP_WFCHANPAGE |
| Manage Workflow Profiles<br>001_APP_MNG_WFPROFILES | + | Workflow Profiles Page<br>001_APP_WFPROFILEPAGE |
| Manage Journal Templates<br>001_APP_MNG_JOURNALS | + | Journal Templates Page<br>001_APP_JOURNALPAGE |
| Manage Form Templates<br>001_APP_MNG_FORMS | + | Form Templates Page<br>001_APP_FORMPAGE |
| Manage Application Workspaces<br>001_APP_MNG_WSAPP | + | Workspace Admin Page<br>001_APP_WSPAGE |
| Manage Task Scheduler<br>001_APP_MNG_TASKSCH<br>Task Scheduler<br>001_APP_TASKSCHEDULER | + | Task Scheduler Page<br>001_APP_TASKSCHPAGE |

Figure 5.6

Now that we have discussed the out-of-the-box application security roles and pages, let's move on to the myriad of objects *within* an application that can be secured.

# Application Objects

After granting application security roles and application user interface roles (001_APP), the next step is to determine how to secure the hundreds of objects that appear within a OneStream application. And when I say hundreds, that is no joke!

Thinking again about securing a home, application security roles and application user interface roles are like securing the windows and doors. They are the first point of entry to a specific application, after being allowed into the community (aka the environment layer).

If application roles are the windows and doors, then **application objects** are all the items found inside a home. As you can imagine, there are hundreds, if not thousands, of individual objects inside one's home!

A OneStream application will have its own set of objects whose numbers are infinitely scalable depending on each company's needs.

Because application objects can be limitless, I like to group them into 13 categories. These 13 categories are not standard OneStream groupings, merely a way to organize objects into more manageable pieces:

1. Metadata (cubes, dimensions, entities, accounts, flow, UD1-8)
2. Business Rules
3. Certifications (groups and profiles)
4. Confirmations (groups and profiles)
5. Cube Views (groups and profiles)
6. Workspaces / Dashboards (maintenance units and profiles)
7. Data Management (groups)
8. Data Sources
9. Explorer (files and folders)
10. Forms (groups and profiles)
11. Journals (groups and profiles)
12. Transformations (groups and profiles)
13. Workflows (profiles)

Within each of these 13 categories, you can have a limitless number of individual objects. For example, your application may have multiple Cube View groups and Cube View Profiles. Each of those can be individually secured if needed.

Or, if you are taking a simple approach to security, you can only secure access to the Cube Views page and thus leave all individual Cube View groups and profiles open to everyone.

The other important item to remember with application object-level security is the naming convention we established in Chapter 3. Application *object* security groups will start with 002 to 009, which helps distinguish them from application role groups (001) discussed in the prior section.

Lastly, let's not forget that application objects have different ways in which they can be secured, as shown in Figure 3.14 in Chapter 3.

There are two primary security groups (access and maintenance) that pertain to *most* application objects, and then additional groups that are specific to metadata and workflows, as shown in Figure 5.7 below.

|  | Access | Maintenance |
|---|---|---|
| Business Rules | Yes | Yes |
| Certification Groups & Profiles | Yes | Yes |
| Confirmation Group & Profiles | Yes | Yes |
| Cubes | Yes | Yes |
| Cube View Group & Profiles | Yes | Yes |
| Dashboard Mnt Unit & Profiles | Yes | Yes |
| Data Mgmt Group | Yes | Yes |
| Data Sources | Yes | Yes |
| Dimensions | Yes | Yes |
| Explorer Files & Folders | Yes | Yes |
| Form Group & Profiles | Yes | Yes |
| Journal Group & Profiles | Yes | Yes |
| Transformation Group & Profiles | Yes | Yes |

|  | Display | Read | Write | Calculate | Manage |
|---|---|---|---|---|---|
| Members - Account, Flow, Uds | Yes | N/A | N/A | N/A | N/A |
| Members - Entity | Yes | Yes | Yes | N/A | N/A |
| Members - Scenarios | N/A | Yes | Yes | Yes | Yes |

|  | Access | Maintenance | Execution | Certification | Journal Process | Journal Approval | Journal Post |
|---|---|---|---|---|---|---|---|
| General Workflows | Yes | Yes | Yes | Yes | N/A | N/A | N/A |
| Adjustment Workflows | Yes | Yes | Yes | Yes | Yes | Yes | Yes |

Figure 5.7

# Application Tables

So, where are all these limitless application objects stored? They are stored in the application database discussed earlier in this chapter, which is accessed from the System > Tools > Database page.

There are over 150 out-of-the-box tables in any given application. That number will grow if any Solution Exchange solutions or custom tables have been added to an application, as they will also appear on the application database page.

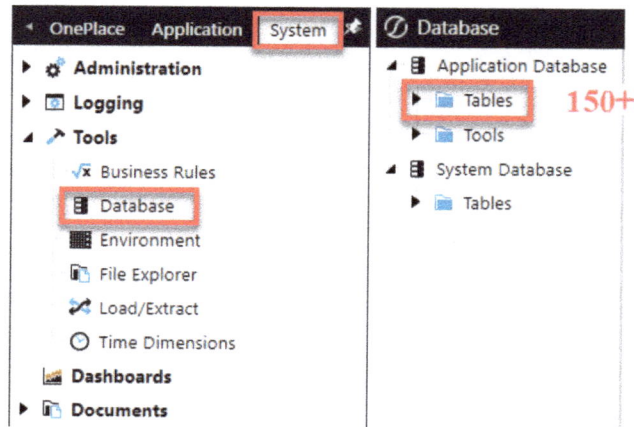

Figure 5.8

These 150+ application tables consist of tables for the following types of items:

- Audit Tables

- Data Tables

- Application Objects Tables

- Hierarchies / Relationships Tables

- Property Tables

- Custom or Solution Exchange Tables

The **audit** and the **application object tables** are important to understand in relation to security and application tables. The audit tables contain who did *what* and *when* within an application. The application object tables contain what security is applied to the 13 different types of application object categories that can be secured.

The remaining application tables containing data, hierarchy relationships, and properties *do not* contain information relevant to security. While they are the backbone of every application, and represent the data and relationships within your application, they do not – in fact – contain any security group information.

It is important to understand the application object tables that *do* contain security information because, if you need to write any custom reports to trace application security, you will be pulling information from these tables.

In the next section, we will focus on the audit and application object tables and delve into what is important to understand about those tables in relation to security.

# Object Tables

Every application table that has security groups will maintain those security groups by a unique ID rather than the security group name. Figure 5.9 shows an example of this from the CubeViewGroup table, where we can see a unique ID for the AccessGroupUniqueID and the MaintenanceGroupUniqueID.

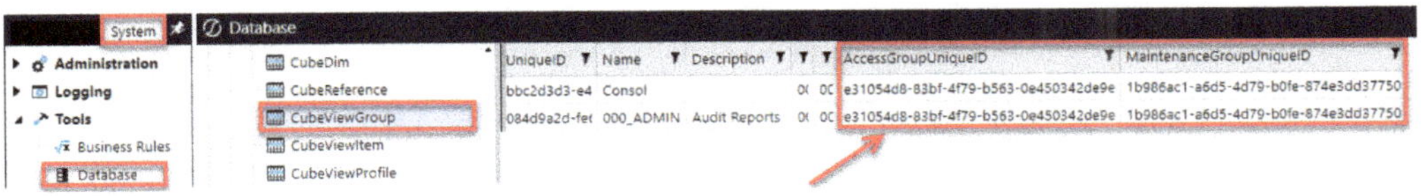

Figure 5.9

There are only three minor exceptions where application tables store the access and maintenance group as the security group name and not the unique ID.

Why is it important to understand security groups are stored by their IDs as opposed to security group names in application tables? Because, to pull back information regarding *which* security groups are assigned to various application objects by *name* – instead of *unique ID* – you need to join application tables with system tables using that unique ID.

This is because security groups exist in the framework database (aka system tables) by their name and ID. And to do that means querying across the application database tables and system database (e.g., framework) tables.

Figure 5.10 provides a list of all application tables that contain security groups stored as unique IDs, which when joined with the system tables, will allow a user to retrieve security group *name* assignments for application objects:

| | |
|---|---|
| BusinessRule | FileInfo |
| CertifyGroups | Folder |
| CertifyProfiles | FormTmpItGroup |
| ConfirmGroups | FormTmpItProfile |
| ConfirmProfiles | JournalTmpItGroup |
| Cube | JournalTmpItProfile |
| CubeViewGroup | Member |
| CubeViewProfile | ParserLayouts |
| DashboardMaintUnit | StageRuleGroups |
| DashboardProfile | StageRuleProfiles |
| DataMgmtGroup | WorkflowProfileAttributes |
| DataMgmtProfile | WorkflowProfileHierarchy |
| Dim | |

Figure 5.10

These tables are consistent from application to application and customer to customer; however, the records contained *within* those tables will be unique to each application and customer. In essence, these tables are blank until a customer starts building and maintaining their application. So, while the table structure is identical from application to application, the members or records existing within these tables are specific to each customer, application, and environment.

It is also worth noting that, as application elements are added during build and new records created in these tables, unless security is assigned to the object, a default security group ID for the `Everyone` group (which is `e31054d8-83bf-4f79-b563-0e450342de9e`) will be assigned as the Access and Maintenance group IDs.

## Audit Tables

While security groups are only stored in the application tables as unique IDs, the same is not true for users within the audit tables. Approximately 75 application audit tables store 'who did what when' within an application by the user name, as opposed to a unique ID.

Why is this relevant? This makes querying and presenting reports displaying audit actions inside OneStream easier than presenting a report that shows what security group is attached to which application object. This is because you do *not* need to query across the application database tables and system database (e.g., framework) tables. All audit tables are self-contained within the application database only.

Because the audit tables store 'who did what when' by the user name (e.g., audit user column in the application audit tables) as opposed to a unique user ID, there is no need to join tables across databases. An example of this is shown in Figure 5.11, where the AuditAppProperty table is displayed with the user name presented in the AuditUser column.

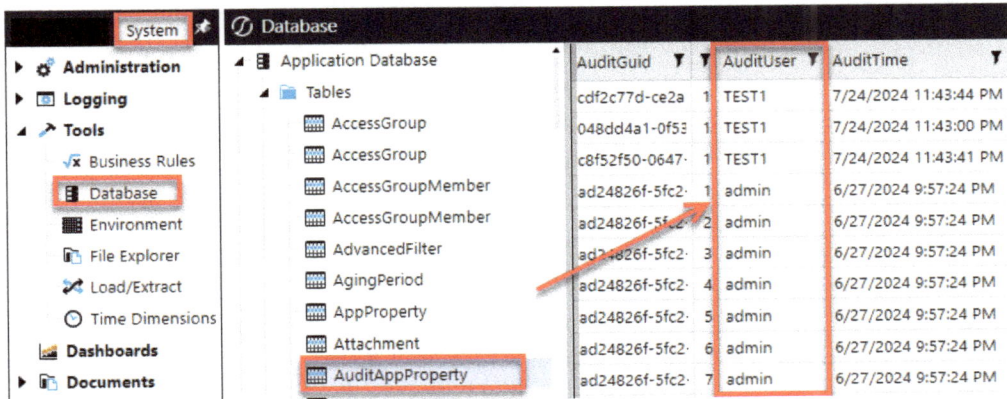

Figure 5.11

This also explains why – in the Solution Exchange Standard Application Reports (RPTA) tool – there are several audit reports that will allow you to see user names, as shown in Figure 5.12.

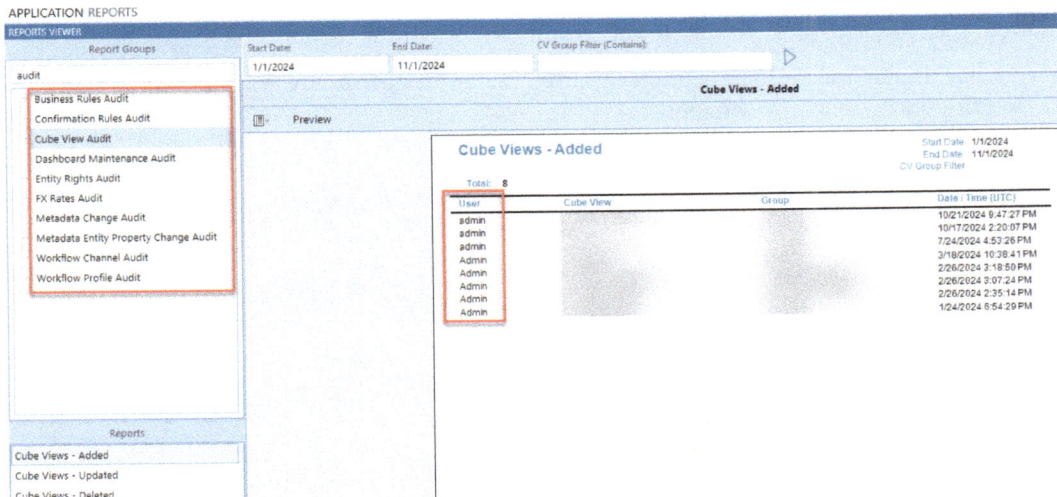

Figure 5.12

There is a consequence of audit tables storing the user name as opposed to the unique ID. This was discussed in Chapter 2 when we talked about deleting versus disabling a user. If you delete a user, that user name is available to be used again.

And because the audit tables store who did what by user name (and not a unique ID), that means you can set up a user with the same name as before, and it will appear as if that new user took action in the audit tables which – in fact – could have been actions taken by the previous, not current, user.

We will touch upon this again in Chapter 8 when we talk about the security audit reports and how you can use all reports together to properly audit user actions.

Now that we have covered the list of 13 distinct categories of application objects that can be secured, the ways in which you can secure those objects (Figure 5.7), and the tables where such security resides (Figure 5.10), let us now delve into some key OneStream application security elements.

# Entity Security

When people think about securing their data, the Entity dimension is one of the first things that comes to mind. The Entity dimension is an integral part of every OneStream application and directly impacts reporting, performance, data loading, and many other elements of your application. When it comes to security, though, I find securing the Entity dimension to be straightforward.

Most companies know who should have read or write access to various entities. Some companies may go quite granular and create read and write entity security groups for each individual base-level entity (e.g., 004_ENT_DE_WRITE). Other companies may choose to secure data at a higher level, like a group of entities such as a region (004_ENT_EMEA_READ) or cost center (004_ENT_GENADMIN_READ) grouping. Companies taking a simpler approach may choose to leave all entities as read access to Everyone and only grant write access to Administrators.

As with all OneStream security, you can go as simple or granular as you wish, and the Entity dimension is no exception. Figure 5.13 shows the many ways in which you can secure your Entity dimension.

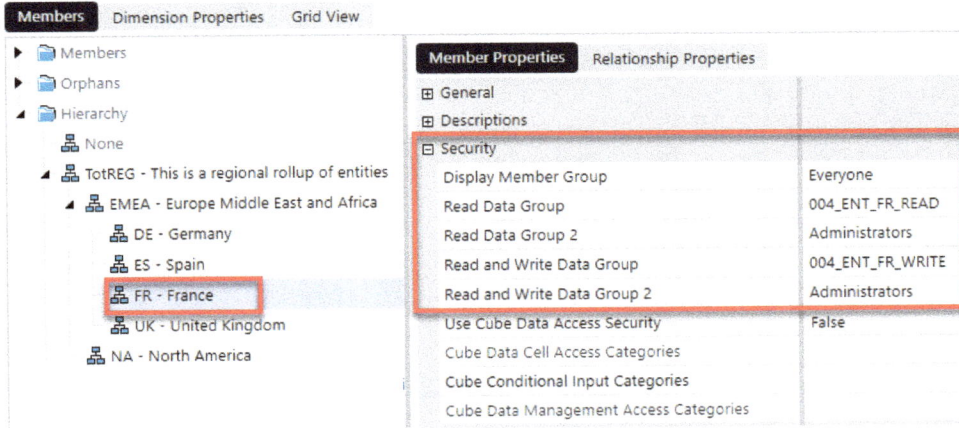

Figure 5.13

In the example above showing entity security, the below is true:

| Entity Security | Description |
|---|---|
| **Read Display Member Group** Everyone | Controls who can see that the entity exists, but does *not* allow a person to see the entity's data. Typically, you will leave this as Everyone. |
| **Read Data Group** 004_ENT_FR_READ | Allows a person to see data for this entity. |
| **Read Data Group 2** Administrators | A second group that can see data for this entity. If using nesting (e.g., 004_ENT_EMEA_READ has rights over 004_ENT_FR_READ), this can be set to Administrators. If you are not nesting entity security groups, then you could set this second group to 004_ENT_EMEA_READ. |
| **Read and Write Data Group** 004_ENT_FR_WRITE | Allows a person to see and modify data for this entity. |
| **Read and Write Data Group 2** ADMINISTRATORS | A second group that can see data for this entity. If using nesting (e.g., 004_ENT_EMEA_WRITE has rights over 004_ENT_FR_WRITE), this can be set to Administrators. If you are not nesting security groups, then you could set this second group to 004_ENT_EMEA_WRITE. |

Figure 5.14

Even though securing the Entity dimension is straightforward, there are a few items I want to highlight.

First, the remaining security applied at the Entity dimension level is shown in Figure 5.15. The Use Cube Data Access Security toggle of True or False pertains to **Data Cell Access** (aka slice) security and will be covered in Chapter 7. But understand that the determination as to whether to use additional slice security – which is set up on the cube admin page – starts with the Entity dimension by toggling this to True and is a setting on each individual entity, as shown in Figure 5.15.

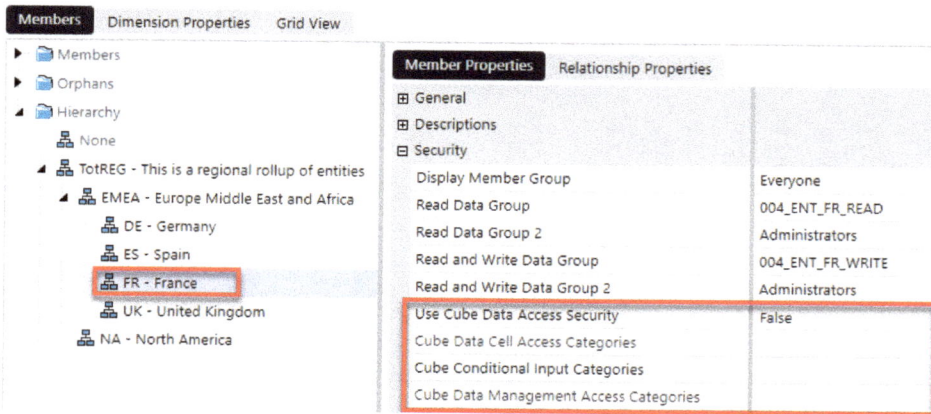

Figure 5.15

## Relationship Security

Next, there is another element of OneStream security that is determined at the cube level and involves the intersection of the Entity (E#) and Consolidation (C#) dimensions. The Use Parent Security for Relationship Consolidation Members security setting is a toggle of True or False, set at the cube level, as shown in Figure 5.16.

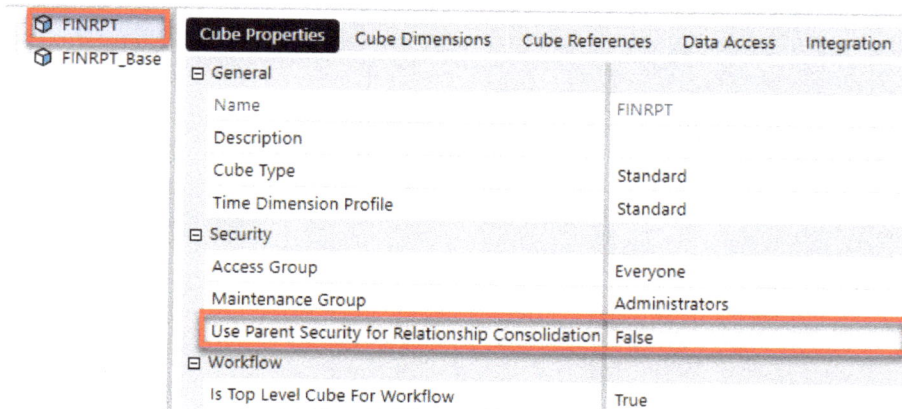

Figure 5.16

If set to False, the user's entity rights control their rights to *all* members of the Consolidation dimension (C#Top). This is the default security model and allows users to see their entity and all the relationship members in the C# dimension.

If set to True, the user's rights to the relationship members of the Consolidation dimension (C#OwnerPostAdj, C#Elimination, C#Share, C#OwnerPreAdj) are determined by their rights to the entity's immediate parent. If a user does not have rights to the immediate parent, they will *not* be able to see the relationship C# members. They will only be able to see their entity for the consolidation members C#Local and C#Translated.

This is shown in Figure 5.17.

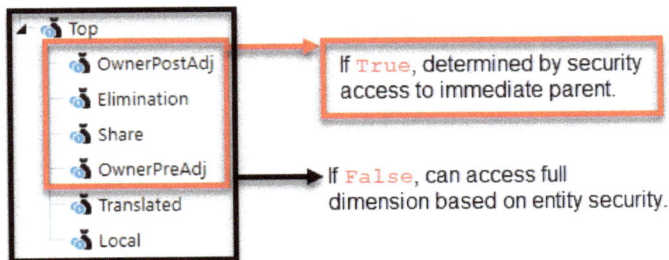

Figure 5.17

It is important to note that although setting to True means a person *cannot* see the C#Elimination member, this will *not* impact that person's ability to reconcile intercompany out-of-balances. There is a built-in exception that will allow a user to see intercompany data of their trading partners, even when this is set to True.

Figure 5.18 shows how the data appears with this cube setting as False versus True from the perspective of a Montreal user. If set to False, the Montreal user will see all C# members, as shown at the top of Figure 5.18. If, however, this is set to True, the Montreal user will only see C#Local and C#Translated for Montreal and get No Access for other consolidation members.

| | | 2011M2 | |
|---|---|---|---|
| Montreal | OwnerPostAdj | (10,000) | |
| | Elimination | | |
| | Share | (4,331,732) | Set to False |
| | OwnerPreAdj | | |
| | Translated | (4,331,732) | |
| | Local | (4,331,732) | |
| | | | |
| Montreal | OwnerPostAdj | No Access | |
| | Elimination | No Access | |
| | Share | No Access | Set to True |
| | OwnerPreAdj | No Access | |
| | Translated | (4,331,732) | |
| | Local | (4,331,732) | |

Figure 5.18

The clearest use case for setting the Use Parent Security for Relationship Consolidation Members to True at the cube level is when you want to prevent a user from seeing any topside adjustments (C#OwnerPostAdj) that may be posted by a corporate function to their entity.

For example, corporate users may post topside adjustments related to restructuring or some other activity. While those journals may be posted to a base entity, they are posted as topside adjustments to a specific parent and child combination. So, while a person may have access to a particular base entity, you may want to restrict them from seeing these topside adjustments.

Another less common use case would be wanting to restrict a user from seeing the C#Share member (another consolidation relationship member), which would allow them to know who owned them and by what percentage of ownership, since those entries post to C#Share in the Consolidation dimension of a base entity.

Again, the default is set to False, which is the most common application. But there can be a handful of rare exceptions as to why your company may want to set this to True at the cube level, so understanding this setting is relevant to entity security.

# Scenario Security

When thinking about securing your OneStream data, the next element that may come to mind is allowing people to view (or not) specific data scenarios. For example, you may want to restrict who can see a long-range Plan scenario or a Forecast scenario versus controlling who can enter Actual data versus Budget data. This is scenario security.

Scenario security consists of Read Data Group, Read and Write Data Group, Calculate from Grids Group, and Manage Data Group security access. The first three, as shown in Figure 5.19, behave much as you would expect. Like entity security, I find scenario security uncomplicated.

However, the Manage Data Group security access is worth calling out as it can impact a user's ability to take certain actions within that scenario.

| ⊟ Security | |
|---|---|
| Read Data Group | 003_SCN_ACTUAL_READ |
| Read and Write Data Group | 003_SCN_ACTUAL_WRITE |
| Calculate From Grids Group | Administrators |
| Manage Data Group | Administrators |
| ⊟ Workflow | |
| Use In Workflow | Select a Security Group to specify which users can execute a 'Reset Scenario' or 'Custom Calculate' Data Management Step for this scenario. It is recommended that this security group is limited to a select list of people since it can be used to clear or modify all of a scenario's data for all entities and all time periods. |
| Workflow Tracking Freq | |

Figure 5.19

A user must be in a security group that is assigned (or inherits rights) to Manage Data Group to take two actions:

1. Run a scenario reset from a data management step

2. Run a custom calculation from a data management step

This is true even for users in the native **Administrators** group. In Chapter 2, we noted that users in the native administrators security group did not need any additional security because administrators have full access to do everything. But we noted there are two exceptions.

> One exception for users in the native **Administrators** group is that to run scenario resets or custom calculations on specific scenarios, those users must also be added to the security group assigned to the Manage Data Group.

Another thing about the Manage Data Group security assignment on a scenario is that it supersedes the other three security group assignments on a scenario: Read Data Group, Read and Write Data Group, and Calculate from Grids Group. By this, I mean a person who is in the Manage Data Group does not need the Read and Write Data Group access to run a scenario reset or custom calculate.

Nor do they need write access to an entity, the application security role to modify data, or any other write data access security. By being in the Manage Data Group alone, a user will be able to perform those two actions on a specific scenario.

This is an exception to security group access, but it is intentional. Since the actions of resetting a scenario or running a custom calculation against a scenario are very narrow and purposeful, it stands to reason that the security allowing a person to do those things is also deliberate and purposeful.

A scenario reset should be used with extreme caution and is rarely used within live applications. It can be used early on during project development cycles to clear all data (cube and Stage) for all time periods for a given scenario. As such, it should be restricted to a very limited number of users.

Custom calculations can be used frequently, especially for Budget and Forecast scenarios. Custom calculations can be used to seed Actual data into a Forecast scenario, run Budget-specific driver-based calculations, and many other calculations that are run on-demand and which are not a part of the standard business rules attached to the cube or as a part of a Data Unit Calculation Sequence (DUCS).

This is important to note because you will want to create a security group specific to each scenario to allow certain users to run custom calculations. The error message that will appear if a user has not been granted **Manage Data Group** access is shown in Figure 5.20.

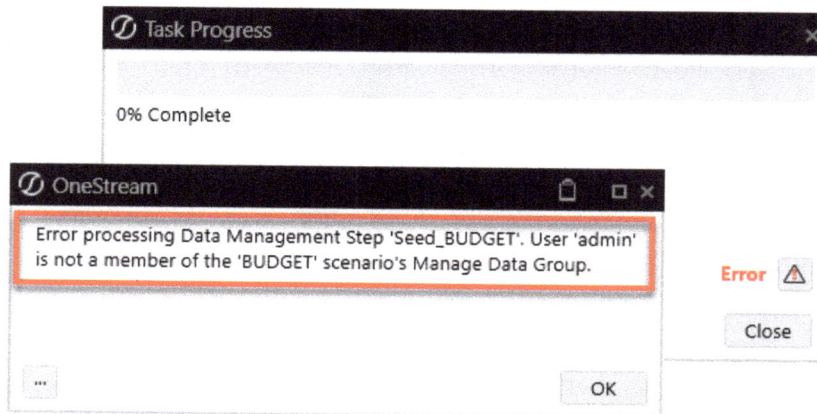

Figure 5.20

# Account, Flow & User Defined Security

The last data object to talk about potentially securing is your Account, Flow, and/or User Defined dimensions. As we all know, in a OneStream application you can have up to eight User Defined dimensions, and Flow and Account dimension(s) that can be extended and used in a multitude of different ways across cubes and Scenario Types.

Account, Flow and all User Defined dimensions have one security group associated with them: a Display Member Group.

Figure 5.21

That's it, one security option for Account, Flow and all User Defined dimensions! Sounds easy, right?

There are a couple of things to keep in mind when securing accounts, flows, and UDs. If a company is taking a simple approach to security and does not need to secure individual UDs or Accounts, it may be good enough to leave the Display Member Group as Everyone and stop there.

If you can take that approach, that is fantastic. This means if a person has access to a cube, entity and scenario, they will see all data associated with that Data Unit.

But if you need to deviate from this simple approach, there are two options with accounts, flows, and UDs:

1.  Use slice security (Chapter 7)

2.  The Display Member Group

We will get into slice security in a subsequent chapter but just understand that if you need to further limit who can see cube data in particular accounts or UDs – because these dimensions go beyond the Data Unit – you will do so by applying slice security.

But let's discuss how you may leverage the **Display Member Group** to your advantage, if needed. Quite often, User Defined dimensions can have a large number of items. And when running reports with prompts or perhaps using forms for data entry in a Budget or Forecast process, you may present your users with a list of these items from which to pick (aka a OneStream parameter).

For example, if you have a User Defined dimension that represents a customer and has thousands of members in that dimension, you can imagine how a person running a report or entering their sales forecast may be overwhelmed if they are presented with a parameter that includes those thousands of members.

Display Member Group security can, therefore, be leveraged to limit the choices people see in a pick list, for example. This security on accounts, flows, and UDs does *not* limit a person from that data rollup through those dimensions. The Account, Flow, and User Defined dimensions aggregate on the fly, so even if you cannot see a particular base member, you can still see how that base member aggregates data.

The Display Member Group *only* limits the member's visibility, but does not limit a user from seeing the data in that member. For example, if a user cannot see a member called U7#DiscOps in a pick list or in the hierarchy, but they type that member name into a Spreadsheet, the user will be able to retrieve that member's data. If you need to control visibility to that data, then slice security (Chapter 7) will need to be employed.

But, when you run a Cube View or enter data into a form, it will not appear in any parameters if you do not have display member group access to a particular Account, Flow, or UD. The most common use case is to leave the Display Member Group on Accounts, Flow, and User Defined dimensions as Everyone. But, just understand that you can add a layer of security to these dimensions if needed, without having to use slice security.

## Workflow Security

Workflows are the backbone of how users interact with OneStream and are key to guiding users in their processes within an application. As such, workflow setup and the application of workflow security are central to the overall end-user experience. We have already touched upon workflow access in this chapter and prior chapters, but let's review this more closely since this is a fundamental OneStream feature.

Workflows have many layers and places where you will have the opportunity to introduce different components of the application. As we will talk about in the next section of this chapter, both Cube Views and dashboards can be presented to users via a workflow. Additional processes, such as importing data, posting journal adjustments, confirmations, certifications, and intercompany matching, are also handled via various workflows.

Most of these processes and components can be secured individually; however, it is strongly recommended that you understand how they all work together before you start creating and applying security to each of them.

Over-securing areas in the workflow can create a web that is sometimes hard to follow and, most times, cumbersome and unnecessary. If the workflow design considers how users access applicable processes, then security should be applied when required and restricted if not needed.

Likewise, under-securing areas in the workflow can lead to end-user confusion, recalling the analogy of entering a community with no street names or house numbers. You can easily get lost as you try to navigate. Workflows can be equally confusing for end-users to navigate if you leave security wide open (aka everyone).

Having the right balance of allowing access when needed, and removing access when not necessary, is a balancing act between ease of maintenance and end-user experience.

Let's start by touching upon the first workflows that are set up within an application as you begin building and implementing OneStream.

# Cube Root & Default Profiles

Workflows are tied to the top-level cube defined for a workflow (therefore, workflows are divided by cube) but are also further divided by workflow suffixes used on a cube, as shown in Figure 5.22.

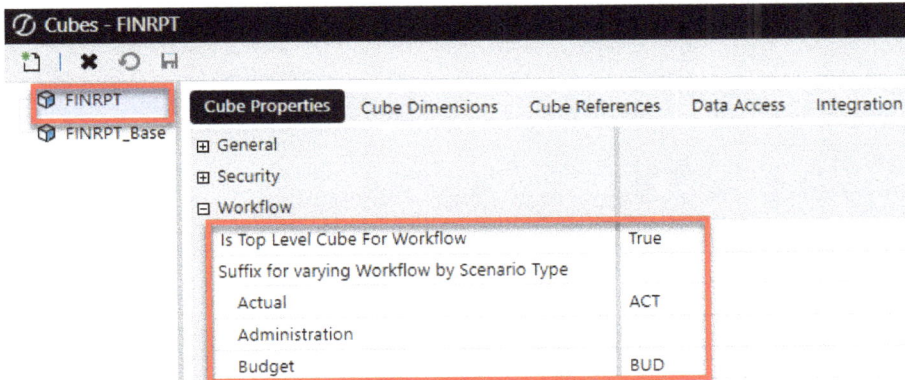

Figure 5.22

This is important to understand from a security perspective because this means you will be able to apply different security not only by cube but also by Scenario Type suffixes, if desired.

The cube root Workflow Profile is always named *CubeName_ ScenarioTypeSuffix*, as shown below in Figure 5.23 (FINRPT_ACT).

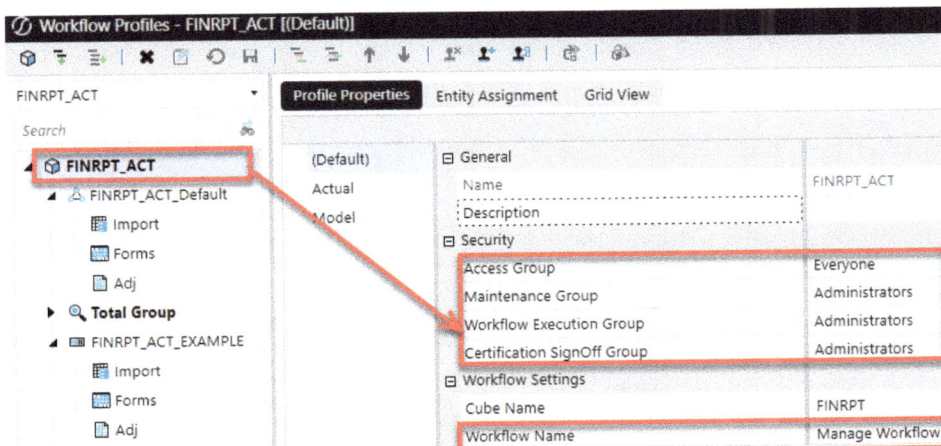

Figure 5.23

Chapter 5

This cube root Workflow Profile is the Manage Workflow dashboard presented when a user navigates to this on the OnePlace tab, as shown in Figure 5.24. This is the dashboard that allows a company to close workflows. Why is this important? Because you almost *never* want to hit the Close Workflow button!

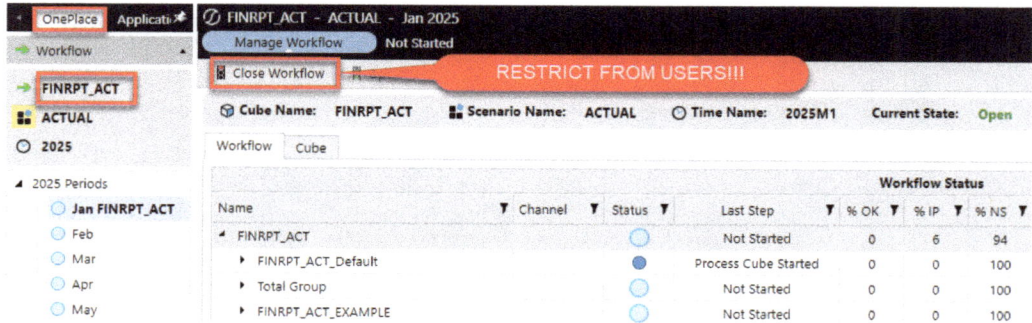

Figure 5.24

To restrict your users from inadvertently closing workflows, one of the first security settings you will want to make within your application is to change the Maintenance Group, Workflow Execution Group, and Certification Sign Off Group access to Administrators on this cube root Workflow Profile (FINPRT_ACT) as shown next.

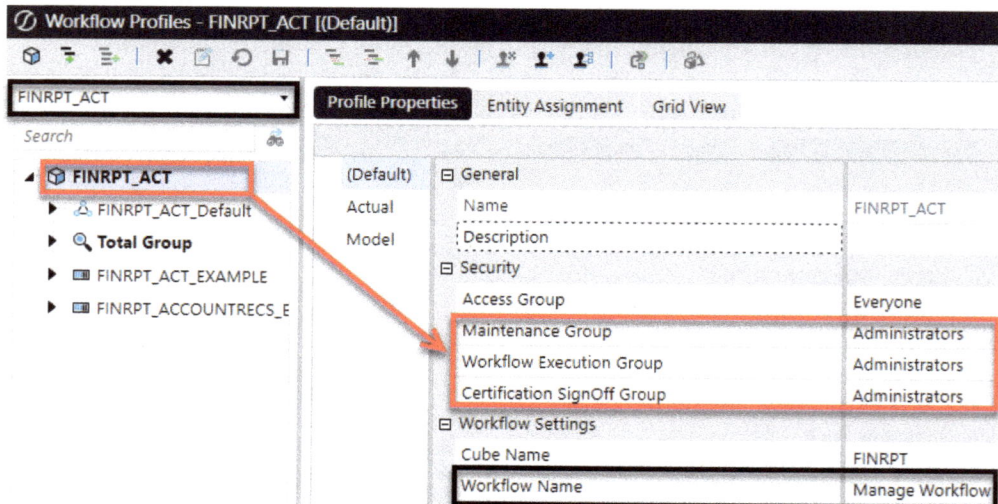

Figure 5.25

You must leave the Access Group open to Everyone because workflows are hierarchical, and for a user to navigate to their processes for this cube and scenario, they will need to *at least* view the cube root Workflow Profile. But by restricting the other security groups on this cube root profile, you will prevent a user from hitting the Close Workflow button in Figure 5.24.

Take, for example, a person who needs to have access to the workflow CORP.Import shown in Figure 5.26 below. That user will need to have access (*not* maintenance, execute, or certify) to the cube root Workflow Profile of FINRPT_ACT in order to be able to navigate to the CORP.Import profile being used to load data. In this case, we can see the access has been set to Everyone on the cube root.

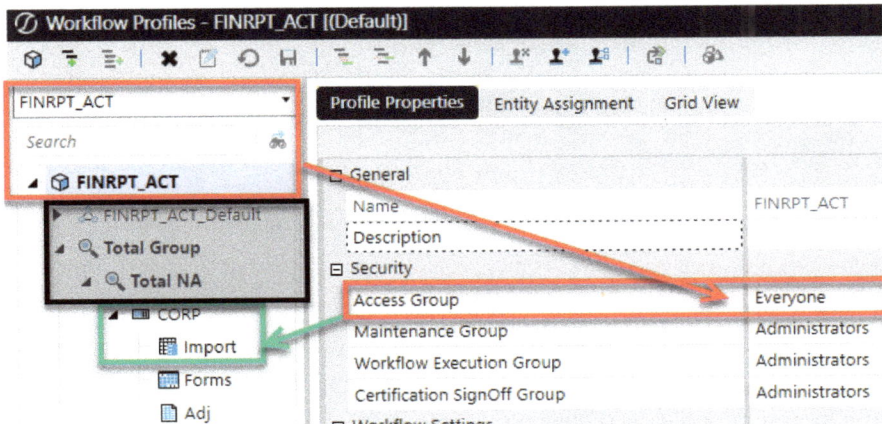

Figure 5.26

The user will *not* need access to the full navigation path (aka all ancestors) above: CORP.Import (e.g., they will not need Total NA and Total Group access). Just having access to the cube root Workflow Profile will allow a user to navigate through any ancestors to reach the Workflow Profile to which they have been granted access.

If the cube root Workflow Profile (e.g., `FINRPT_ACT`) has been restricted to an access group to which a user does not have access, they will not be able to navigate to `CORP.Import` to which they have been granted access, as shown in Figure 5.27.

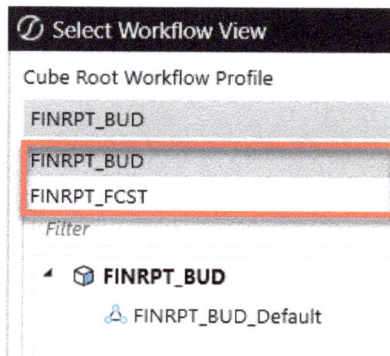

Figure 5.27

`FINRPT_ACT` is not in their pick list, so they cannot navigate the rest of the cube root workflow hierarchy to get to the workflow to which they have been granted access. This only applies to the cube root Workflow Profile, and not all other intermediate parents or ancestors in the rest of the workflow hierarchy.

As a rule of thumb, any cube root Workflow Profiles will need to have the Access Group set to Everyone. This is to allow users to navigate to any other workflows to which they have been granted access. You will want to ensure the cube root Workflow Profiles Maintenance Group, Workflow Execution Group, and Certification Sign Off Group are set to Administrators so that a user cannot close a workflow inadvertently!

Now that we have talked about the basic security assigned to the cube root Workflow Profile let's next review the default Workflow Profile that is also created for every cube and Scenario Type named *CubeName_ScenarioTypeSuffix_Default*, as shown below in Figure 5.28 (`FINRPT_ACT_Default`).

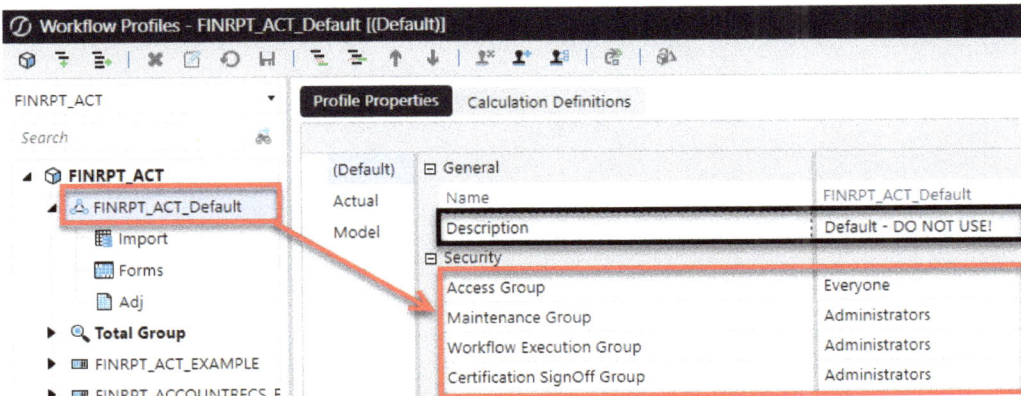

Figure 5.28

The purpose of this default Workflow Profile is to serve as a placeholder for all other Workflow Profiles that are created and used in your application. It holds default values for things like workflow channels, unassigned entities, etc. Just like the cube root Workflow Profile serves as a starting point of navigation for all workflows relating to this cube and Scenario Type(s), so too does the default Workflow Profile.

Therefore, you will also want to leave the Access Group open to Everyone so users have a starting point in their workflow navigation. Because this workflow serves merely as a placeholder for default values, you *do not* want to use this Workflow Profile to load any data or run any processes within your application.

Therefore, as shown in Figure 5.28, you want to restrict the Maintenance Group, Workflow Execution Group, and Certification Sign Off Group access to Administrators. Also, I like to go the extra step – as shown in Figure 5.28 – and update the description of this default profile to DO NOT USE!, which serves as a further warning to users.

As for the default Import, Forms, and Adj child Workflow Profiles that exist under the parent default profile, you will want to make the changes as shown in Figure 5.29. Because users will not need to navigate to these default base-level workflows to perform their work, I set the Access Group, Maintenance Group, Workflow Execution Group, and Certification Sign Off Group all to Administrators once again to prevent users from seeing unnecessary items, and that they will never need to use.

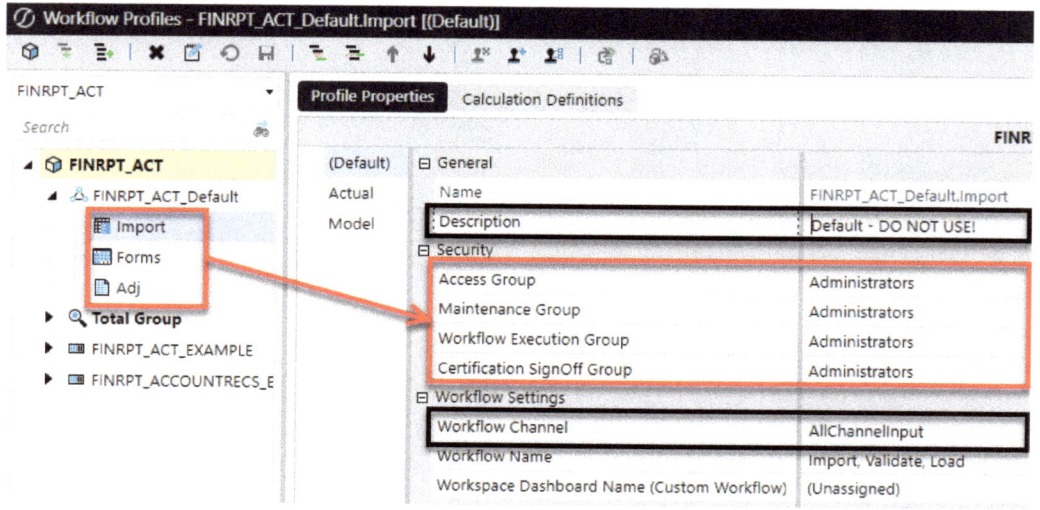

Figure 5.29

Lastly, regarding the Import, Forms, and Adj child Workflow Profiles shown in Figure 5.29, I also like to update the Workflow Channel to be AllChannelInput on these three base workflows. This is a proactive measure to prevent errors if workflow channels are used within your application. Once again, I like to go the extra step and update the description of this default profile to DO NOT USE! (Figure 5.29).

Where you go from the cube root and default workflows that exist in every application for every top-level cube and Scenario Type suffix will entirely depend on your company's needs, processes, and how you want users to interact with OneStream.

The key thing to remember with workflow security, as shown earlier (Figure 5.7), is that there are many types of security groups that you can apply to workflows. This is shown again in the following figure.

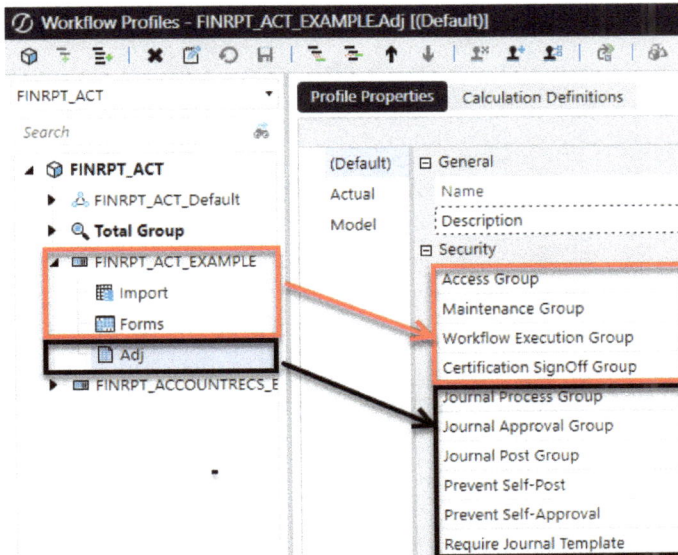

Figure 5.30

There is no one-size-fits-all, as workflows and processes are unique to each company. You will want to adhere to naming conventions and nesting for security groups laid out in Chapter 3 as you apply security groups to your company's workflows.

> The key to workflow security is the *less-is-more* approach. If a user does not need to see or access a workflow to do their role, restrict access to administrators or a limited group of users. This will prevent end-user confusion and make user navigation far simpler!

# Reporting Security

Now that we have covered entity, scenario, and workflow security, let's get into how to secure reporting in OneStream. In Chapter 3, we talked about how the intersection of a person's object security (a Cube View or dashboard), in addition to their data security (cube, scenario, and entity), will allow a user to see data in OneStream (Figure 3.2).

Because data and reporting are integral to every OneStream application, let's dive a little deeper into report security.

# Cube View Security

A person may have access to view a particular Cube View (008_CV_), but as we already learned, they will also need cube (002_CUBE_), scenario (003_SCN_), and entity (004_ENT_) access to view data on that Cube View.

In addition to that security, there are a handful of settings that can be applied at the individual Cube View level to further restrict what a person can do from that Cube View.

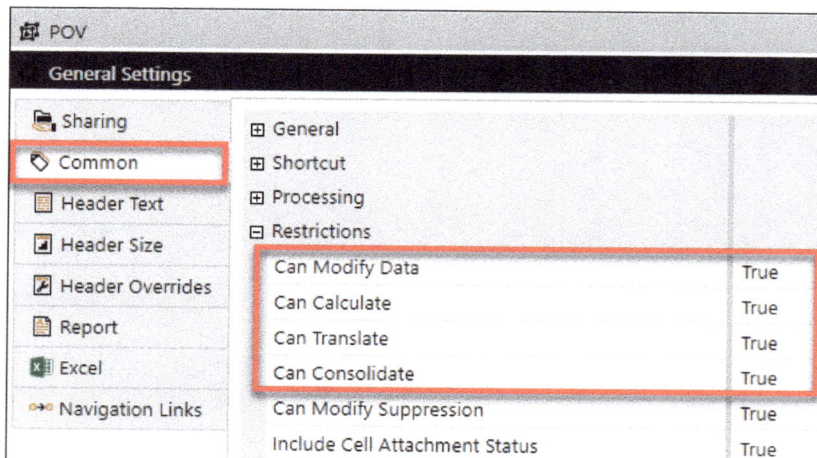

Figure 5.31

These True or False toggles at the Cube View level can further restrict a person from being able to enter data, right-click and calculate, translate, or consolidate data from a particular Cube View.

These are important because they *supersede* a user's access to modify data. For example, if you have a user who can modify data, but to do so, they run a Cube View and the Cube View itself has Can Modify Data set to False, they will not be able to enter data via that Cube View.

> As a rule of thumb, if a Cube View is not used in a form, workflow, or dashboard, Can Modify Data and Can Calculate should be set to False. Additionally, if you want to control consolidations and translations from workflow "process" steps, Can Translate and Can Consolidate should also be set to False.

When setting up Cube View group, Cube View Profile, and Cube View page security, you want to think about where the user will access this report.

Typically, your end-user will not need access to the Cube View page, as that is not where they access and run reports. The only users needing access to the Cube View page are typically your native administrators *or* users with the **Manage Cube Views** security role.

If that is the case, you can take a simple approach and leave your Cube View group access open to everyone. With this approach, you are relying on the fact that users will not be able to navigate to the Cube Views page, and thus, you do not need to restrict access to your potentially hundreds of Cube View groups. This is a case of "Less is More" or "K-I-S-S" (Keep It Simple, Stupid) when it comes to applying security. And who does not love a kiss?

Your end-user will typically access Cube Views by one of these methods:

1. OnePlace
2. Dashboards
3. Excel
4. Forms
5. Workflow

Therefore, you will rely on the Cube View Profile security access to determine who can see what reports and from where. Figure 5.32 shows the types of visibility you can apply to Cube View Profile(s) that will determine who can see what reports.

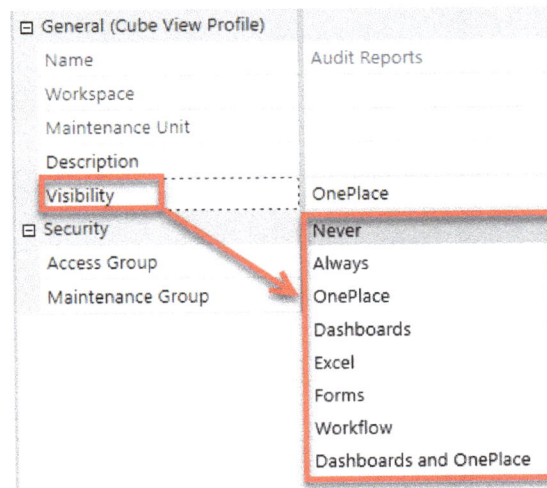

Figure 5.32

If you want a user to access a report from the OnePlace tab, you will select OnePlace as the Visibility setting on the profile. That, in conjunction with the Access Group of that Cube View Profile, will allow a person to see those reports from the OnePlace tab.

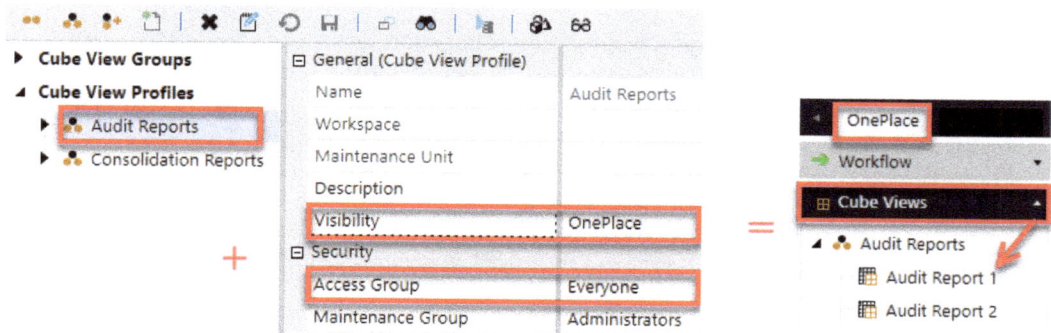

Figure 5.33

If, however, a Cube View will be presented to the end-user via a dashboard, Excel, form, or workflow, then you will select one of those options as the Visibility setting in Figure 5.32, and thus restrict the user to navigating to that set of Cube Views by one of those other methods. Again, you are putting guardrails around your end-users, illuminating the path along which you want them to access various reports.

As an example, if a user gains access to a Cube View via a workflow, then access to the report is controlled by setting up a Cube View Profile with Visibility set to Workflow, granting access to that workflow (005_WF_CORP_A). In this way, the user will navigate to that workflow, as shown in Figure 5.34, to gain access to those reports.

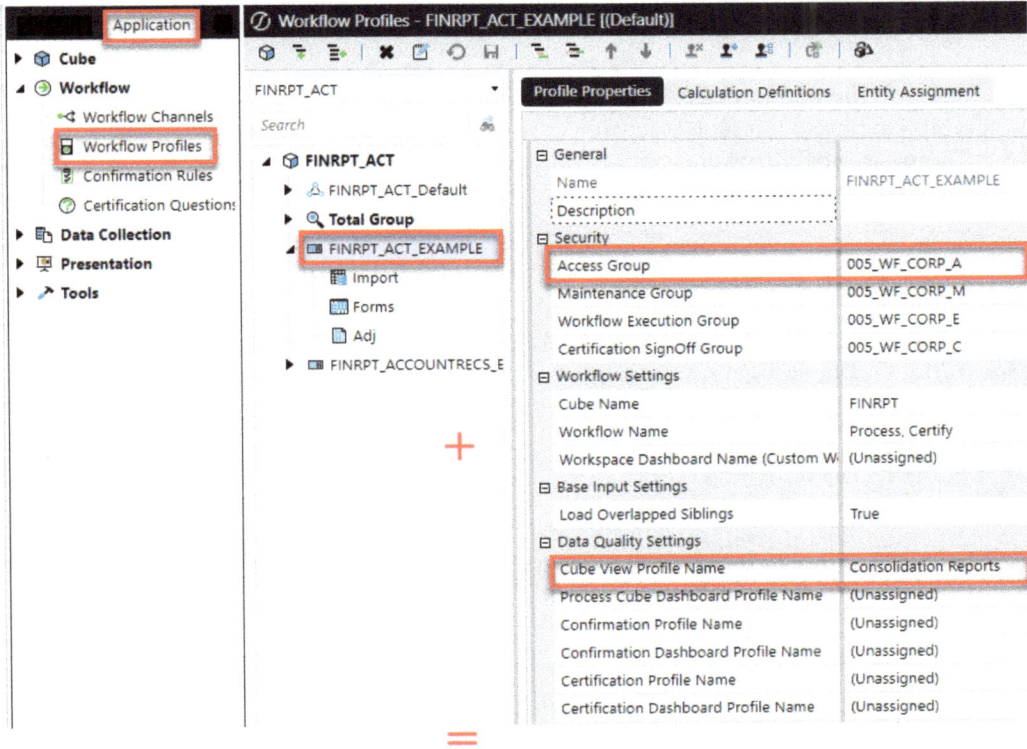

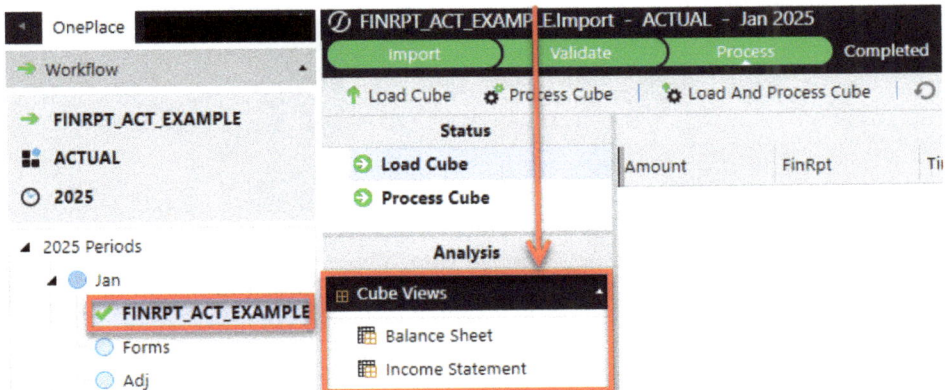

Figure 5.34

> The key to Cube View (or dashboard) security is to determine how your users will interact with various reports (OnePlace, dashboards, Excel, forms, or workflow) and set up your Cube View (or dashboard) profile security accordingly.

## Dashboard Security

Like Cube Views, your end-users will also not need access to the dashboard page itself (the Workspace admin page) as that page is where dashboards are developed and maintained, but *not* where dashboards are consumed.

The only users needing access to the dashboard page are typically your native administrators *or* users with the Administer Application Workspace Assemblies or Manage Application Workspaces security roles.

Dashboards are typically presented to end-users in one of two ways:

1. OnePlace
2. Workflow

Therefore, you will rely on Dashboard Profile security access to determine who can see what dashboards and from where. Figure 5.35 shows the types of Visibility you can apply to dashboard profiles, determining who can see what dashboards.

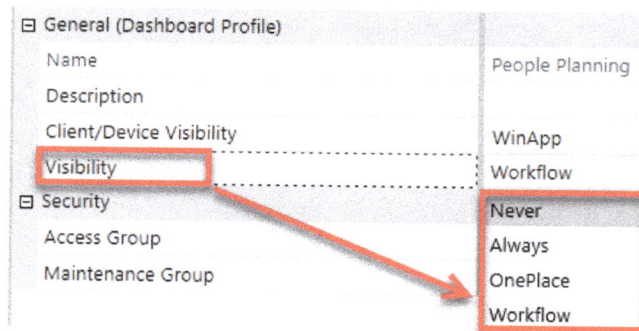

Figure 5.35

If you want a user to access a dashboard from the OnePlace tab, you will select OnePlace as the Visibility setting on the profile. That, in conjunction with the Access Group of that dashboard profile, will allow a person to see those dashboards from the OnePlace tab as shown in Figure 5.36.

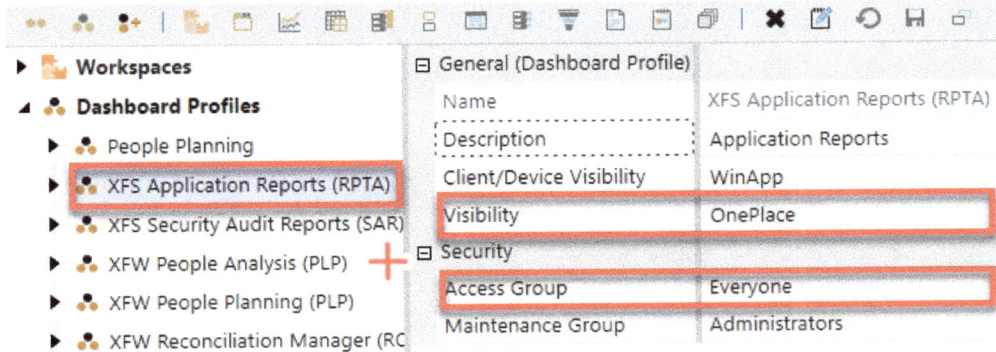

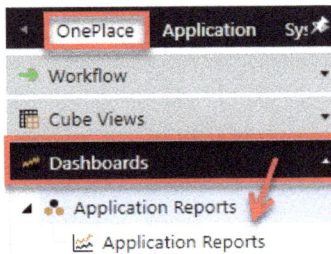

Figure 5.36

If, however, a dashboard will be presented to the end-user via a workflow, then you will select that option as the Visibility setting, restricting the user to only navigating to that dashboard via a workflow.

As an example, if a user gains access to a dashboard via a workflow, then access to the dashboard is controlled by setting up a dashboard profile where Visibility is set to Workflow, granting access to that workflow (005_WF_PLP_A). In this way, the user will navigate to that workflow – as per the bottom of Figure 5.37 – to gain access to that dashboard.

# Chapter 5

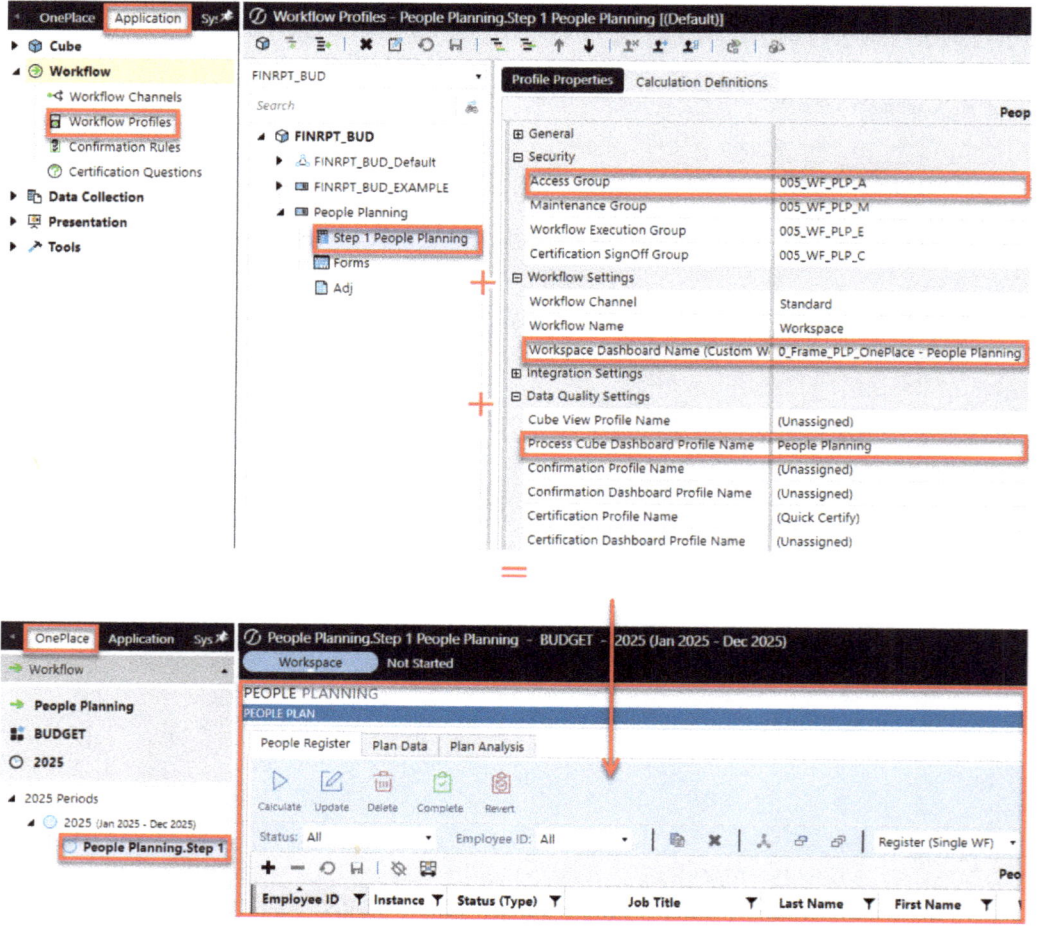

Figure 5.37

> 💡 As a rule of thumb, users will not need access to the Cube View page or Workspace admin page because you will typically grant access to reports and dashboards via other methods.

# Data Integration Security

Let us end the chapter on application security by talking about the security you will place around **loading data** into OneStream. This is a case of ending with the beginning in mind… bringing data into a OneStream application. As we have all heard before, "Data, Data, Data."

There are four primary ways to import data into OneStream:

1. Imports

2. Forms

3. Journals

4. Consolidations/Calculations

When you talk about any of these four methods, we must remember that the starting point for anyone modifying data in OneStream is the out-of-the-box application security role of Modify Data, discussed earlier in this chapter. Then, additionally, that individual will need appropriate cube, scenario, entity, and workflow execution access as well. This is shown in Figure 5.38.

| Application Security Role | Pre-requisites / + Additions |
|---|---|
| Modify Data<br>001_APP_MODIFYDATA | + 002_CUBE_<br>+ 003_SCN_X_WRITE<br>+ 004_ENT_X_WRITE<br>+ 005_WF_X_A/E |

Figure 5.38

So, a prerequisite for anyone loading data in OneStream will be, at a minimum, the above security (unless, of course, you have left any of these elements open to Everyone).

In this section, we are going to focus on users who will bring in data via an import process, whether importing data to OneStream via a file load or by directly connecting to a source system. I am not going to delve into other data integration methods, such as forms or journals, but those will follow a similar logic as we will discuss below.

Before we start talking about applying security to individuals who will import data to OneStream, we first need to revisit the design questions we asked in Chapter 3. The answer to these questions will help determine your overall security strategy around data integration in OneStream:

- Is your load process centralized or distributed?

- Who will maintain data mappings?

- Who will maintain what metadata?

- Who can consolidate and calculate data?

For example, are you going to allow the person who is responsible for importing data into OneStream access to update any mappings and add the new metadata required to load such data?

Will your data loads be centralized and even scheduled so that your process is automated? Or will individual locations and users be responsible for loading their own data?

Once the data is loaded, do you want the person who loaded the data to run consolidations, aggregations, and/or calculations, or will you instead schedule routine consolidations?

As you answer these questions, you can start to layer in the additional pieces of security a person needs to import data. There are several application objects that relate to the overall data import process in OneStream:

- Data Sources

- Connector and Parser Business Rules

- Workflows

- Transformation Profiles

- Metadata

Data sources, connector and parser business rules, and workflows are typically established upfront and only maintained if there are changes to an existing or a new process. As such, security to maintain these items is normally limited to your OneStream Administrators security group. A person responsible for data loading will not need to access these application pages to perform their data load actions.

Therefore, access to those objects can be set to administrators for the maintenance group, and everyone for the access group. Again, this means you will rely on the fact that a person cannot get to those application pages and thus leave their access open to everyone.

Likewise, your typical data load individual will not need access to navigate to the application user interface roles shown in Figure 5.39.

| Application User Interface Role | User Responsible for Data Imports |
|---|---|
| Business Rules Page<br>001_APP_BRPAGE | *Access is not needed for users to perform established data load processes.* |
| Data Sources Page<br>001_APP_DSPAGE | |
| Workflow Profiles Page<br>001_APP_WFPROFILEPAGE | |

Figure 5.39

So that leaves us asking what access people who are going to load data need. The answer depends on whether you want to allow your data loaders to maintain mappings and metadata.

If the answer is yes, then you are going to grant that person not only the application security role of Modify Data, as already discussed, but you will want to grant them the roles shown in Figure 5.40.

| Application Security Role | Pre-requisites / + Additions |
|---|---|
| Manage Metadata<br>001_APP_MNG_METADATA | + 001_APP_DIMPAGE |
| Manage Transformation Rules<br>001_APP_MNG_MAPPING | + 001_APP_MAPPINGPAGE<br>+ 002_CUBE_ |

Figure 5.40

The above security roles and pages will give your data loaders the ability to manage mapping changes and add any new dimension members as needed to address the data load process.

For example, if during a data load a new account arises which has not been mapped and/or does not yet exist in OneStream, by granting the security from Figure 5.40, the person responsible for loading data will be able to add the new account, update mapping, and then reprocess the load to see the process through end-to-end.

If, however, you want to control metadata maintenance through a centralized OneStream administrator, then you may only want to grant the person responsible for loading data the access shown in Figure 5.41.

| Application User Interface Role | User Responsible for Data Imports |
|---|---|
| Dimension Library Page<br>001_APP_DIMPAGE | Everyone for the Access Group |
| Transformation Rules Page<br>001_APP_MAPPINGPAGE | |

Figure 5.41

This will allow a person responsible for data loading to view mappings and dimensions to help them understand the data load process, but will *not* allow them to modify any mappings or update any metadata (e.g., add new entities, accounts, etc.).

This goes back to the point we made early on in this chapter that you want to keep your application security roles separate from your application user interface roles for this very reason of granting one person the ability to make changes (doer) and another person only the ability to see pages (viewer).

The final key is to ensure that once on these pages – the **Dimension Library Page** or **Transformation Rules Page** – individual application objects on those pages have a Maintenance Group of Administrators, as shown in Figure 5.42.

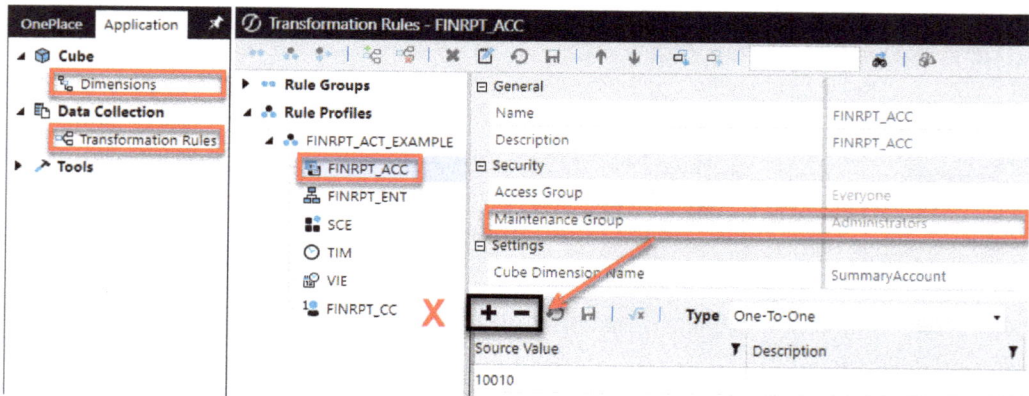

Figure 5.42

As you can see in the figure above, this user has been granted access to *see* the Dimensions page and the Transformation Rules page; however, they *cannot* modify these pages, as is evidenced by the Name, Description, and other properties being greyed out.

It is worth noting that a person who is *allowed* to update mappings does not necessarily need access to the **Transformation Rules Page** in application user interface roles. Mappings can also be updated directly from the Validate step of a workflow import. But, as shown in Figure 5.43, unless that user has Maintenance

Group rights to the transformation profile and mapping group shown previously, they will receive the error message shown in Figure 5.43, even when trying to update mappings from the Validate step directly on the workflow import.

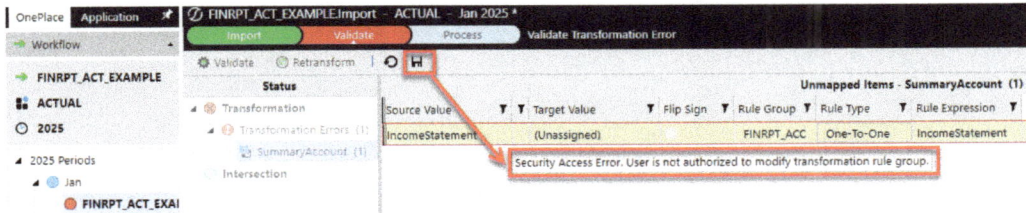

Figure 5.43

> If you are going to allow users to navigate to specific application pages (application user interface roles), the key is to ensure that the application objects on those pages are restricted as to their maintenance group. This is what will allow users to get to those pages but prevent them from modifying the objects on those pages.

We have now covered in detail everything you can find inside every OneStream application, from out-of-the-box security roles and pages to all the different application objects and ways you may want to approach securing these myriad objects. We covered the basic table structure and went into key elements around entity, scenario, workflow, reporting, and data integration security.

What is important to keep in mind is that securing your application(s) can be as simple or complex as your company needs. While it may seem overwhelming in the beginning to determine your security approach, just remember that it can change over time. You may start out with a simple approach and find – during implementation, or even years after go-live – that you want to take a different approach. Your application security is not set in stone and can change to meet evolving business needs.

In the next chapter, we will zoom out of application security to security that applies across an entire environment and go into system security in detail. If application security is like individual homes (there are lots of them!), system security can be likened to postal codes. Postal codes are still important, but there are far fewer postal codes than individual home addresses.

# 6
# System Security

In this chapter, we will take a deep dive into the security elements inside the system layer. Contrary to the application security layer (discussed in Chapter 5), which has a direct impact on end-users' experiences within OneStream, the system security layer is almost exclusively limited to your OneStream administrators and perhaps a small group of other users (e.g., IT users).

The items we will cover in this chapter, while important for overall security, will have a limited impact on end-users. It is safe to say that most, if not all, end-users will never need to navigate to the System tab shown in Figure 6.1. This chapter, therefore, focuses on concepts important to OneStream administrators and limited IT individuals who will need to interact with the System tab.

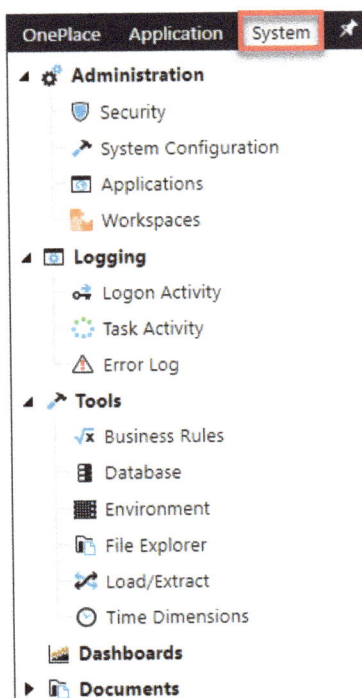

This tab is almost exclusively limited to your administrators.

In rare cases, you may grant your end-users the ability to navigate to this tab for a very limited number of use cases.

Figure 6.1

# System Database

As noted in prior chapters, there is one system database (aka the framework) per environment. All system-specific tables reside in that database.

You can see this by going to the System > Tools > Database page within an environment.

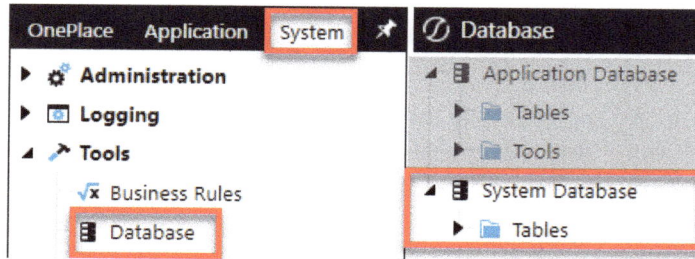

Figure 6.2

On this Database page, you will see that you have Application Database tables, and directly below, you have your System Database tables. These two databases contain all the tables necessary to support your application and system security. In this chapter, we will focus on the system database.

If you were to log out of a particular application, (e.g., OneStream Production application), and log into another application within the *same* environment, (e.g., OneStream Development), you would notice that the System Database tables remain constant on this Database page.

This speaks to what we touched upon in Chapter 2; your framework database, aka the system database, applies to an *entire* environment. There is only one framework database per environment. If you were to log out of a particular environment (e.g., PRD1) and into another environment (e.g., DEV1), it is only then that you would see a different framework database.

In Chapter 8, we will cover how to migrate your security framework from one environment to another. This is an important process as most companies need to copy applications between environments, and in doing so, they will also need to ensure that as they copy applications (which have security group assignments), those application copies (application databases) retain their security groups (framework database).

# System Roles & Pages

Similar to how we have application security roles and application user interface roles (that we learned about in the prior chapter), there are also a handful of out-of-the-box system security roles and system user interface roles. Let us review all of these in detail.

These can be found on the System > Administration > Security > System Security Roles page, as seen in Figure 6.3. There are 18 out-of-the-box **System Security Roles** and 16 **System User Interface Roles**.

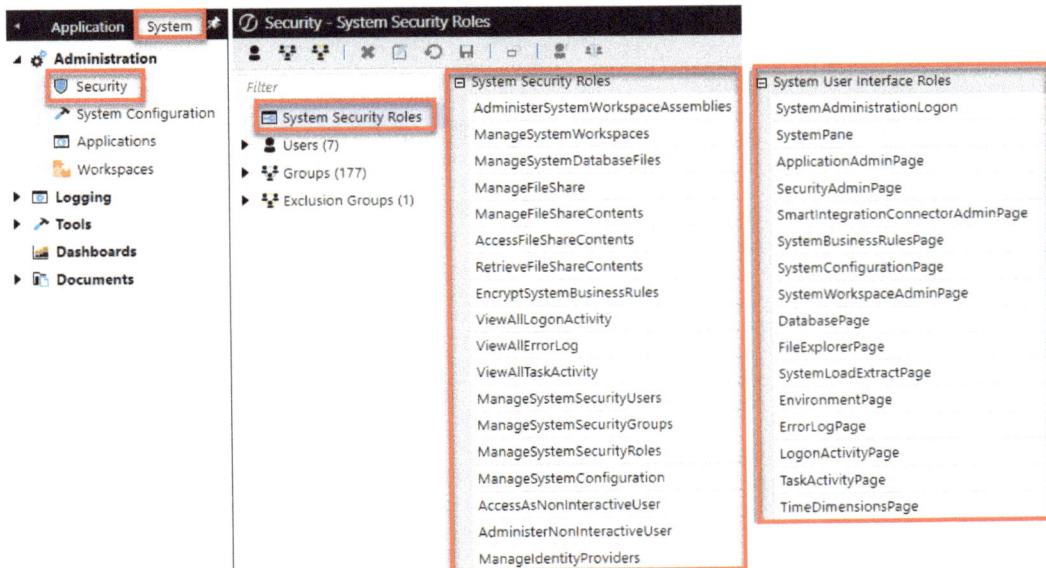

Figure 6.3

## System Security Roles

System security roles are standard (aka out-of-the-box) roles that exist in every customer environment, allowing you to manage different aspects of a OneStream environment. As we learned in the last chapter, these roles answer the question "Can I do X?" across an environment.

Some of these roles, when granted, will require additional security in order to do "X". For example, a user may have access to the security role Administer System Workspace Assemblies (001_SYS_WSADMIN), but that person will still need additional dashboard maintenance group access (008_DMU_X_M) to modify any Workspace assemblies. This is like the concepts covered in Chapter 5, where application roles still – sometimes – require additional security.

However, there are some system roles that, when granted, supersede the need for additional security, which is also similar to some application roles covered in Chapter 5. For example, a user granted access to the security role Manage System Workspaces (`001_SYS_MNG_WS`) will not need any additional dashboard maintenance group or profile access in order to modify Workspaces.

The tables below go over the functionality of each of these 18 system security roles and point out which ones supersede the need for additional security versus which ones are a prerequisite to do something but still require additional security to complete their functionality.

| System Security Role | Description | Pre-requisites / + Additions |
|---|---|---|
| Administer System Workspace Assemblies<br>`001_SYS_WSADMIN` | Allows a user to edit any system assemblies. This applies to all dashboard groups within the generic default Workspace and all non-default Workspaces.<br><br>Maintenance unit security determines access. | + `001_SYS_SYSPANE`<br><br>+ `008_DMU_X_M` |
| Manage System Workspaces<br>`001_SYS_MNG_WS` | Allows a user to create new system dashboards and manage dashboard groups and profiles.<br><br>**Supersedes** dashboard profile and group access. | + `001_SYS_SYSPANE`<br><br>+ `001_SYS_WSPAGE` |
| Manage System Database Files<br>`001_SYS_MNG_DBFILES` | By default, a user has full access to their user folders and files in the application file explorer.<br><br>This role **supersedes** all access, allowing users read and write access to all System Data files and folders. | N/A<br> |
| Manage File Share<br>`001_SYS_MNG_FILESHARE` | The `File Share` is a Windows folder that application servers can read and write. It is configured in the `XFAppServerConfig.xml` file using the file share root folder setting. It is a server-side storage area where external systems or IT can stage and upload files.<br><br>Users with this role can edit these folders and files using File Explorer. | N/A<br> |

| System Security Role | Description | Pre-requisites / + Additions |
|---|---|---|
| Manage File Share Contents<br>001_SYS_MNG_FILECONTENT | Exposes the Contents folder in File Explorer > File Share under Applications and System.<br><br>Grants full rights to create, upload, download, and delete folders. | N/A<br> |
| Access File Share Contents<br>001_SYS_ACC_FILECONTENT | Exposes the Contents folder in File Explorer > File Share under Applications and System.<br><br>Allows only viewing the Contents folder and its files, and allows downloading. | N/A |
| Retrieve File Share Contents<br>001_SYS_RET_FILECONTENT | The Contents folder is not exposed to the user in the File Share for Applications or System using the File Explorer.<br><br>All files are accessible through the OneStream application, such as through dashboards and business rules. | N/A |
| Encrypt System Business Rules<br>**Nobody** | Allows a user to encrypt/decrypt a rule from the Business Rule screen in the System tab to obfuscate the contents of the rule from all users. | Nobody **supersedes** Administrators |
| View All Logon Activity<br>001_SYS_VIEW_LOGON | Users can see the logon activity for all users in the environment. | + 001_SYS_SYSPANE<br><br>+ 001_SYS_LOGONPAGE |
| View All Error Log<br>001_SYS_VIEW_ERROR | Users can see the error log for all users in the environment. | + 001_SYS_SYSPANE<br><br>+ 001_SYS_ERRORPAGE |
| View All Task Activity<br>001_SYS_VIEW_TASK | Users can view the tasks and detailed child steps through the Task Activity icon in the toolbar. | + 001_SYS_SYSPANE<br><br>+ 001_SYS_TASKPAGE |
| Manage System Security Users<br>001_SYS_MNG_USERS | Allows a user to create, modify, delete, and disable users<br><br>Users with this role cannot create, modify, or delete Administrators, directly or indirectly. Also, they cannot:<br><br>• Add or remove themselves to or from groups or roles.<br><br>• Delete themselves.<br><br>• Add other users to Manage System Security privileges.<br><br>• Add or remove groups they are members of from roles. | + 001_SYS_SYSPANE |

Chapter 6

| System Security Role | Description | Pre-requisites / + Additions |
|---|---|---|
| Manage System Security Groups<br><br>001_SYS_MNG_GROUPS | Allows a user to create, modify, copy, and delete groups and exclusion groups. You can also add or remove members and users to or from groups and exclusion groups.<br><br>Users with this role cannot:<br><br>• Modify the Administrators group.<br><br>• Assign users to a group that establishes Administrator privileges.<br><br>• Modify your membership in other groups.<br><br>• Modify the parent group of a group that the user is a member of. | + 001_SYS_SYSPANE |
| Manage System Security Roles<br><br>001_SYS_MNG_ROLES | Allows a user to manage system security roles. However, you cannot:<br><br>• Modify the Manage System Security Role itself.<br><br>• Assign the Everyone or Nobody groups.<br><br>• Add a group to the role of which you are a member. | + 001_SYS_SYSPANE |
| Manage System Configuration<br>001_SYS_MNG_CONFIG | Allows a user to adjust system configurations. Note: native administrators will also need access to this group. | + 001_SYS_SYSPANE<br><br>+ 001_SYS_CONFIGPAGE |
| Access as Non-Interactive User<br>**Nobody** | Allows a user to create, revoke, and access PATs (Personal Access Tokens) for use in API calls. More information can be found in the **Identity and Access Management Guide** under OneStream's support documentation online. | N/A |
| Administer Non-Interactive User<br>**Nobody** | Allows a user to revoke another user's PATs and access information about all PATs related to API calls. More information can be found in the **Identity and Access Management Guide**. | N/A |
| Manage Identity Providers<br>001_SYS_MNG_IP | Allows a user to manage identity providers and add, test, view, edit, and remove OIDC and SAML 2.0-compliant identity providers. | + 001_SYS_SYSPANE<br><br>+ 001_SYS_SICPAGE |

Figure 6.4

There are fewer (18) out-of-the-box system security roles in the table above than application security roles (35) covered in Chapter 5. This is because there are far fewer items a person would need access to from the System tab, and far fewer users needing to get to these roles at all.

In Chapter 2, we discussed two exceptions to the native administrators group having full application access. One was noted in the prior chapter involving the Manage Data Group on the scenario, and the second is below.

> The second exception for users in the native **Administrators** group is that to change access to ancillary table security groups, the admin must also be added to the security group assigned to the Manage System Configuration.

Next, let us talk about the different pages to which a person can (or cannot) navigate within the System tab, which will go together with the system security roles above.

## System User Interface Roles

I like to think of system user interface roles simply as pages. While system security roles answer "Can I do X?", system user interface roles answer "Can I *get to* X?" This is very similar to what we learned in Chapter 5 with application roles and pages.

You may want to allow some admin or IT users to view X, but you do not want to allow them to manage X. So while system roles and system pages *can* go hand-in-hand (meaning that if a person can do X, they will also need to get to X) they can also be separate in the case of allowing certain users to view but not manage X.

Therefore, as mentioned in Chapter 3, when applying security to both system security roles and system pages (001_SYS), you will want to use distinct groups for each so that you can separate the viewer from the doer.

Suppose you want to grant certain pages to subsets of users. In that case, you will set up corresponding security groups (001_SYS_XPAGE), assign the groups to those pages, and then nest these group(s) into your various admin or IT groups (000_GRP).

Once a user has access to reach a page, then additional layers of security (including the manage security roles discussed in the prior section) will apply that will determine *what* the person can see or do once they get to that page. Figure 6.5 lists all the system user interface roles and what access they will grant.

# Chapter 6

| System User Interface Role | Description of Access |
|---|---|
| **System Administration Logon**<br><br>001_SYS_ADMINPAGE | Allows a user to log in to the System Administration only page upon logon, seen here:<br><br>User Name<br><br>admin<br><br>Password<br><br>••••••••<br><br>■ Remember User<br><br>Logon   Logoff<br><br>Application<br><br>(System Administration)<br>(System Administration) |
| **System Pane**<br><br>001_SYS_SYSPANE | Allows access to the System tab, where other page access is defined as per additional system user interface roles:<br><br>◄ OnePlace   Application   System<br>▸ 🗗 Administration<br>▸ 🗔 Logging<br>▸ ↗ Tools<br>   📊 Dashboards<br>▸ 🗎 Documents |
| **Application Admin Page**<br><br>001_SYS_APPPAGE | Grants **view only** access to the following page:<br><br>◄ OnePlace   Application   System<br>▾ 🗗 Administration<br>  🛡 Security<br>  ↗ System Configuration<br>  🖥 Applications<br>  🖳 Workspaces<br>▸ 🗔 Logging<br>▸ ↗ Tools<br>  📊 Dashboards<br>▸ 🗎 Documents |
| **Security Admin Page**<br><br>001_SYS_SECPAGE | Grants **view only** access to the following page:<br><br>◄ OnePlace   Application   System 📌   ⊘ Security<br>▾ 🗗 Administration    👤 👥 👥 ✕ 🗐 🔄<br>  🛡 Security<br>  ↗ System Configuration   *Filter*<br>  🖥 Applications    🖥 System Security Roles<br>  🖳 Workspaces    ▸ 👤 Users (7)<br>▸ 🗔 Logging    ▸ 👥 Groups (177)<br>▸ ↗ Tools    ▸ 👥 Exclusion Groups (1)<br>  📊 Dashboards<br>▸ 🗎 Documents |

| | |
|---|---|
| **Smart Integration Connector Admin Page**<br>001_SYS_SICPAGE | Grants access to this page:<br>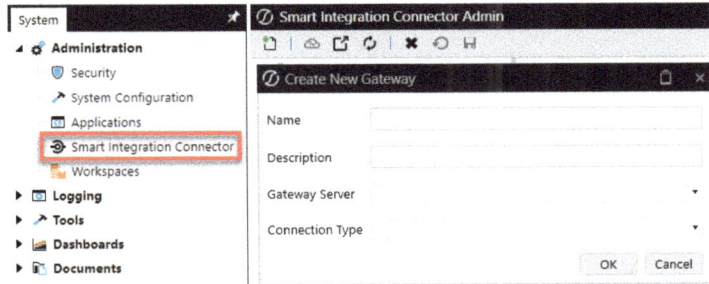 |
| **System Business Rules Page**<br>001_SYS_BRPAGE | Grants access to the System Business Rules page for Extender BRs. Access to BRs once on this page is dependent on Access & Maintenance Groups for each BR:<br>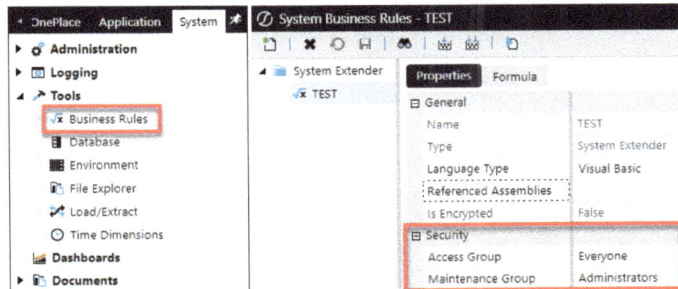 |
| **System Configuration Page**<br>001_SYS_CONFIGPAGE | Grants **view only** access to the following page:<br>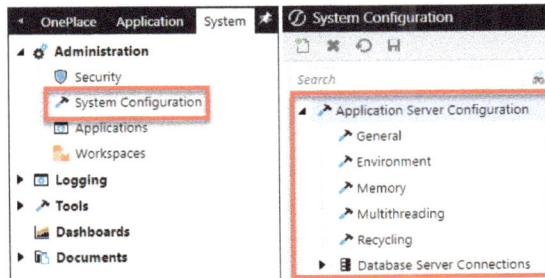 |
| **System Workspace Admin Page**<br>001_SYS_WSPAGE | Grants access to the System Workspaces page. Access to dashboards once on this page is dependent on Access & Maintenance Groups for each dashboard maintenance unit:<br>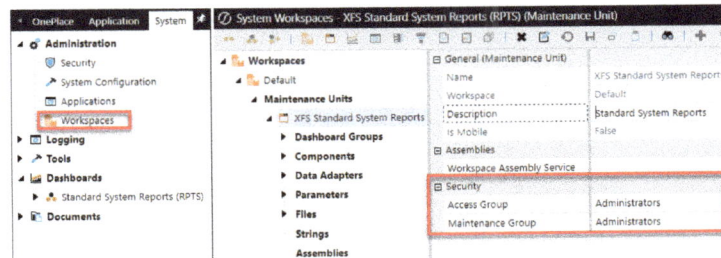 |

# Chapter 6

| | |
|---|---|
| **Database Page**<br>Administrators | **Administrators,** by default, have access to this page. This is under evaluation for future use. |
| **File Explorer Page**<br>001_SYS_FILEPAGE | Grants access to the File Explorer page. Access to files and folders on this page is dependent on Access & Maintenance Groups for those items:<br><br> |
| **System Load Extract Page**<br>Administrators<br>001_SYS_LOADEXTRAC TPAGE | Grants access to the page below. Once on this page, a person's ability to load or extract information will be determined by their additional System Security "Manage" Roles. For example, if a person does not have access to View All Task Activity, then that choice will be grayed out.<br><br>As such, this system user interface role is typically limited to **administrators**.<br><br> |
| **Environment Page**<br>001_SYS_ENVPAGE | Grants access to the following page:<br><br> |

| | |
|---|---|
| **Error Log Page**<br>001_SYS_ERRORPAGE | Grants access to the following page. A person will only see their own error log unless they have also been granted the View All Error Log security role.<br><br>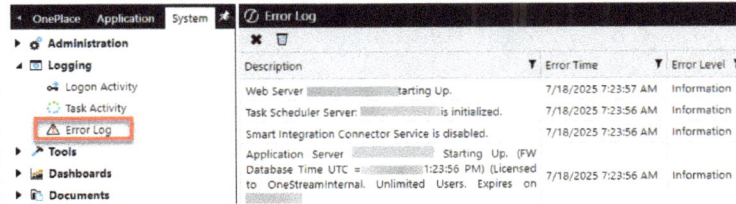 |
| **Logon Activity Page**<br>001_SYS_LOGONPAGE | Grants access to the following page. A person will only see their own logon attempts unless they have also been granted the View All Logon Activity security role. You can view all users but cannot log them off. By default, only administrators have access to this section.<br><br>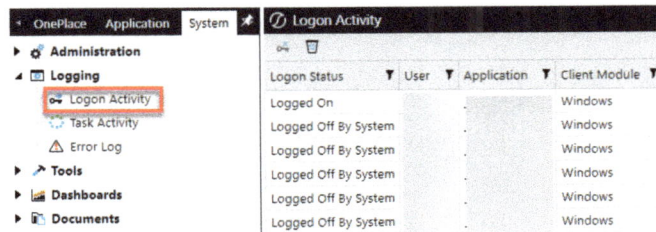 |
| **Task Activity Page**<br>001_SYS_TASKPAGE | Grants view access to the following page. A person will only see their own tasks unless they have also been granted the View All Task Activity security role.<br><br>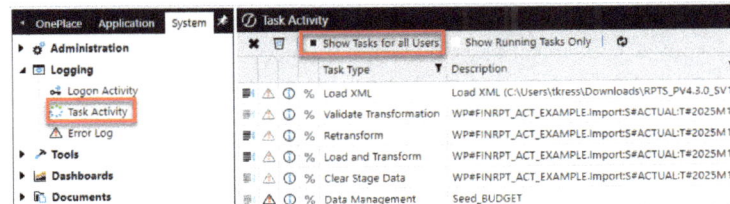 |

| Time Dimension Page 001_SYS_TIMEDIMPAGE | Grants access to the following page: 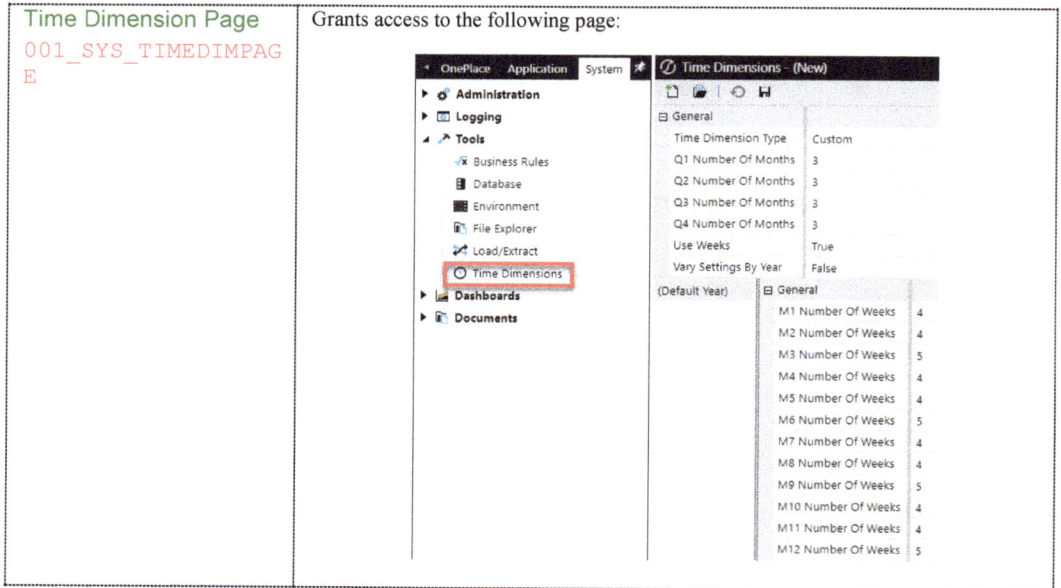 |
| --- | --- |

Figure 6.5

A common theme with system user interface roles is that they will allow a user to get to a specific application page; however, *other* security access will determine what that user can see and do once on that page.

As mentioned previously, of the 18 system security roles, over half (10) of them require additional page access via a corresponding system user interface role. This means if a person can do X, they will naturally also need to be able to navigate to X.

To bring all these out-of-the-box roles together, Figure 6.6 shows the correlation between system security roles (*doer*) and system user interface roles (*viewer*).

| System Security Role | + | System User Interface Role |
|---|---|---|
| Administer System Workspace Assemblies<br>001_SYS_WSADMIN | + | System Pane<br>001_SYS_SYSPANE |
| Manage System Workspaces<br>001_SYS_MNG_WS | + | System Pane<br>001_SYS_SYSPANE<br>System Workspace Admin Page<br>001_SYS_WSPAGE |
| View All Logon Activity<br>001_SYS_VIEW_LOGON | + | System Pane<br>001_SYS_SYSPANE<br>Logon Activity Page<br>001_SYS_LOGONPAGE |
| View All Error Log<br>001_SYS_VIEW_ERROR | + | System Pane<br>001_SYS_SYSPANE<br>Error Log Page<br>001_SYS_ERRORPAGE |
| View All Task Activity<br>001_SYS_VIEW_TASK | + | System Pane<br>001_SYS_SYSPANE<br>Task Activity Page<br>001_SYS_TASKPAGE |
| Manage System Security Users<br>001_SYS_MNG_USERS | + | System Pane<br>001_SYS_SYSPANE |
| Manage System Security Groups<br>001_SYS_MNG_GROUPS | + | System Pane<br>001_SYS_SYSPANE |
| Manage System Security Roles<br>001_SYS_MNG_ROLES | + | System Pane<br>001_SYS_SYSPANE |
| Manage System Configuration<br>001_SYS_MNG_CONFIG | + | System Pane<br>001_SYS_SYSPANE<br>System Configuration Page<br>001_SYS_CONFIGPAGE |
| Manage Identity Providers<br>001_SYS_MNG_IP | + | Smart Integration Connector Admin Page<br>001_SYS_SICPAGE |

Figure 6.6

Now that we have discussed the out-of-the-box system security roles and pages, let us discuss which ones of these – if any – you may want to allow your end-users to access.

As a general rule of thumb, basic end-users of OneStream will not need to access the System tab. The types of activities found on this tab span the entire environment and are not limited to just one application. So, if you are taking the "less is more approach", you may not grant the majority of your end-users access to get to the System tab.

But as with everything, there are exceptions. Circling back to the pin we placed in Figure 6.1, in some cases, you may want to grant users the ability to see the Logging activities on the System tab. These activities are shown in Figure 6.7.

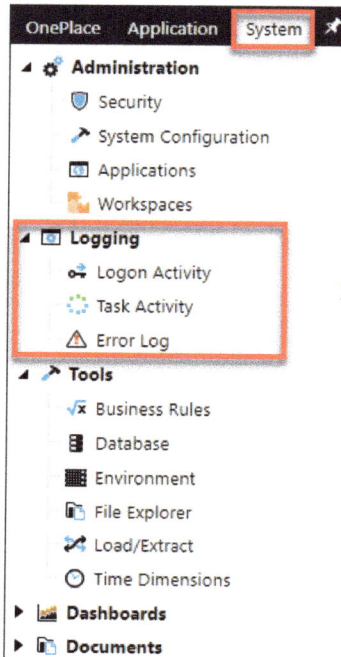

Figure 6.7

If this is the case, remember the concepts discussed in Chapters 2 and 3. You will create a user group (000_GRP_LOGACTIVITY), place users into that group, and then embed the appropriate 001_SYS security roles and pages into this group, as shown in Figure 6.8.

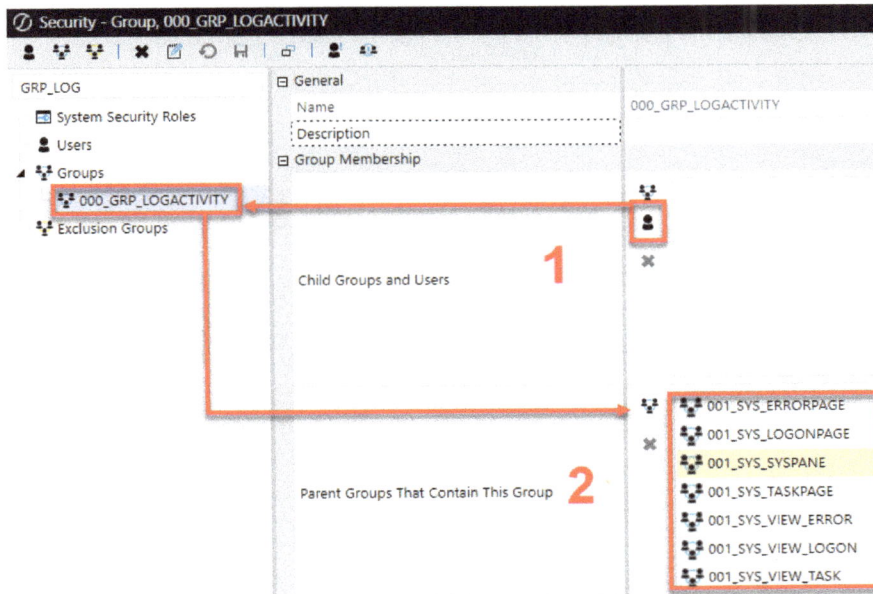

Figure 6.8

# System Objects

After granting system security roles and system user interface roles (001_SYS), the next step is to determine how to secure the other limited number of objects that appear on the System tab. Unlike with application objects, of which we said there are almost a limitless number of application objects grouped into 13 categories, the same is not true for system objects.

System objects fall into three categories:

1. **Business Rules**

2. **Workspaces / Dashboards** (maintenance units & profiles)

3. **Explorer** (files & folders)

Everything else on the System tab is a page that allows you to review or manage certain items, but these three categories of objects – as shown in Figure 6.9 – are pages that themselves can contain a limitless number of individual objects. If desired, you can secure them individually.

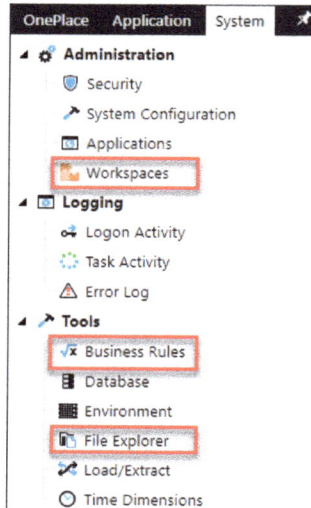

Figure 6.9

There are two security groups associated with securing these three sets of system objects: **Access** and **Maintenance**, as shown in Figure 6.10. If you are taking the "less is more" or simpler approach to your system security, you may control their access by limiting who can get to these three pages via their system user interface roles, discussed earlier in this chapter.

But if you need to limit security further, you can secure individual sets of business rules, dashboards, or files and folders on these system pages via their access or maintenance groups.

|  | Access | Maintenance |
|---|---|---|
| Business Rules | Yes | Yes |
| Workspace / Dashboard Profiles | Yes | Yes |
| Explorer Files & Folders | Yes | Yes |

Figure 6.10

# System Tables

So, where are all these system objects stored? They are stored in the system database discussed earlier in this chapter, which is accessed from the System > Tools > Database page.

There are approximately 80 out-of-the-box tables in any given framework database. That number will grow if any Solution Exchange tools or custom tables have been added to the framework database. Any additional tables will also appear on the System Database page, as shown in Figure 6.11.

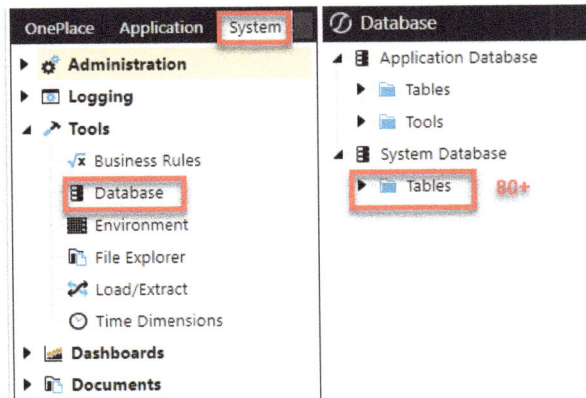

Figure 6.11

These 80+ system tables consist of tables for the following types of items:

- Audit Tables

- System Objects Tables

- Security Group & User Tables

- Server Configuration Tables

- Custom or Solution Exchange Tables (e.g., OSD tables)

The most important tables within the system tables are those that contain your security groups and users. The security group tables form a direct link between the framework database and your application database. As we discussed in Chapter 5, it is the unique ID associated with each security group that is the ID that is stored within all tables in your application database.

In the next section, let us explore your security group and user tables in more detail.

## Security Group Tables

As we learned in Chapter 5, every application table with security groups will maintain those groups by a unique ID in the application database rather than the security group name. Figure 6.12 shows an example of this from the Cube View Group application table, where we can see a unique ID for the Access Group Unique ID and the Maintenance Group Unique ID.

Figure 6.12

The link between our application tables, such as the Cube View group table above, and the system framework tables is, therefore, the unique ID (as shown by the first set of arrows in Figure 6.13).

By creating that first link based on the unique ID from the application tables (e.g., the CubeViewGroup table) to the SecGroup (or SecExclGroup) system table, we can pull back the security group name, which is what is recognizable to everyone in OneStream.

Then, if you need to dive deeper into nested security groups, you can make the second link, again based on the unique ID, to go from the SecGroup (or SecExclGroup) table to the SecGroupChild (or SecExclGroupChild) table, all contained within the framework database.

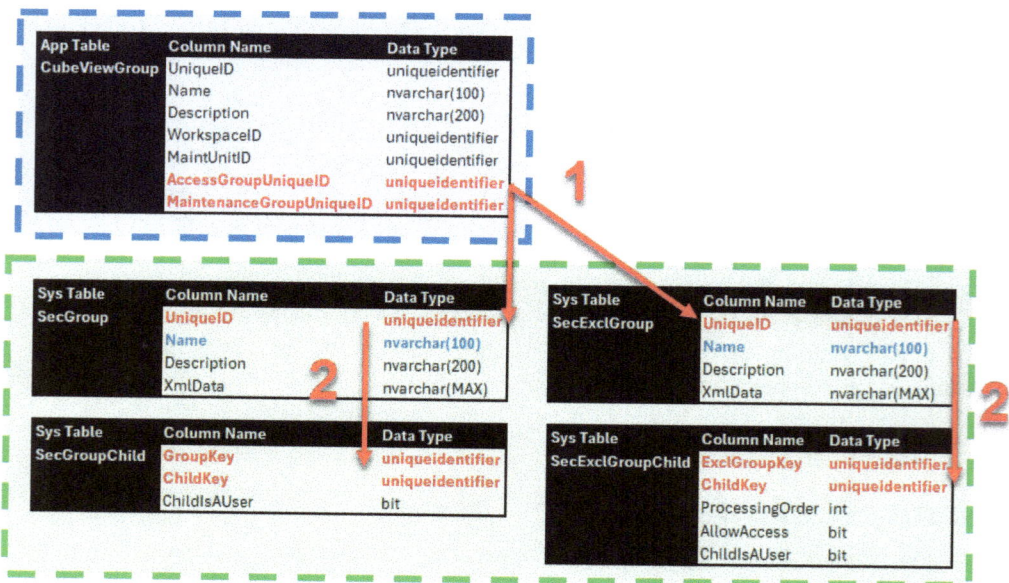

Figure 6.13

What is key to understanding all of this is that the link between application tables containing application object security, and the system security tables is all based on the unique identifier being the security group ID. To get a list of security groups attached to application objects by security group name, you have to make this link.

The other key thing to remember is that Azure will not natively let you run SQL against two databases (application and framework). That is a native Azure restriction. Therefore, to run queries against both databases, you will have to do so via a business rule, whereby you open two separate database connections and join tables within the construct of that business rule.

## Security User Tables

While security groups are only stored in the application tables as unique IDs, the same is not true for users within the application audit tables. There are approximately 75 application audit tables that store "who did what when" within an application by the user name, as opposed to a unique ID.

Why is this relevant? This makes querying and presenting reports displaying audit actions inside of OneStream easier than presenting a report that displays what security group is attached to which application object. This is because you do *not* need to query across the application database tables and system database (e.g., framework) tables. All audit tables are self-contained within the application database only.

Because the audit tables store "who did what when" by the user name (e.g., `AuditUser` column in the application audit tables) as opposed to a unique user ID, there is no need to join tables across databases. An example of this is shown in Figure 6.14, where the `AuditAppProperty` table is displayed with the user name presented in the `AuditUser` column.

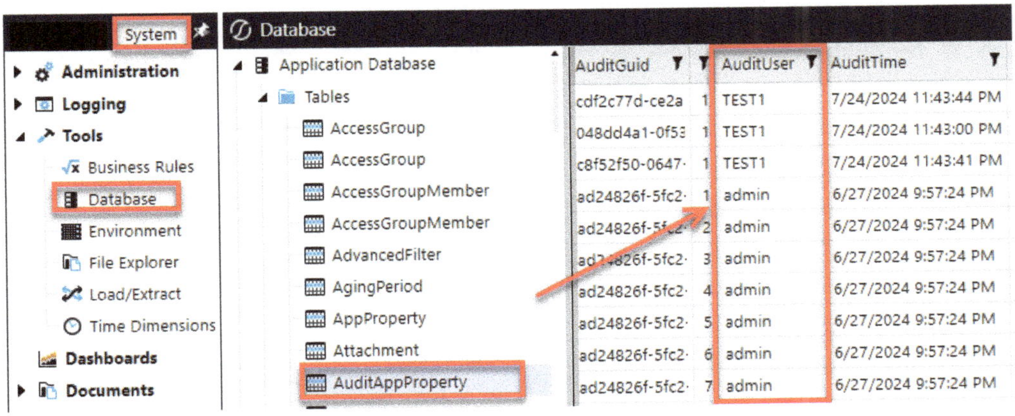

Figure 6.14

There is a consequence of audit tables storing the user name as opposed to the unique ID. This was discussed in Chapter 2 when we talked about deleting versus disabling a user. If you delete a user, that user name is available to be used again.

And because the audit tables store "who did what when" by user name (and not a unique ID), that means you can set up a user with the same name as before, and it will appear as if that new user took action in the audit tables which – in fact – could have been actions taken by the previous, not current, user.

We touched upon this in the prior chapter and will revisit it in Chapter 8 when we talk about the security audit reports and how you can use all the reports together to audit user actions properly.

## Ancillary Tables

In this chapter and the prior chapter, we have covered all the out-of-the-box or standard application and system tables. These tables are found in every customer application and environment and *cannot* be edited or altered as they are fundamental to OneStream functionality.

So, what about any custom tables you created in your OneStream application? Or tables that are installed as part of the Solution Exchange tools? Those are considered ancillary tables in OneStream. They are additional database tables (either within the application or framework database) that can be created and edited to support various customizations and additional functionality with OneStream.

These tables can be key to supporting your OneStream applications and functionality, but access to these tables is not automatic because they are custom additions to your out-of-the-box application and framework tables.

Granting access to ancillary tables is important because it allows users to view, edit, and maintain the data within these tables. You can grant security to these ancillary tables by going to the System tab > System Configuration Page > OneStream Database Server, as shown in Figure 6.15.

Do not forget the exception we mentioned earlier in that, whatever security group you have assigned to the Manage System Configuration role, the user will also need to be in that group to reach the screen in Figure 6.15, even native **Administrators**!

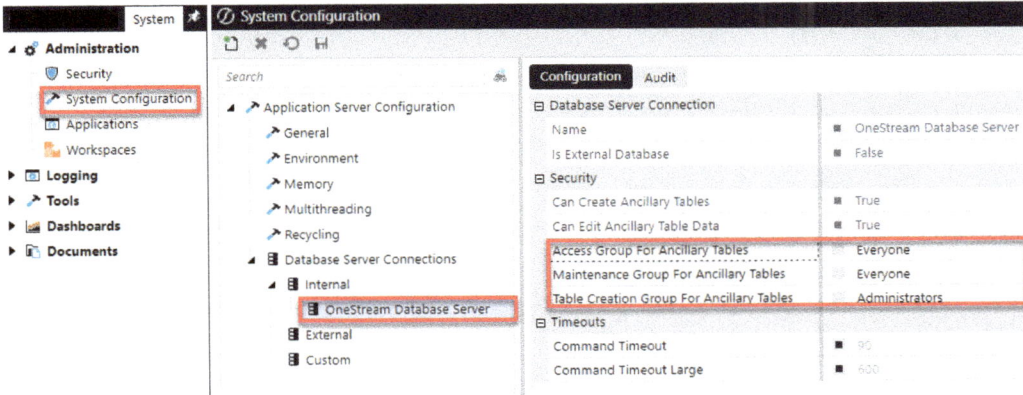

Figure 6.15

The three security groups I want to highlight are:

- Access Group for Ancillary Tables
- Maintenance Group for Ancillary Tables
- Table Creation Group for Ancillary Tables

First, the only people who should be allowed to *create* custom tables will typically be your native administrators group. This is the group that can create custom tables to support functionality within your application, or the group that can download, load, and use "setup tables" functionality for Solution Exchange tools.

The other two groups for access and maintenance will be needed by users requiring access and/or interactions with any Solution Exchange tools. Think of Account Reconciliations (XFW_RCM tables) or People Planning (XFW_PLP tables) in which you will have users who will need to view and make changes within these solutions.

As a rule of thumb, I suggest setting the Access to Ancillary Tables and Maintenance to Ancillary Tables to Everyone. This will allow users to get to, and interact with, any custom or Solution Exchange tools. Their workflow security will further control access to Solution Exchange tools.

Now that we have covered *how* and *what* you can secure on the System tab, let us delve into the final piece of system security: security APIs (Application Programming Interfaces). Admit it, you might have heard about APIs but never knew what that acronym means until now, right?

# Security APIs

An API, or Application Programming Interface, is a set of rules that allows software applications to communicate with each other. APIs are used to share data, functionality, and services between applications, systems, and devices.

Figure 6.16 shows all the security APIs currently available in OneStream.

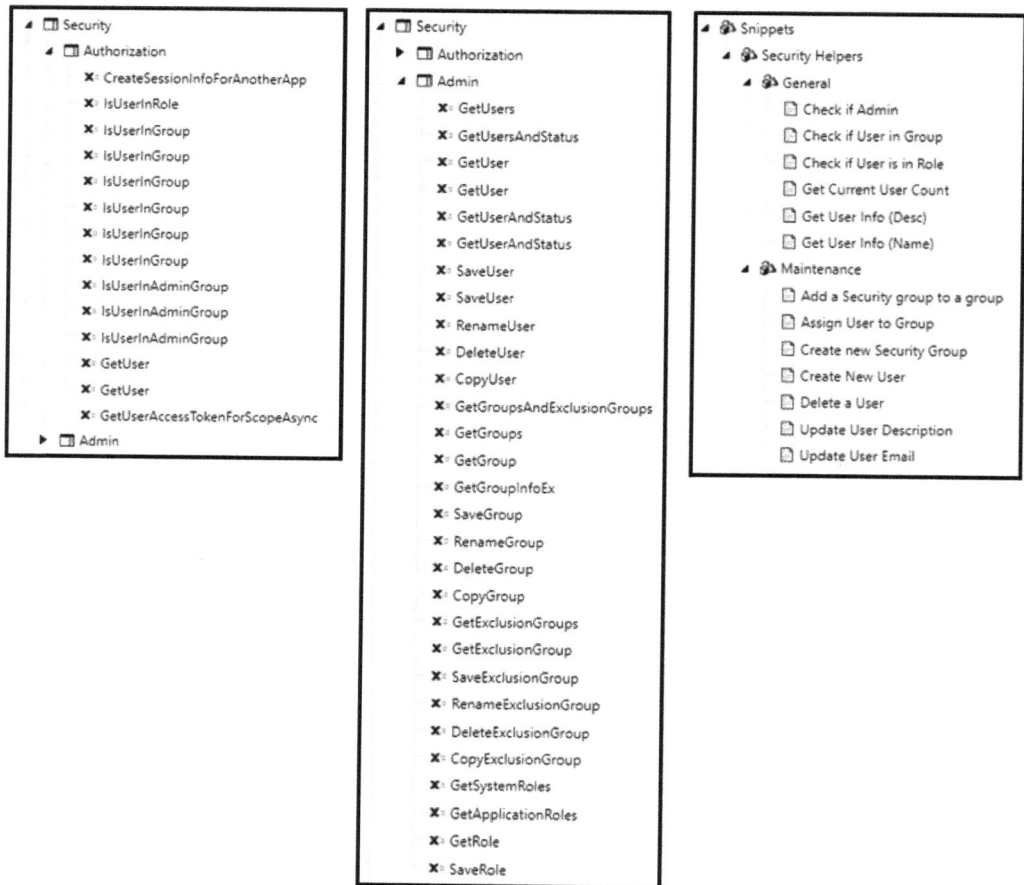

Figure 6.16

The BRApi.Security.Authorization functions are listed in Figure 6.17 below.

| FUNCTION | EXAMPLE |
|---|---|
| Create Session Info For Another App | Dim si As SessionInfo = BRApi.Security.Authorization.CreateSessionInfoForAnotherApp(siSource, appName, openAppResult) |
| Is User In Role | Dim bValue As Boolean = BRApi.Security.Authorization.IsUserInRole(si, roleTypeId) |
| Is User In Group | Dim bValue As Boolean = BRApi.Security.Authorization.IsUserInGroup(si, groupName) |
| | Dim bValue As Boolean = BRApi.Security.Authorization.IsUserInGroup(si, groupID) |
| | Dim bValue As Boolean = BRApi.Security.Authorization.IsUserInGroup(si, userName, groupName, allowAccessIfInAdministratorsGroup) |
| | Dim bValue As Boolean = BRApi.Security.Authorization.IsUserInGroup(si, userID, groupName, allowAccessIfInAdministratorsGroup) |
| | Dim bValue As Boolean = BRApi.Security.Authorization.IsUserInGroup(si, userName, groupID, allowAccessIfInAdministratorsGroup) |
| | Dim bValue As Boolean = BRApi.Security.Authorization.IsUserInGroup(si, userID, groupID, allowAccessIfInAdministratorsGroup) |
| Is User In Admin Group | Dim bValue As Boolean = BRApi.Security.Authorization.IsUserInAdminGroup(si) |
| | Dim bValue As Boolean = BRApi.Security.Authorization.IsUserInAdminGroup(si, userName) |
| | Dim bValue As Boolean = BRApi.Security.Authorization.IsUserInAdminGroup(si, userID) |
| Get User | Dim objUserInfo As UserInfo = BRApi.Security.Authorization.GetUser(si, userName) |
| | Dim objUserInfo As UserInfo = BRApi.Security.Authorization.GetUser(si, userID) |
| Get User Access Token For Scope Async | Dim objSystem.Threading.Tasks.Task`1[[OneStream.Shared.Wcf.OISAccessToken, OneStream.SharedWcfContract, Version=1.0.0.0, Culture=neutral, PublicKeyToken=null]] As System.Threading.Tasks.Task`1[[OneStream.Shared.Wcf.OISAccessToken, OneStream.SharedWcfContract, Version=1.0.0.0, Culture=neutral, PublicKeyToken=null]] = BRApi.Security.Authorization.GetUserAccessTokenForScopeAsync(si, scopes) |

Figure 6.17

The BRApi.Security.Admin functions are listed in Figure 6.18 below.

| FUNCTION | EXAMPLE |
|---|---|
| Copy Exclusion Group | BRApi.Security.Admin.CopyExclusionGroup(si, uniqueID, newName, copyListOfChildPrincipals) |
| Copy Group | BRApi.Security.Admin.CopyGroup(si, uniqueID, newName, copyListOfChildPrincipals, copyListOfParentGroups) |

| Copy User | BRApi.Security.Admin.CopyUser(si, uniqueID, newName, copyListOfParentGroups) |
|---|---|
| Delete Exclusion Group | BRApi.Security.Admin.DeleteExclusionGroup(si, exclusionGroupName) |
| Delete Group | BRApi.Security.Admin.DeleteGroup(si, groupName) |
| Delete User | BRApi.Security.Admin.DeleteUser(si, userName) |
| Get Application Roles | objList = BRApi.Security.Admin.GetApplicationRoles(si) |
| Get Exclusion Group | Dim objExclusionGroupInfo As ExclusionGroupInfo = BRApi.Security.Admin.GetExclusionGroup(si, exclusionGroupName) |
| | objList = BRApi.Security.Admin.GetExclusionGroups(si) |
| Get Group | Dim objGroupInfo As GroupInfo = BRApi.Security.Admin.GetGroup(si, groupName) |
| Get Group Info Ex | Dim objGroupInfoEx As GroupInfoEx = BRApi.Security.Admin.GetGroupInfoEx(si, uniqueID) |
| Get Groups | objList = BRApi.Security.Admin.GetGroups(si) |
| Get Groups And Exclusion Groups | objList = BRApi.Security.Admin.GetGroupsAndExclusionGroups(si) |
| Get Role | Dim objRoleInfo As RoleInfo = BRApi.Security.Admin.GetRole(si, roleName) |
| Get System Roles | objList = BRApi.Security.Admin.GetSystemRoles(si) |
| Get User | Dim objUserInfo As UserInfo = BRApi.Security.Admin.GetUser(si, userName) |
| | Dim objUserInfo As UserInfo = BRApi.Security.Admin.GetUser(si, userID) |
| | objList = BRApi.Security.Admin.GetUsers(si) |
| Get User And Status | Dim objUserInfoAndStatus As UserInfoAndStatus = BRApi.Security.Admin.GetUserAndStatus(si, userName) |
| | Dim objUserInfoAndStatus As UserInfoAndStatus = BRApi.Security.Admin.GetUserAndStatus(si, userID) |
| | objList = BRApi.Security.Admin.GetUsersAndStatus(si) |
| Rename Exclusion Group | BRApi.Security.Admin.RenameExclusionGroup(si, uniqueID, newName) |
| Rename Group | BRApi.Security.Admin.RenameGroup(si, uniqueID, newName) |
| Rename User | BRApi.Security.Admin.RenameUser(si, uniqueID, newName) |
| Save Exclusion Group | BRApi.Security.Admin.SaveExclusionGroup(si, exclusiongroupInfo, isNew) |
| Save Group | BRApi.Security.Admin.SaveGroup(si, groupInfo, updateListOfParentGroups, parentGroupIDs, isNew) |
| Save Role | BRApi.Security.Admin.SaveRole(si, role) |
| Save User | BRApi.Security.Admin.SaveUser(si, user, updateListOfParentGroups, parentGroupIDs, isNew) |
| | BRApi.Security.Admin.SaveUser(si, user, newInternalProviderPW, updateListOfParentGroups, parentGroupIDs, isNew) |

Figure 6.18

Below, in Figure 6.19, are some snippet examples.

| SNIPPET | EXAMPLE |
|---|---|
| Check if Admin | 'Check to see if the current user is an administrator (Returns True/False)<br>Dim userIsAdmin As Boolean = BRApi.Security.Authorization.IsUserInAdminGroup(si) |
| Check if User in Group | 'Check to see if the current user is in a specified security group (Returns True/False)<br>Dim secGroup As String = "Everyone" '<--Enter name Of the security Group To test for current user<br>Dim isUserInGroup As Boolean = BRApi.Security.Authorization.IsUserInGroup(si, secGroup) |
| Check if User in Role | 'Check to see if the current user is in a specified security role (Returns True/False)<br>Dim roleTypeID As onestream.Shared.Wcf.RoleTypeId = onestream.Shared.Wcf.RoleTypeId.ManageData '<-- Specify the RoleTypeID to test<br>Dim isUserInRole As Boolean = BRApi.Security.Authorization.IsUserInRole(si, roleTypeID) |
| Get Current User Count | 'Get current security user count (Returns datatable)<br>Dim isEnabled As Integer = 1 '<- specify if disabled users should be included in the count (True = 1, False = 0)<br>Dim intUserCount As Integer = 0<br>'Define SQL Query<br>Dim sql As New Text.StringBuilder<br>sql.AppendLine("Select COUNT([Name]) as UserCount ")<br>sql.AppendLine("From [SecUser] ")<br>sql.AppendLine("Where IsEnabled = " & isEnabled)<br>'Execute Query on App DB<br>Using dbConnFw As DBConnInfo = BRApi.Database.CreateFrameworkDbConnInfo(si)<br>  Dim dtCount As DataTable = BRAPi.Database.ExecuteSql(dbConnFw, sql.ToString, True)<br>  If Not dtCount Is Nothing Then<br>    For Each row As DataRow In dtCount.Rows<br>      intUserCount = row("UserCount")<br>    Next<br>  End If<br>End Using |
| Get User Info (Desc) | 'Get current user description<br>Dim userDesc As String = String.Empty<br>Dim objUser As UserInfo = BRApi.Security.Authorization.GetUser(si, si.AuthToken.UserName)<br>If Not objUser Is Nothing Then<br>  userDesc = objUser.User.Description<br>End If |
| Get User Info (Name) | 'Get current user name<br>Dim userName As String = si.AuthToken.UserName |

# Chapter 6

| | |
|---|---|
| Add a Security Group to a Group | ```vbnet
'Add a group to another group.
Dim groupAddingTo As String = "Administrators"
Dim groupBeingAdded As String = "Test Group"
'Add a group to another group.
Dim objGroup1Info As GroupInfo = BRApi.Security.Admin.GetGroup(si, groupAddingTo)
Dim objGroup2Info As GroupInfo = BRApi.Security.Admin.GetGroup(si, groupBeingAdded)
If Not objGroup1Info Is Nothing And Not objGroup2Info Is Nothing Then
    Dim objOtherGroupInfoEx As GroupInfoEx = BRApi.Security.Admin.GetGroupInfoEx(si, objGroup2Info.Group.UniqueID)
    If Not objOtherGroupInfoEx Is Nothing Then
        If (Not objOtherGroupInfoEx.ParentGroups.ContainsKey(objGroup1Info.Group.UniqueID)) Then
            Dim parentGroupIDs As List(Of Guid) = objOtherGroupInfoEx.ParentGroups.Keys.ToList()
            parentGroupIDs.Add(objGroup1Info.Group.UniqueID)
            BRApi.Security.Admin.SaveGroup(si, objGroup2Info, True, parentGroupIDs, TriStateBool.Unknown)
        End If
    End If
End If
``` |
| Assign User to Group | ```vbnet
'Get Group Info
Dim secGroupName As String = "Administrators"
'User Info
Dim userName As String = "TestUser1"
'Get a Group And UserInfo Object And add the Group To the user's list of parent groups.
Dim objGroupInfo As GroupInfo = BRApi.Security.Admin.GetGroup(si, secGroupName)
If Not objGroupInfo Is Nothing Then
    Dim objUserInfo As UserInfo = BRApi.Security.Admin.GetUser(si, userName)
    If Not objUserInfo Is Nothing Then
        If (Not objUserInfo.ParentGroups.ContainsKey(objGroupInfo.Group.UniqueID)) Then
            Dim parentGroupIDs As List(Of Guid) = objUserInfo.ParentGroups.Keys.ToList()
            parentGroupIDs.Add(objGroupInfo.Group.UniqueID)
            BRApi.Security.Admin.SaveUser(si, objUserInfo.User, True, parentGroupIDs, TriStateBool.Unknown)
        End If
    End If
End If
``` |
| Create New Security Group | ```vbnet
'Get Group Info
Dim newGroupName As String = "Test Group"
'Create a New Group
Dim objGroup As Group = New Group()
objGroup.Name = newGroupName
Dim objGroupInfo As GroupInfo = New GroupInfo()
objGroupInfo.Group = objGroup
BRApi.Security.Admin.SaveGroup(si, objGroupInfo, False, Nothing, TriStateBool.Unknown)
``` |
```

| | |
|---|---|
| Create New User | ```
'Get User Info
Dim newUserName As String = "TestUser1"
Dim newUserDesc As String = "Test User 1"
Dim newUserText1 As String = "User Text"
'Create a New user
Dim objUser As User = New User()
objUser.Name = newUserName
objUser.Description = newUserDesc
objUser.Text1 = newUserText1
BRApi.Security.Admin.SaveUser(si, objUser, False, Nothing,
TriStateBool.Unknown)
``` |
| Delete a User | ```
Get User Info
Dim userToDelete As String = "TestUser1"
'Delete user
BRApi.Security.Admin.DeleteUser(si, userToDelete)
``` |
| Update User Description | ```
'Get a UserInfo Object And change the user's description.
Dim userToUpdate As String = "TestUser" '<--Enter user name to update
Dim updatedDescription As String = "User Description"  '<-- Enter new user description
Dim objUserInfo As UserInfo = BRApi.Security.Admin.GetUser(si, userToUpdate)
If Not objUserInfo Is Nothing Then
    objUserInfo.User.Description = updatedDescription
    BRApi.Security.Admin.SaveUser(si, objUserInfo.User, False, Nothing,
TriStateBool.Unknown)
End If
``` |
| Update User Email | ```
'Get a UserInfo Object And change the user's email address
Dim userToUpdate As String = "TestUser" '<--Enter user name to update
Dim updatedEmail As String = "UserEmailAddress@provider.com"  '<-- Enter user email address
Dim objUserInfo As UserInfo = BRApi.Security.Admin.GetUser(si, userToUpdate)
If Not objUserInfo Is Nothing Then
    objUserInfo.User.Email = updatedEmail
    BRApi.Security.Admin.SaveUser(si, objUserInfo.User, False, Nothing,
TriStateBool.Unknown)
End If
``` |

Figure 6.19

At this point, we have covered the foundational building blocks to security and your end-user experience in OneStream: the framework and environment (Chapter 2), design concepts and naming conventions (Chapter 3), common roles (Chapter 4) and took a deep dive into the application (Chapter 5) and framework (aka system) databases in this chapter.

In the remaining two chapters, let us turn our attention to some equally important security concepts that are most relevant to OneStream administrators. In Chapter 7, we will cover slice security, No Input BRs, and some common Solution Exchange tools and their security.

We will end with all the things administrators will want to understand about reporting, testing, maintaining, migrating and auditing security.

# 7

# Other Security

At this point, we have taken a tour around the OneStream neighborhood, including the application and system databases, users and groups, objects and data, roles and pages, and the hundreds of tables supporting all those items. We are now ready to leave the confines of our neighborhood and branch out to 'other' security.

Other security goes beyond these fundamental building blocks of all customers' OneStream security. While the prior chapters covered security that can be found in *every* customer environment and application, this chapter will delve into security that can be extended or added to your OneStream application or environment. The concepts covered in this chapter may not be used on every project or in every customer application; however, they are important enough to be covered in a book on OneStream security.

## Slice Security

Many people may have heard of slice security, like a buzzword, but do not fully understand what it is, or have had the opportunity to leverage it. First, you will want to understand what it is and why you *may* want to leverage it on your project or in your application.

Slice security, known formally as **Cube Data Access** security, allows you to grant security to *any or all* 18 OneStream cube dimensions at a granular level of detail:

- Entity & Parent
- Consolidation
- Scenario
- Time
- View
- Account, Flow & UD1-8
- Origin
- IC

As we learned in prior chapters, there are out-of-the-box data security groups associated with the cube, entity, and scenario, as shown in Figure 7.1. And these data security groups work in conjunction with each other, meaning if you have Access Group to a cube, along with Read and Write Data Group to an entity, but have *only* Read Data Group to a particular scenario, then you will have the lesser of those rights, or read-only access, to that cube, entity, and scenario combination.

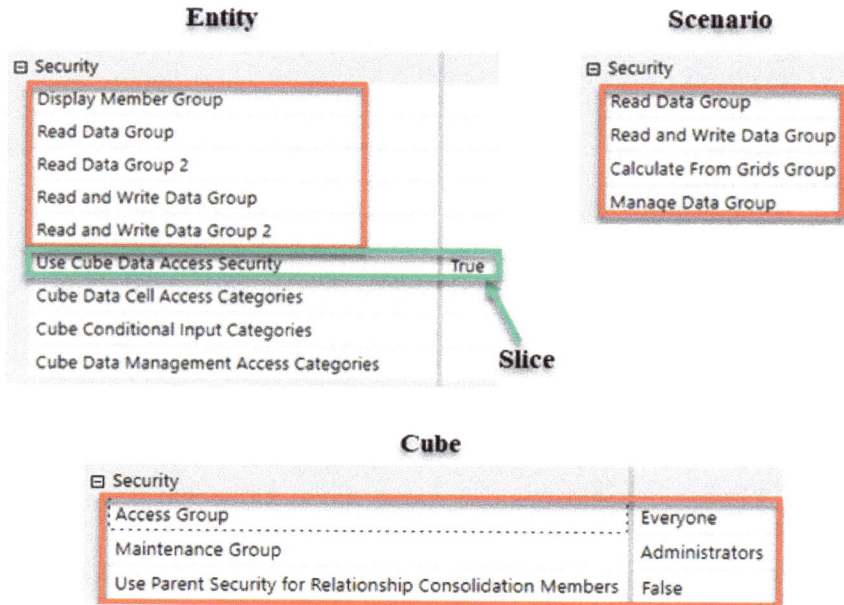

Figure 7.1

But what happens when securing your data by cube, entity, and scenario alone is not enough? Or when perhaps you want to be more granular or dynamic in how you apply your entity or scenario security? This is where **Slice Security** comes into play.

Slice security is set up on the cube (as we will see later in this section), but the starting point for turning on slice security resides within the Entity dimension. The True/False toggle switch (in Figure 7.1) that tells OneStream to continue to look at the cube for additional access rights is set at each entity.

If you are not using slice security, this setting should be False across all entities at all levels. By setting this to false, OneStream stops after applying the Display Member Group, Read Data Group and Read and Write Data Group listed on each entity, rather than continuing to the cube for further data access application.

To turn on slice security at the cube level, you will start by setting this to True across all entities where you want to apply more granular slice security. This means you can determine, *by entity*, whether you want OneStream to look to the cube for additional security, as shown in Figure 7.2.

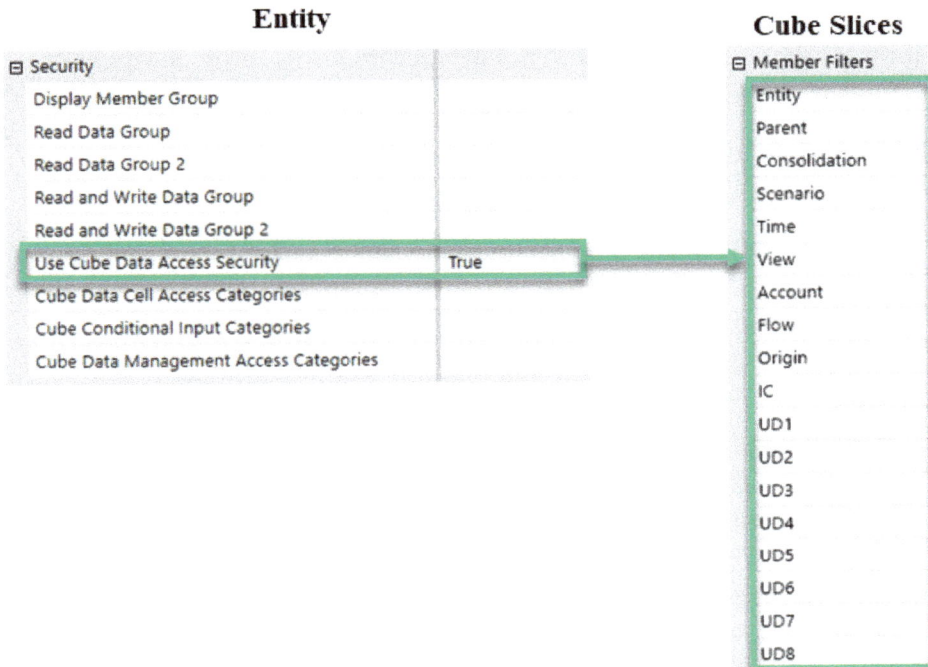

Figure 7.2

In general, if you are using slice security to apply a more granular level of data access by Account, Flow, or UD1-8, you will want to do so for all entities. But just know that does not have to be the case.

Say, for example, that you only need additional data security at a base entity level to control data entry by Account, Flow, or UDs. You can, therefore, set this toggle to true only for base entities, as base entities are where data entry happens. For all parent entities, you could leave this set to false.

📌 Why is this important to understand? Because enabling slice security *can* have performance implications. Let us stick a pin in this for now, but just know that, unless you need an entity to look to the cube for additional data security access, it is best to leave those entities set to false.

## Use Cases

The most common use case for applying slice security is when you have a User Defined dimension (UD1-8) to which you want to restrict access. If you recall from Chapter 5, Account, Flow, and the User Defined dimensions have only one security group associated with them, a Display Member Group, as shown again in Figure 7.3.

Figure 7.3

This display member group only controls whether people can see this member or not. It does not allow you to control whether a user has read or write access to a particular UD member. Therefore, if you need to secure a User Defined dimension, you will need to use slice security.

Another less often considered use case can be applying dynamic security to any of your 18 dimensions. Let us walk through two use cases around dynamic security – using slices – to get a better understanding.

For the first use case, imagine you have an entity hierarchy that is often changing: say your Entity dimension represents sales regions, and those regions are often reorganized. Applying slice security to your Entity dimension can help reduce overall security maintenance.

Changing your Entity dimension necessitates the need for re-consolidations or re-aggregations of historical data, but some companies may make frequent entity hierarchy changes. If you are only using the read and write groups at the entity level, and/or relying upon nesting your security groups to control entity access, you could be left with a maintenance nightmare of constantly updating security groups and security group nesting as your entity structure changes.

Let us walk through an example to understand this use case better. Imagine that your entity hierarchy appears as on the left (Figure 7.4), and you want to grant read access to users responsible for Territory 1 to the cities in Territory 1. If you were *not* using slice security, your security group nesting may appear as per Figure 7.4 on the right.

**Entity Hierarchy**                    **Security Group Nesting**

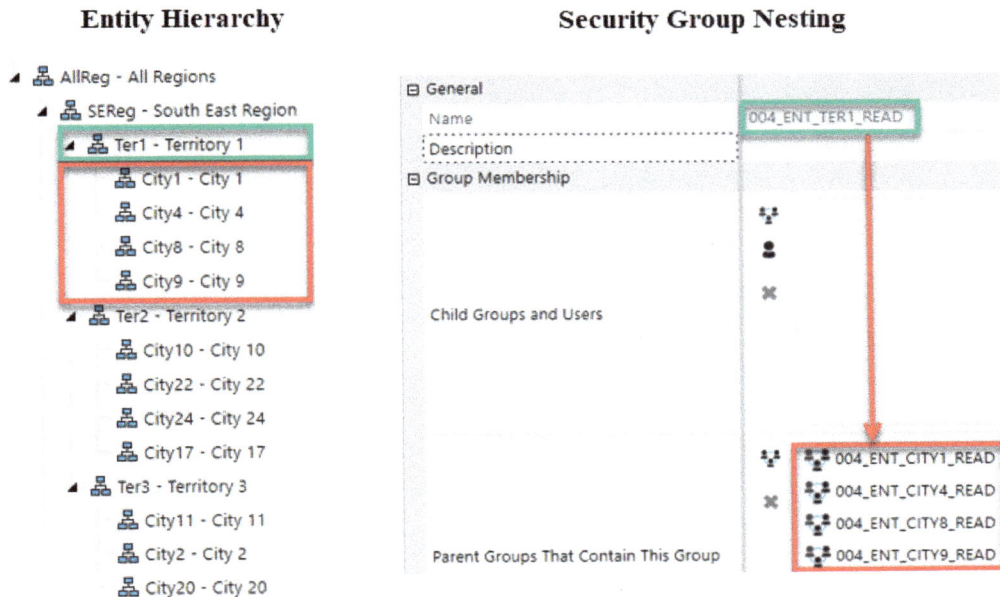

Figure 7.4

As you can see in the entity hierarchy on the left, Territory 1 includes Cities 1, 4, 8, and 9. To achieve the goal of granting read access to all cities in Territory 1 to users who are allowed to read Territory 1, *without* slice security, your nesting would include the read entity security groups (004_ENT_CITY1/4/8/9_READ) for each of those four cities in the Parent Group box of the Territory 1 read group (004_ENT_TER1_READ), as shown on the right of Figure 7.4.

So, what happens when changes are made to that entity hierarchy? Say, for example, you move City 8 to Territory 2 due to a sales reorganization. What needs to then be done with your security groups to reflect this entity hierarchy change?

You will need to not only update your entity hierarchy (as shown on the left in Figure 7.5) but *also* update your security group nesting as shown on the right. You will want to remove 004_ENT_CITY8_READ from being nested within the 004_ENT_TER1_READ security group, and instead add 004_ENT_CITY8_READ to the 004_ENT_TER2_READ security group.

**Entity Hierarchy After**　　　　**Security Group Nesting After**

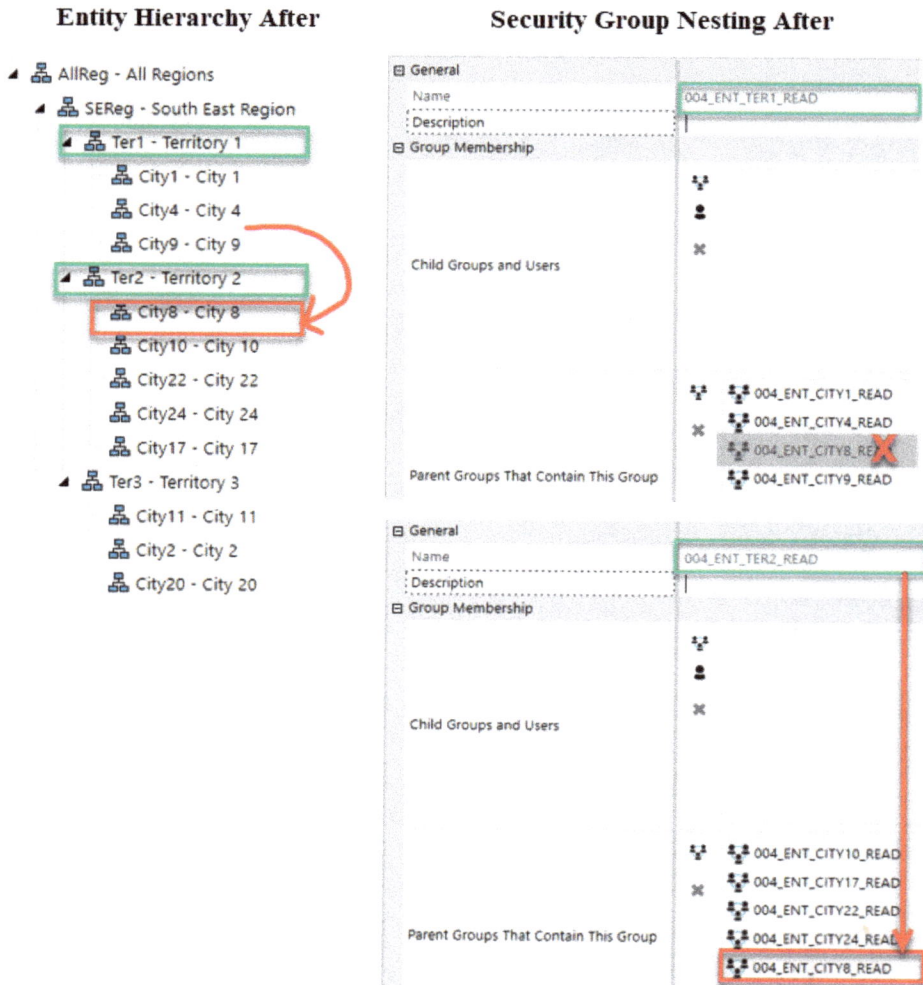

Figure 7.5

Every time your sales regions are reorganized, you will need to constantly update the security group nesting if you want to control who can read and write to the various members within a region. You can see how this can become a security nightmare over time if the sales regions are constantly changing.

To avoid this, you can apply slice security to your Entity dimension. Slice security allows you to create a Member Filter that can include `.TreeDescendants` to a parent entity. This means that, as your entity hierarchy changes, the slice security filter (which includes, for example, `Ter1.TreeDescendants` or `Ter2.TreeDescendants`) will dynamically update security rights.

For the same sales reorganization discussed above, no changes would need to be made to security. The act of changing the entity hierarchy alone, to move City 8 from

Territory 1 to Territory 2, would be enough. This is because slice security can be used to apply member security to entities in a *dynamic* fashion.

Let us talk about another possible use case for using slice security dynamically. Imagine that you have a group of users (000_GRP_CORPUSERS) that are only allowed to view Actual data after it has been finalized by the regions.

Effectively, you want to block these corporate users from seeing Actual data for a given month, until the regions have completed their work. In this example, you can use slice security – combining both the Actual scenario with your Time dimension – so that, at the beginning of a closing cycle, the Actual data for that month (and subsequent months) is not visible to a subset of users (000_GRP_CORPUSERS).

A set of 12 slices, each focusing on the Time dimension for a given month and year (T#YYYY.TreeDescendantsInclusive.Remove(YYYYM1)), combined with scenario, can be used to achieve this goal. In the next section, we will walk through how to apply slice security to achieve goals such as these use cases and beyond.

## Applying Slice Security

As noted in Figure 7.1, the first action in setting up slice security is setting the applicable entities to True. Then what?

Every cube (whether stand-alone, linked base, or top-level cube) has a Data Access tab. This Data Access tab controls access to all data that resides within a particular cube once you have set the entity toggle to True.

As shown in Figure 7.6, the Data Access tab contains three sections:

1. Data Cell Access Security
2. Data Cell Conditional Input
3. Data Management Access Security

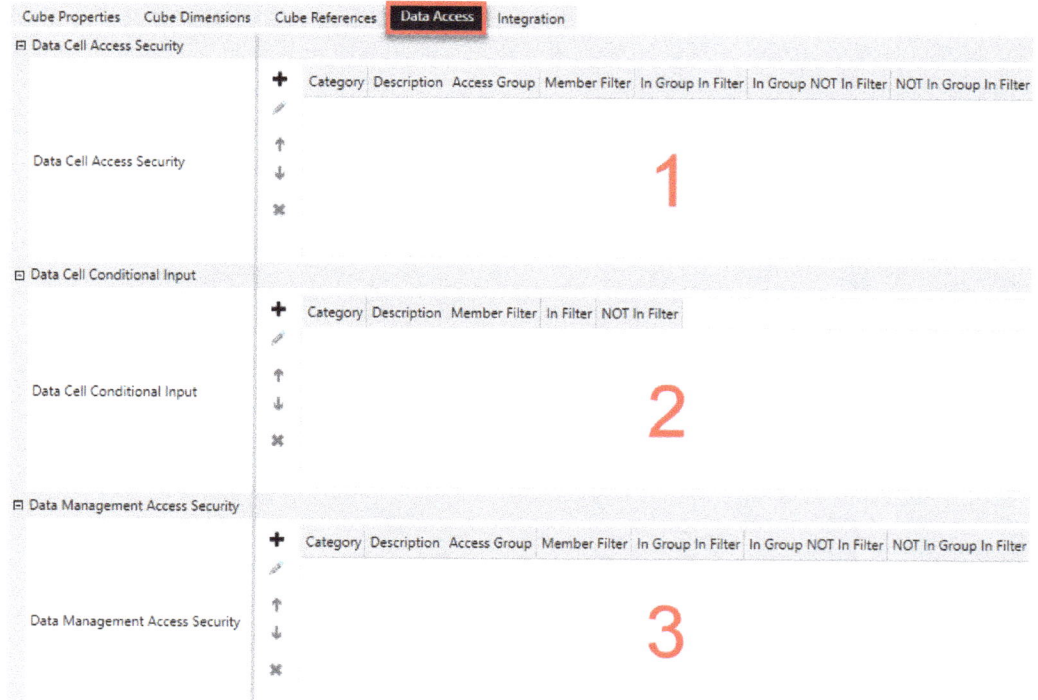

Figure 7.6

## Data Cell Access Security

This section is where rules can be created to decrease or increase access to data at a more granular level than Application > Cube > Entity > Scenario.

No Access, Read Only, or All Access (aka modify or write access) can be granted to a group of data cells down to a single data cell.

To be able to view or modify an entity's data, a user must have read or write access to the entity through standard entity security (shown in Figure 7.1). If the Use Cube Data Access Group for that entity has been set to False, the user will have access to *every* single data cell for that particular entity (combined with their scenario security).

If, however, the entity's Use Cube Data Access Group has been set to True, OneStream will look to the cube's Data Access tab to further determine how security is applied. If set to True and you do not define anything on the Cube Data Access tab, the user will retain full access to all data cells for that entity. This is the equivalent of having that entity set to False for Use Cube Data Access Group. But, as mentioned earlier, if you do not have any slices, then you want to leave the entity as False, as that is more performant.

Let us look at how you can create slices of data to refine the security for a particular entity. The starting point for creating data cell slices is shown in Figure 7.7.

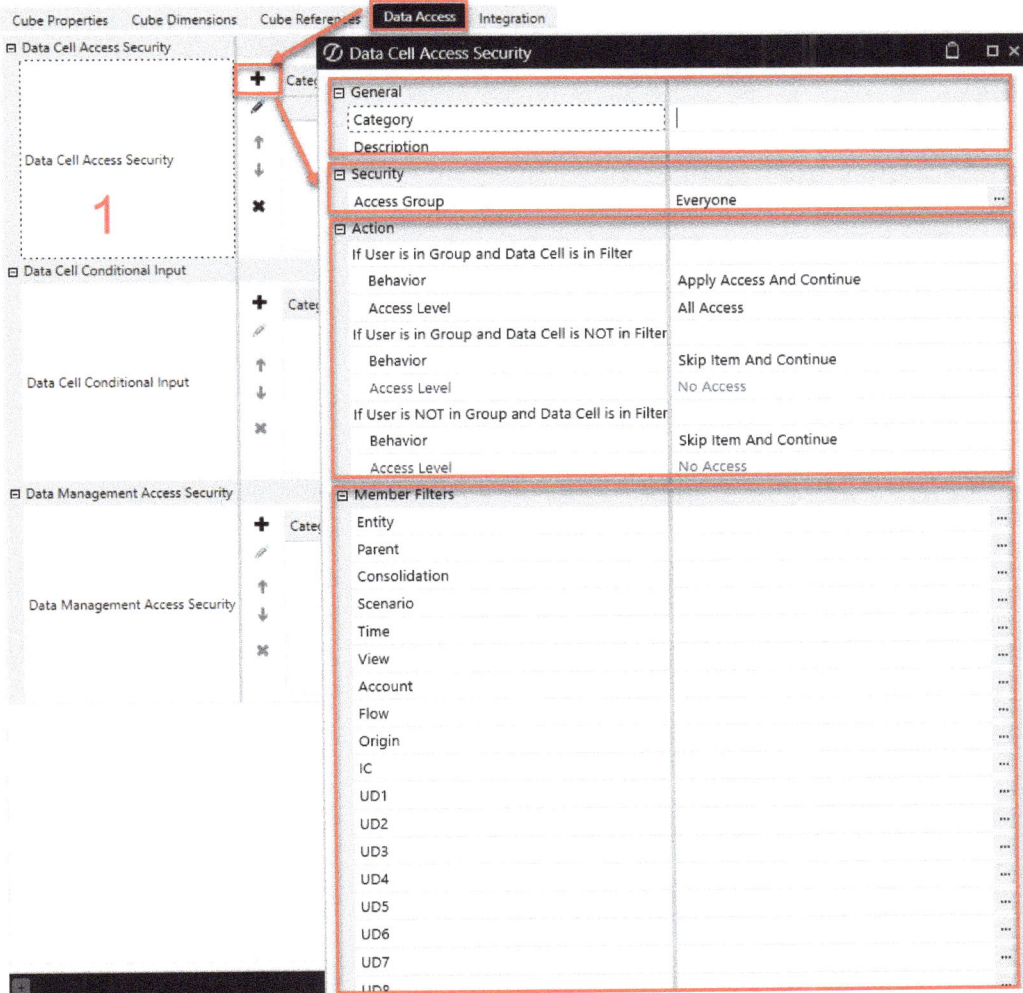

Figure 7.7

There are four parts to creating a data cell slice:

1. General
2. Security
3. Action
4. Member Filters

## General

The Category is an optional free-form field (limited to 100 characters) that exists at the entity level, and also on any slices you create on the cube.

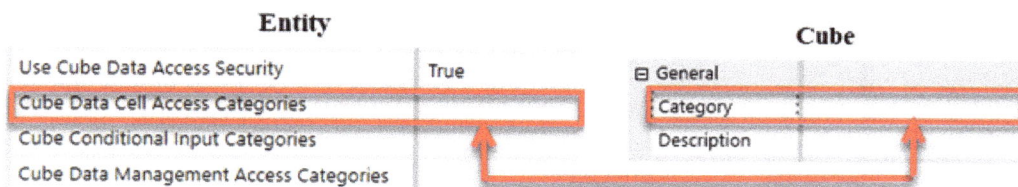

Figure 7.8

Categories allow you to create broad groupings of slices, and then potentially only apply relevant slices to certain entities. For example, if you have 200 slices on the cube but maybe those fit into 20 broad categories, you could then decide – *entity by entity* – which categories of slices need to be evaluated for a particular entity. Therefore, you can improve performance by only having each entity look to *those* slices that are required to determine access.

The Description is an optional free-form field (limited to 200 characters) to add a description for the data access rule.

## Security

Access Group is a security group that is set up on the System > Security tab. Here, users are assigned, and Data Cell Access security roles applied. Using the naming convention established in Chapter 3, it may be 006_UD1_FINANCE_READ or 006_UD1_FINANCE_WRITE if you are securing UD1, which may represent cost centers, as an example.

## Action

The most important part of creating slice security is in the "Action" section. It is here that you will define how security is applied depending on three criteria:

1. User is *in* Group, and Data Cell is *in* Filter

2. User is *in* Group, and Data Cell is *NOT in* Filter

3. User is *NOT in* Group, and Data Cell is *in* Filter

It is the application of these actions that will have the most impact on the performance of your slice security. As mentioned previously, a performance cost is associated with applying slice security.

In applying slice security, you are asking OneStream to take an extra step in evaluating *each intersection* of data, whether in a Cube View, Excel, Workflow import, form, journal, or dashboard, to decide whether that intersection is read, write, or no access for that user.

Without slice security, the Data Unit dimensions of Cube, Entity, and Scenario control access to *all* data intersections. This is a quicker evaluation process because you are not asking OneStream to be any more granular in applying security than to the entire Data Unit as a whole.

How significant the performance implications of applying slice security will be largely depends on two factors: how you define the three actions, *and* the order of operation in which you create your slices.

> As a rule of thumb, you will want to create your slices in the order they will be applied to the most users first (cast the widest net first) and apply the STOP action (exit the evaluation process) when possible.

There are eight Behaviors in the Action section that will determine how each intersection of data is treated:

1. Skip Item and Continue: Default if user is *in* group and data cell is *not in* filter, or if user is *not in* group and data cell is *in* filter.

2. Skip Item and Stop: Skip a slice and stop evaluating the remaining slices.

3. Apply Access and Continue: Default if user is *in* group and data cell is *in* filter.

4. Apply Access and Stop: Apply access to a slice and stop evaluating the remaining slices.

5. Increase Access and Continue: Increase access to a slice and continue evaluating the remaining slices.

6. Increase Access and Stop: Increase access to a slice and then stop evaluating the remaining slices.

7. Decrease Access and Continue: Decrease access to a slice and then continue evaluating the remaining slices.

8. Decrease Access and Stop: Decrease access to a slice and then stop evaluating the remaining slices.

There are three Access Levels associated with the behaviors above:

1. No Access: Prevents users from read or write access to cells in the filter.

2. Read Only: Allows users to read cells in the filter.

3. All Access: Allows users to write to cells in the filter.

Chapter 7

## Member Filter

This section is used to define the dimension members required as part of Data Cell Access to allow or deny access to specific intersections of data.

The filter can be a singular dimension and dimension member(s), *or* a combination of multiple dimensions and members. For example, if your security applies to a particular scenario in conjunction with a particular UD, it will be the combination of those two dimensions within a single slice that will be applied to the data access (e.g., both filter conditions need to be met before slice is applied).

If, however, you want specific UD security applied to all scenarios, then you will only fill out the UD dimension by itself for a single slice. Thus, it will stand on its own, meaning that slice will apply to *all* scenarios of data.

As shown in Figure 7.9, the Member Filter box employs the same syntax as used throughout the application.

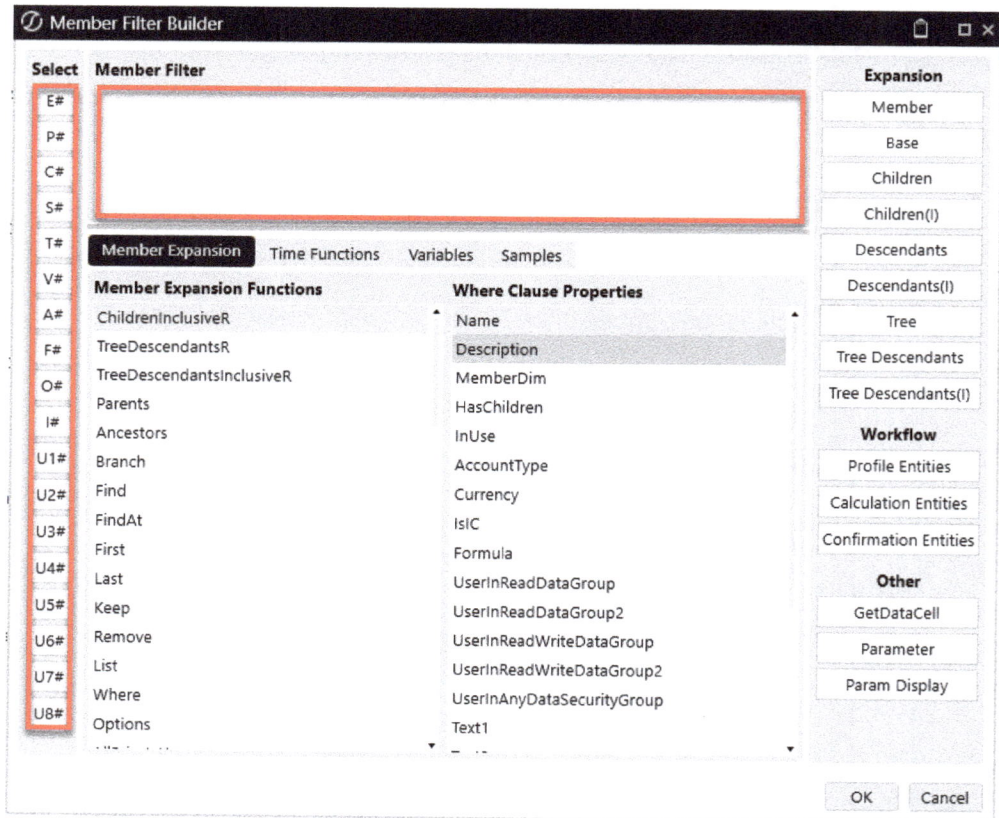

Figure 7.9

As you can imagine from the Member Filter builder, you can apply filters for specific intersections of data in almost a limitless number of combinations. You can use `.Remove()`, `.Where()`, `.Descendants(I)`, etc., to build out your filters to very granular intersections or data cells. When doing so, keep in mind that you want to apply the filters and slices in the most efficient way possible (capturing most use cases first and using STOP when possible).

The easiest way to understand how to construct slices is to walk through an example. So, let's do so.

Suppose you have a Cost Center dimension (U1) that appears as per Figure 7.10.

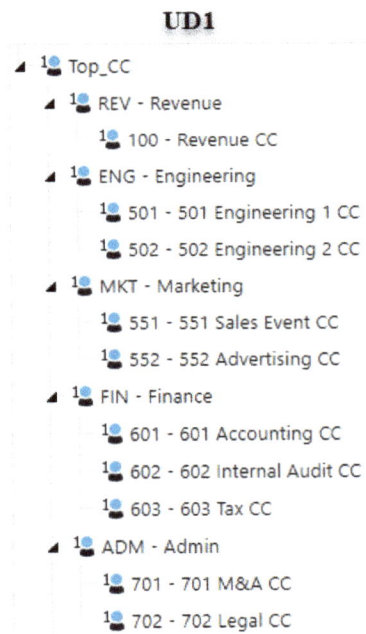

**UD1**

```
▲ Top_CC
    ▲ REV - Revenue
        100 - Revenue CC
    ▲ ENG - Engineering
        501 - 501 Engineering 1 CC
        502 - 502 Engineering 2 CC
    ▲ MKT - Marketing
        551 - 551 Sales Event CC
        552 - 552 Advertising CC
    ▲ FIN - Finance
        601 - 601 Accounting CC
        602 - 602 Internal Audit CC
        603 - 603 Tax CC
    ▲ ADM - Admin
        701 - 701 M&A CC
        702 - 702 Legal CC
```

Figure 7.10

Now, let us suppose that you have the following security requirements:

- For the Budget scenario, you want to control write access to cost centers
- For the Budget scenario, you also want to control read access to cost centers
- For the Budget scenario, you have some users who can write to all cost centers
- For the Budget scenario, you have some users who can read all cost centers
- These rules will not apply to the Actual scenario of data

Chapter 7

How will you achieve this? In the next section, we will go over the basic steps to set up slice security to achieve the above goals. Keep in mind that the steps detailed can apply to dynamic entity security, dynamic time security, or any other combination of 18 dimensions for which you want to apply granular security.

## Step 1

First, you will want to create the security groups needed to achieve the desired access on the System > Security tab. Using the naming conventions established in Chapter 3, this may look like Figure 7.11:

| Security Group from System Tab | Description of Access |
|---|---|
| 006_UD1_ALL_READ / WRITE | Group for users that will have access to all cost center(s). |
| 006_UD1_REV_READ / WRITE | Group for users that will have access to revenue cost center(s). |
| 006_UD1_ENG_READ / WRITE | Group for users that will have access to engineering cost center(s). |
| 006_UD1_MKT_READ / WRITE | Group for users that will have access to marketing cost center(s). |
| 006_UD1_FIN_READ / WRITE | Group for users that will have access to finance cost center(s). |
| 006_UD1_ADM_READ / WRITE | Group for users that will have access to admin cost center(s). |

Figure 7.11

As seen in Figure 7.12, we will assume you have already set up the following groups, which apply to other security rules discussed in prior chapters:

| Security Group from System Tab | Description of Access |
|---|---|
| 001_APP_VIEWALLDATA | Security group applied to Application Security Role to grant view to all data |
| 001_APP_MODIFYDATA | Security group applied to Application Security Role to allow modification of data (when coupled with other security) |
| 002_CUBE_FINPRT | Security group granting access to the FinRpt cube |
| 003_SCN_ACTUAL_READ / WRITE | Security group granting access to read or write to Actual data. |

| Security Group from System Tab | Description of Access |
|---|---|
| 003_SCN_BUDGET_READ / WRITE | Security group granting access to read or write to Budget data. |
| 004_ENT_ALLCOMPANY_READ / WRITE | Security group granting access to read or write to all entities data. |
| 005_WF_ACTUAL_E | Security group granting workflow execution rights to an Actual WF. |
| 005_WF_BUDGET_E | Security group granting workflow execution rights to a Budget WF. |

Figure 7.12

Once your security groups are set up on the System > Security tab and users have been appropriately embedded into those groups, you are ready to move on.

## Step 2

Next up, go to your Entity dimension(s) and set all entities – for which you want this additional layer of security to apply – as True for their Use Cube Data Access Security.

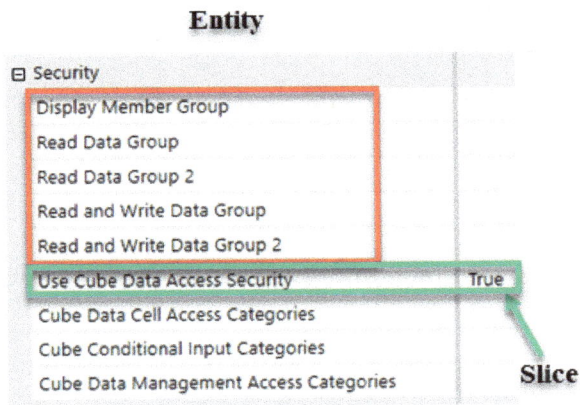

Figure 7.13

## Step 3

The third step to applying slice security is to go to the Data Access tab for whatever cube(s) you want to apply slice security to. If you have vertically integrated (aka **linked cubes**), you will want to set up your slice security across *all* linked cubes. The reason for this extra step with linked cubes is because the Entity dimension can be shared among cubes; therefore, to accurately apply data access security, the same slices need to be set up across all cubes to which those entities are shared. I recommend starting with one cube first, and once tested, extract those slices to an XML file and copy the same slices into the remaining linked cubes.

I like to start slice security with the users who are in the `006_UD1_ALL_READ` or `006_UD1_ALL_WRITE` groups first. My assumption is that the majority of users will fall into one of these two security groups, so to prevent OneStream from unnecessarily continuing to evaluate additional slices, I build these two broad slices first and then apply the "stop" action.

Then, the remaining slices (`006_UD1_XXX_READ / WRITE`) can be built to increase access based upon the filter criteria. Since the remaining slices are granting security back (that was removed in the first slice) and are all "continue" slices (since people could exist in multiple slices), these can appear in any order.

Figure 7.14 shows the culmination of how slice security can be set up on the cube(s) to achieve the desired results.

| A | B | | C | D | | E | | F | |
|---|---|---|---|---|---|---|---|---|---|
| Slice | Security Group Name | Scenario Filter | UD1 Filter | *In* Group *In* Filter | Access Group | *In* Group *Not In* Filter | Access Group | *Not In* Group *In* Filter | Access Group |
| 1 | 006_UD1_ALL_READ | S#BUDGET | U1#Root.DescIncl | Apply Stop | Read Only | Skip Continue | No Access | Decrease Continue | No Access |
| 2 | 006_UD1_ALL_WRITE | S#BUDGET | U1#Root.DescIncl | Increase Stop | All Access | Skip Continue | No Access | Skip Continue | No Access |
| 3 | 006_UD1_REV_WRITE | S#BUDGET | U1#REV.DescIncl | Increase Continue | All Access | Skip Continue | No Access | Skip Continue | No Access |
| 4 | 006_UD1_REV_READ | S#BUDGET | U1#REV.DescIncl | Increase Continue | Read Only | Skip Continue | No Access | Skip Continue | No Access |
| 5 | 006_UD1_ENG_WRITE | S#BUDGET | U1#ENG.DescIncl | Increase Continue | All Access | Skip Continue | No Access | Skip Continue | No Access |
| 6 | 006_UD1_ENG_READ | S#BUDGET | U1#ENG.DescIncl | Increase Continue | Read Only | Skip Continue | No Access | Skip Continue | No Access |
| 7 | 006_UD1_MKT_WRITE | S#BUDGET | U1#MKT.DescIncl | Increase Continue | All Access | Skip Continue | No Access | Skip Continue | No Access |
| 8 | 006_UD1_MKT_READ | S#BUDGET | U1#MKT.DescIncl | Increase Continue | Read Only | Skip Continue | No Access | Skip Continue | No Access |
| 9 | 006_UD1_FIN_WRITE | S#BUDGET | U1#FIN.DescIncl | Increase Continue | All Access | Skip Continue | No Access | Skip Continue | No Access |
| 10 | 006_UD1_FIN_READ | S#BUDGET | U1#FIN.DescIncl | Increase Continue | Read Only | Skip Continue | No Access | Skip Continue | No Access |
| 11 | 006_UD1_ADM_WRITE | S#BUDGET | U1#ADM.DescIncl | Increase Continue | All Access | Skip Continue | No Access | Skip Continue | No Access |
| 12 | 006_UD1_ADM_READ | S#BUDGET | U1#ADM.DescIncl | Increase Continue | Read Only | Skip Continue | No Access | Skip Continue | No Access |
| 13 | 006_UD1_HR_WRITE | S#BUDGET | U1#HR.DescIncl | Increase Continue | All Access | Skip Continue | No Access | Skip Continue | No Access |
| 14 | 006_UD1_HR_READ | S#BUDGET | U1#HR.DescIncl | Increase Continue | Read Only | Skip Continue | No Access | Skip Continue | No Access |

Figure 7.14

Column A shows the order of operation of how the slices will be applied. Again, the first two slices are capturing all read or all write users and thus apply the Stop behavior in column D. If a user is not in the first slice, then all access is removed in column F with Decrease to No Access. If a user is in the first or second slice, that access is granted via column D and Stop can be used as the remaining slices do not need to be evaluated.

If a person is not in the first two slices, now the process of evaluating the remaining slices (numbers 3 to 14 in column A) begins. For all remaining slices, the assumption is that a user *may be* in one or more security groups to Increase access to various cost centers; thus, all remaining slices are Continue behavior.

What is key to point out in Figure 7.14 is also how the Member Filter is applied (column C). Because one of the requirements for this example is that we wanted this behavior to apply to the Budget scenario, but not the Actual scenario, you can see that the filter is a combination of both S# and U1# filters (column C). This will make sense when we move to the last step of setting up slice security… testing!

## Step 4

The last step to applying slice security is to evaluate that it is working as designed and meets the requirements discussed previously. When in doubt, test and retest!

Let us take an example user in the groups shown in Figure 7.15. This user has write access to both the Budget and Actual scenarios as well as write access to the Finance Cost Centers.

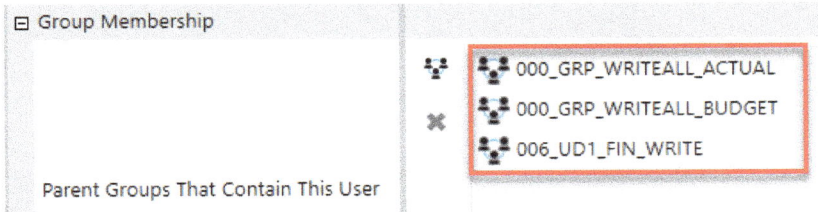

Figure 7.15

We will assume that access for the two user groups (000_GRP) shown in Figure 7.15 are as listed in Figure 7.16, below. Recalling our prior chapters, these 000 user groups contain 001-005 nested groups, which grant them group access to the various data and objects as needed.

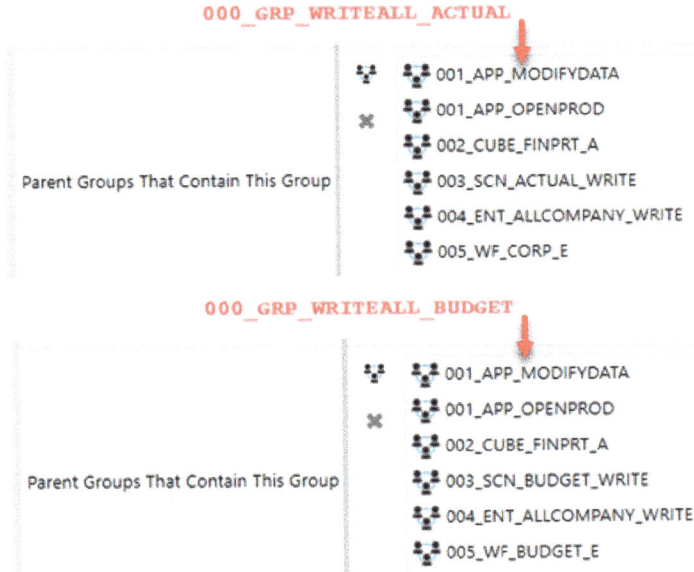

Figure 7.16

Chapter 7

To test that slice security is working as designed, I like to set up a spreadsheet with the relevant intersections of data and then log in with the same security as this user and refresh the spreadsheet, as shown in Figure 7.17. Column A shows our cost center U1 dimension. Column B contains the Actual scenario, and Column C contains the Budget scenario.

Based on this user's membership, slice security is working as designed. The No Access cells in the Budget column are the result of this user not appearing in slices 1 and 2 on the cube (Figure 7.14). Because this user is not in the all read or write U1 security groups, their access has been set to No Access in the first slice.

Because the user has been included in the security group `006_UD1_FIN_WRITE`, we can see that in the Budget scenario, column C, they have input access (white cells) for the base Finance Cost Centers.

Lastly, because we mentioned that this slice security *only* applies to the Budget scenario in our use case, we can see for the Actual scenario of data (column B), they have full write access based upon the `000_GRP_WRITEALL_ACTUAL` security group membership, as evidenced by all base cost centers appearing as white input intersections.

| | A | B | C |
|---|---|---|---|
| | | ACTUAL | BUDGET |
| | | Entity CO 1 | Entity CO 1 |
| | Top_CC | | No Access |
| | Revenue | | No Access |
| | Revenue CC | | No Access |
| | Engineering | | No Access |
| | 501 Engineering 1 CC | | No Access |
| | 502 Engineering 2 CC | | No Access |
| | Marketing | | No Access |
| | 551 Sales Event CC | | No Access |
| | 552 Advertising CC | | No Access |
| | Finance | | |
| | 601 Accounting CC | | |
| | 602 Internal Audit CC | | |
| | 603 Tax CC | | |
| | Admin | | No Access |
| | 701 M&A CC | | No Access |
| | 702 Legal CC | | No Access |
| | Human Resources | | No Access |
| | 801 Recruiting CC | | No Access |
| | 802 Training CC | | No Access |

Figure 7.17

Let's take another step and add this person into the slice to grant read access to engineering departments (006_UD1_ENG_READ), as shown in Figure 7.18.

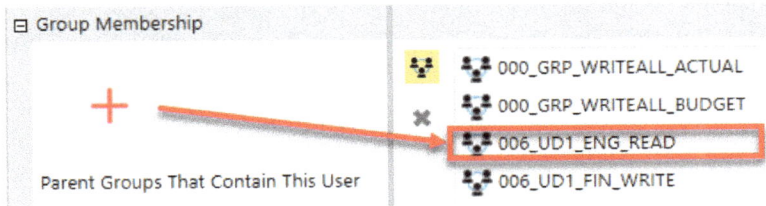

Figure 7.18

What does the spreadsheet look like now, when refreshed as that user? As you can see in Figure 7.19, this user has green cells (aka read-only) for the Engineering Cost Centers, which were previously No Access, while retaining white cells (input) for the Finance Cost Centers in the Budget column.

This is due to the Continue behavior we applied in Figure 7.14 on slices 3-14. Because we said a person *may be* in more than one cost center slice, as the remaining slices 3-14 are applied, they are Increase and Continue, which is what allows the security shown in Figure 7.19.

| | A | B | C |
|---|---|---|---|
| | | ACTUAL | BUDGET |
| | | Entity CO 1 | Entity CO 1 |
| | Top_CC | | No Access |
| | Revenue | | No Access |
| | Revenue CC | | No Access |
| | Engineering | | |
| | 501 Engineering 1 CC | | |
| | 502 Engineering 2 CC | | |
| | Marketing | | No Access |
| | 551 Sales Event CC | | No Access |
| | 552 Advertising CC | | No Access |
| | Finance | | |
| | 601 Accounting CC | | |
| | 602 Internal Audit CC | | |
| | 603 Tax CC | | |
| | Admin | | No Access |
| | 701 M&A CC | | No Access |
| | 702 Legal CC | | No Access |
| | Human Resources | | No Access |
| | 801 Recruiting CC | | No Access |
| | 802 Training CC | | No Access |

Figure 7.19

The above steps are one example of applying slice security to a combination of U1 and Scenario members. As discussed previously, the possible combinations of access across the 18 dimensions are almost limitless.

Figure 7.20 shows an additional example of how you may create 12 slices to apply time-based dynamic security to grant a set of users access to each closed month as the year progresses. As each month is closed and the Corporate users (000_GRP_CORPUSERS) are allowed to see a specific month's data, each successive slice group (e.g., 006_TIME_M1_12NOACCESS) would be removed as a restriction on the Corporate users, allowing them to view each month's data as it is closed.

| A | B | C | | D | | E | F |
|---|---|---|---|---|---|---|---|
| Slice | Security Group Name | Scenario Filter | TimeFilter | *In* Group *In* Filter | Access Group | *In* Group *Not In* Filter | *Not In* Group *In* Filter |
| 1 | 006_TIME_M1_12NOACCESS | S#ACTUAL | T#YYYY.TreeDescIncl | Apply Stop | No Access | Skip Continue | Skip Continue |
| 2 | 006_TIME_M2_12NOACCESS | S#ACTUAL | T#YYYY.TreeDescIncl.Remove(YYYYM1) | Apply Stop | No Access | Skip Continue | Skip Continue |
| 3 | 006_TIME_M3_12NOACCESS | S#ACTUAL | T#YYYY.TreeDescIncl.Remove(YYYYM1,YYYYM2) | Apply Stop | No Access | Skip Continue | Skip Continue |
| 4 | 006_TIME_M4_12NOACCESS | S#ACTUAL | T#YYYY.TreeDescIncl.Remove(YYYYM1,...,YYYYM3) | Apply Stop | No Access | Skip Continue | Skip Continue |
| 5 | 006_TIME_M5_12NOACCESS | S#ACTUAL | T#YYYY.TreeDescIncl.Remove(YYYYM1,...,YYYYM4) | Apply Stop | No Access | Skip Continue | Skip Continue |
| 6 | 006_TIME_M6_12NOACCESS | S#ACTUAL | T#YYYY.TreeDescIncl.Remove(YYYYM1,...,YYYYM5) | Apply Stop | No Access | Skip Continue | Skip Continue |
| 7 | 006_TIME_M7_12NOACCESS | S#ACTUAL | T#YYYY.TreeDescIncl.Remove(YYYYM1,...,YYYYM6) | Apply Stop | No Access | Skip Continue | Skip Continue |
| 8 | 006_TIME_M8_12NOACCESS | S#ACTUAL | T#YYYY.TreeDescIncl.Remove(YYYYM1,...,YYYYM7) | Apply Stop | No Access | Skip Continue | Skip Continue |
| 9 | 006_TIME_M9_12NOACCESS | S#ACTUAL | T#YYYY.TreeDescIncl.Remove(YYYYM1,...,YYYYM8) | Apply Stop | No Access | Skip Continue | Skip Continue |
| 10 | 006_TIME_M10_12NOACCESS | S#ACTUAL | T#YYYY.TreeDescIncl.Remove(YYYYM1,...,YYYYM9) | Apply Stop | No Access | Skip Continue | Skip Continue |
| 11 | 006_TIME_M11_12NOACCESS | S#ACTUAL | T#YYYY.TreeDescIncl.Remove(YYYYM1,...,YYYYM10) | Apply Stop | No Access | Skip Continue | Skip Continue |
| 12 | 006_TIME_M12NOACCESS | S#ACTUAL | T#YYYY.TreeDescIncl.Remove(YYYYM1,...,YYYYM11) | Apply Stop | No Access | Skip Continue | Skip Continue |

Figure 7.20

Because the possibilities are many, it is important to always keep in mind that you want to balance ease of use, control, and maintenance, as we mentioned in Chapter 2. The more slices and Member Filters you add, not only can there be performance implications, but maintenance becomes more challenging as well.

Advice for creating data slices in the most optimal manner are:

✓ Use categories so each entity only checks the applicable slices.

✓ Try defining the slices using the "STOP" behavior instead of "Continue" whenever possible.

✓ Determine the most likely cases and define them first.

✓ If there are entities where you do not need slice, turn to "False."

✓ Administrators bypass **Data Cell Access** so they may see better performance.

✓ Applies to Cube Views, Excel, Dashboards; e.g., anywhere data is being pulled.

# Data Cell Conditional Input Security

The second section of a cube's Data Access tab allows the ability to conditionally provide access for *all* users to input data (or not) for a group of data cell(s).

**Data Cell Conditional Input** security is similar to the prior section on data cell access security with two key differentiators. Data cell conditional input is *not* tied to a security group because slices in this section apply to *all* users (including administrators), not a group of users. It is all users or no one! And this security is to strictly apply write security only; e.g., you cannot apply read and/or write using this slice security. As the name suggests, it is conditional "input" only!

Therefore, when configuring slices for a data cell conditional input rule, all users will either have access (or not have access) to input data to the data cells defined in the Member Filter. The starting point for setting up conditional slices is shown in Figure 7.21.

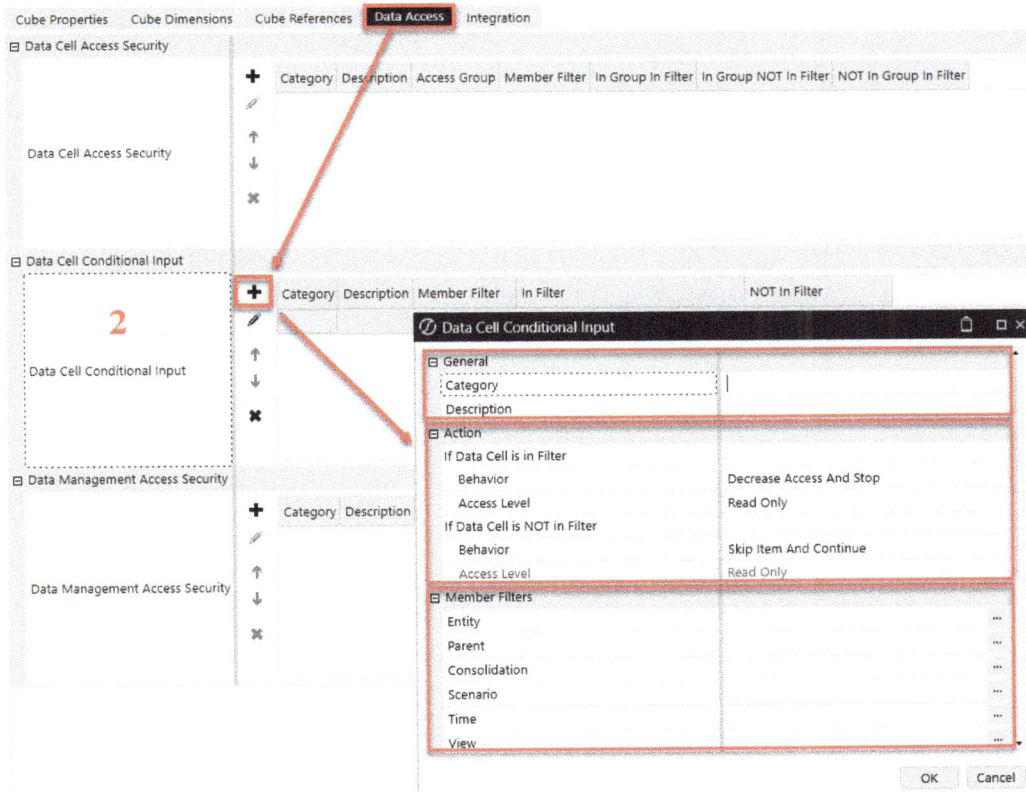

Figure 7.21

There are three parts (as opposed to four for data cell access) to creating a conditional slice:

1. General

2. Action

3. Member Filters

## General

The Category and Description fields for conditional slices behave in the same manner as explained in the prior section for data access slices.

## Action

There are only two items (as opposed to three for data cell access) in the Action section for conditional input security:

1. If Data Cell is *in* Filter

2. If Data Cell is *NOT in* Filter

And there are only two Access Levels associated with the behaviors above (again, as opposed to three for data cell access):

1. Read Only: Allows users to read cells in the filter.

2. All Access: Allows users to write to cells in the filter.

The same eight Behaviors apply to conditional slices as data access slices in the Action section. These eight items determine how each intersection of data is treated with no link to a security group (as it is all users or no one) for conditional input. All eight behaviors are the same as for Data Cell Access Security, with two exceptions:

1. Skip Item and Continue: Default if data cell is *not in* filter. All users or no one.

2. Skip Item and Stop: Same as prior section.

3. Apply Access and Continue: Default if data cell is *in* filter. All users or no one.

4. Apply Access and Stop: Same as prior section.

5. Increase Access and Continue: Same as prior section.

6. Increase Access and Stop: Same as prior section.

7. Decrease Access and Continue: Same as prior section.

8. Decrease Access and Stop: Same as prior section.

## Member Filter

A Member Filter for data cell conditional input security is defined in the same way as explained in the prior section for data access slices (Figure 7.9).

Again, the conditional input slices behave much in the same way as the data access slices, except that conditional slices are not tied to a security group on the System > Security tab, which just means that conditional slices apply to all users the same. And, whereas native administrators bypass data cell access slices, they *do not* bypass conditional input slices.

Lastly, you can only grant Read Only or All Access via conditional slices. The ability to grant No Access is not an option in this section since this section is focused on conditional input access for cells, not whether a person cannot see the cell altogether. No Access can only be achieved through the first data access section discussed previously.

---

Tips about conditional input data slices:

✓ Will *not* affect read-only Cube Views and dashboards.

✓ Will affect the Excel add-in.

✓ Determine the most likely cases and define them first, along with using the "STOP" behavior instead of "Continue" whenever possible.

✓ Administrators do *not* bypass data cell conditional input slices.

---

# Data Management Access Security

This third and final section of a cube's Data Access tab provides a level of security when running processes from a data management (DM) sequence or step.

Before we get into the properties and behaviors of this section, it is important to review the other security that may impact a user's ability to run a DM process.

Data management sequences can be launched from a number of different areas within OneStream:

- Workflows
- Dashboards
- Data Management page
- Other BRs that launch DM sequences

No matter where a person launches a data management sequence from, there are other pieces of security that must be in place.

Assuming you have granted the proper access to the Manage Data Group in the Scenario dimension, as well as access to the data management group, and write access to the Cube, Entity and Scenario dimensions (all previously covered in Chapter 5 of this book), then you can move on to applying a slice to data management access in this section.

So, what does the Data Management Access security slice on the Data Access tab of a cube give you beyond those items? It is used to control who has access to read or modify cube data during various data management processes.

DM sequences are focused on the cube Data Unit or the workflow Data Unit and not individual data cells. Data management access security is crucial for maintaining data integrity and ensuring that only authorized modifications are made to the cube data during specific processes.

Data management access security shares the same properties and behaviors as data cell access security described earlier in this chapter, with one minor exception. The only Member Filters available are for Entity and Scenario, as can be seen in Figure 7.22.

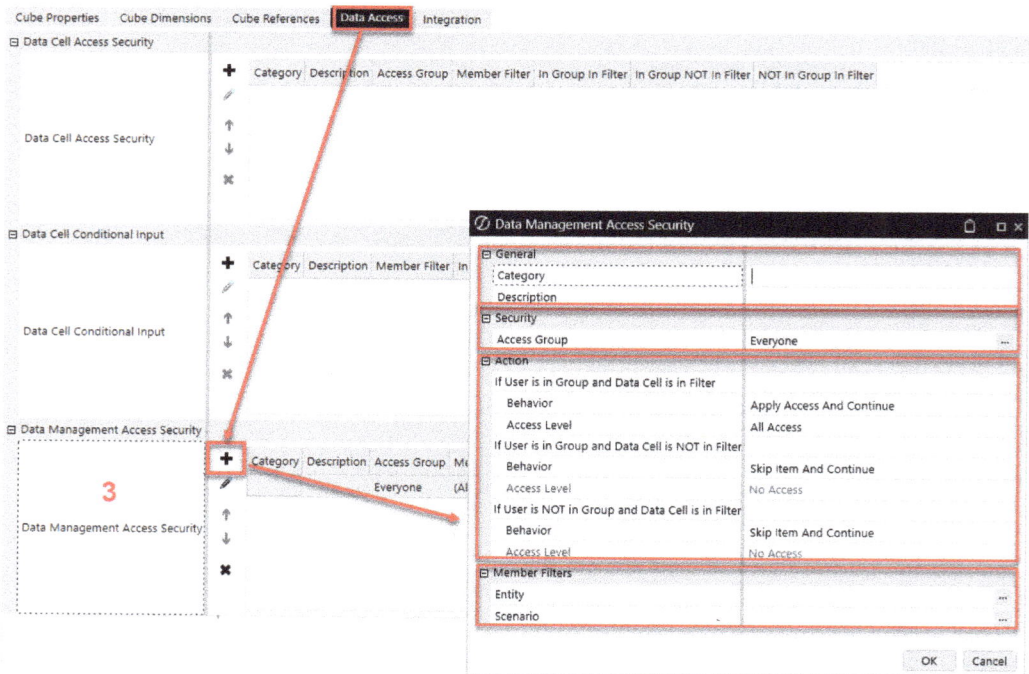

Figure 7.22

## General

The Category and Description fields for data management slices behave in the same manner as explained in the prior sections.

## Security

The Access Group is a security group that is set up on the System > Security tab, into which users are assigned and where data management access security roles apply. Once more, you will want to use the naming convention established in Chapter 3 (e.g., 006_DM_BUDGETCALC, as an example).

## Action

Once again, and similar to the first section of slice security already discussed (data cell access security), the most important part of creating your slices is in the Action section. Here, you will define how security is applied depending on the same three criteria as with data cell access security:

1. User is *in* Group, and Data Cell is *in* Filter
2. User is *in* Group, and Data Cell is *NOT in* Filter
3. User is *NOT in* Group, and Data Cell is *in* Filter

The same eight Behaviors apply to data management slices as data access slices. These eight items determine how each intersection of data is treated when running a data management sequence in the same way as the Data Cell Access Security section:

1. Skip Item and Continue
2. Skip Item and Stop
3. Apply Access and Continue
4. Apply Access and Stop
5. Increase Access and Continue
6. Increase Access and Stop
7. Decrease Access and Continue
8. Decrease Access and Stop

There are three Access Levels associated with the behaviors, and are also identical to those for the Data Cell Access Security section:

1. No Access
2. Read Only
3. All Access

## Member Filter

The difference between Member Filters in data management access security and data cell access security or data cell conditional access security is that Entity and Scenario dimensions are the only options to which you can apply filters. The Member Filter focus is not at the data cell level but at the Data Unit level instead.

This concludes the section on Slice Security. Let's move on to another way in which you can control how people input data.

# No Input BRs

Another way to control who has access to intersections of data is to apply a finance business rule to a cube(s) and use the ConditionalInput section to define rules around data cell input capability. These finance rules, often called **No Input BRs** or **Conditional Input Rules**, are set up as finance BRs, as shown in Figure 7.23.

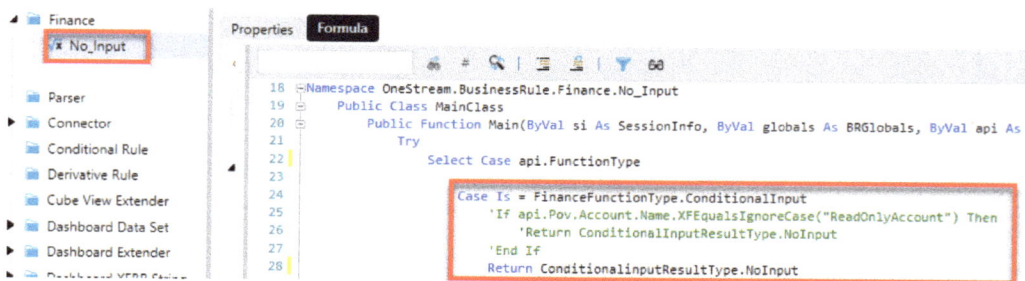

Figure 7.23

You will set up this finance BR and attach it to the cube where you want this condition to apply through BR 1-8.

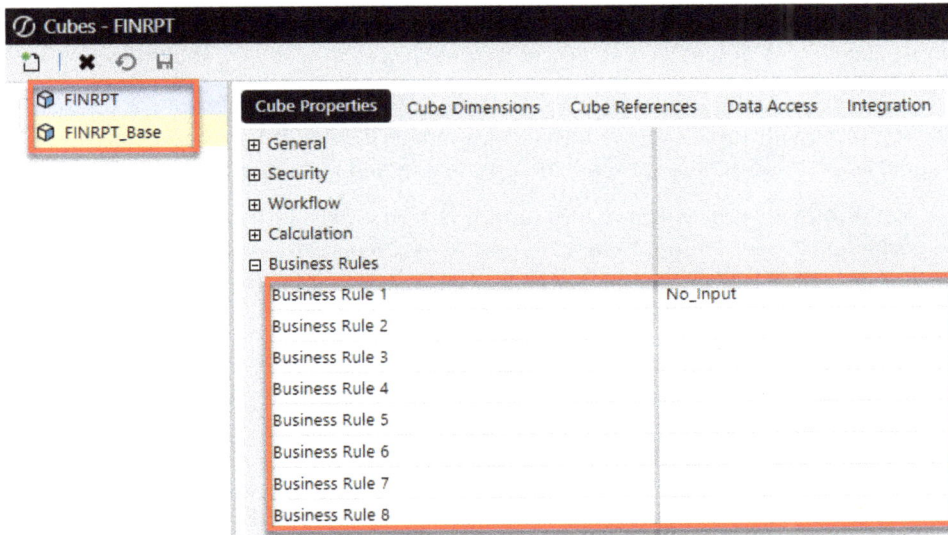

Figure 7.24

Within the `Case Is = FinanceFunctionType.ConditionalInput` section of a finance BR, you will write the conditions to which you want to apply no input access.

In a No Input BR, you have code to define criteria around who will be able to input (or not) to certain intersections of data:

- `IF, ELSE, END IF, ANDALSO, ORELSE`

- `>=`

- `<`

- `Api, args, and BRApi calls`

All of the coding options available in a finance BR can be used to ultimately determine whether to flip a specific intersection to read-only. For example, you can use a No Input BR to check if a user is in a specific security group or not, before limiting their access to read-only.

Once you have gone through a series of `IF` statements to evaluate whether an intersection should be read-only, the last step in a No Input BR is to flip the cell status to read-only with a `Return` statement as follows:

`Return ConditionalInputResultType.NoInput`

You may be asking yourself, what is the difference between using a No Input BR attached to a cube versus applying data cell conditional input security slices on the cube?

If you recall from the earlier section, conditional slice security is *not* tied to a security group. These slices either allow or deny input access for *all* users, including native administrators.

However, the conditional input section of a finance BR can be used to check if a particular user belongs to a specific security group and *then apply* the conditions.

If the conditions are met within the No Input BR, you can only set the intersection to read. You cannot use No Input BRs to grant All Access or No Access, as you can with a conditional slice. Likewise, in a No Input BR, you cannot increase or decrease access as you can with conditional slice behaviors.

Using a No Input BR, as opposed to a conditional slice, requires coding. You are working with a BR and VB.NET or C# to create the conditions in which you want to restrict access to read-only. In setting up conditional slices on the cube, no coding is involved as the standard Member Filter builder applies.

Lastly, while conditional slices can have a negative impact on performance, using a No Input BR may have a greater negative performance impact. This is because No Input BRs are attached to the cube and run as part of the DUCS (Data Unit Calculation Sequence), whereas conditional no input slices will only run when a user is retrieving data in a Cube View, dashboard, or Excel.

So again, we come back to why you might choose one option over the other. With security, you always want to think about the ease of use and maintenance. If you have other data access security that you will apply to the cube, then perhaps you will want to keep your conditional input security also in the Data Access tab on the cube. In this way, an administrator does not have to look in multiple places to determine how security is being applied.

However, if you have no other data access needs involving slice security, or very few use cases in which this needs to apply, then you may want the flexibility that a No Input BR provides. And certainly, if you need to tie your conditional no input security to security groups or other items using API or BRAPI calls, then you will have to use a No Input BR because those conditions are not available in slices. Remember, slices do not involve code.

Like everything in OneStream, there is always more than one way to achieve a goal. It is up to you – as the consultant or administrator – to determine whether a conditional slice or conditional BR suits your business needs. Figure 7.25 summarizes the pros and cons of each of these security options.

| | Conditional Slice | Conditional BR |
|---|---|---|
| Negative Impact to Performance | Medium | High |
| Can Apply No Access or All Access | Yes | No |
| Can Apply Read Only Access | Yes | Yes |
| Can Increase or Decrease Access | Yes | No |
| Requires Coding | No | Yes |
| Can Vary By User and/or Security Group | No | Yes |
| Can be based on logic like IF, >=, ANDALSO, ORELSE, API. Args, BRApis, data values,etc | No | Yes |

Figure 7.25

Now that we have covered additional data security (that you may choose to apply to your cube data), let us branch out again to security not involving cube data, but involving table-based and/or dashboard-based solutions available on the Solution Exchange.

# Solution Exchange Security

There are over 100 (and growing!) OneStream, Partner, and Community-developed solutions available on OneStream's Solution Exchange. I cannot cover the security involved with all these tools, but I will cover the most popular tools and some security basics around using them.

First, nearly all Solution Exchange tools will require users who have access to ancillary tables. Why is this the case?

The tables that come with every customer application (the application tables discussed in prior chapters) are not considered ancillary tables. These tables are native tables within every customer application and environment. However, when you download and install a Solution Exchange tool, if these tools set up custom tables within your application, they are considered *ancillary* tables. They are not part of the core application tables that make up every customer application.

As such, OneStream users – other than users in the native administrators group – will not inherently have access to custom tables added into your application/environment. Therefore, the first step in allowing your user base to access any Solution Exchange tools will be to grant access to these ancillary tables.

In Chapter 6, we covered how to grant ancillary table access to your user base, so I will not cover that again. But just understand that users who *view* Solution Exchange tools will need access to the Access Group for Ancillary Tables.

For users who will be *updating* data in Solution Exchange tools (interacting and updating People Planning, account recs, etc.), those users will also need Maintenance Group for Ancillary Tables access.

Chapter 7

The only group that will need Table Creation Group for Ancillary Tables will likely be your administrators, who are the ones who do the initial download and setup of these tools. This access is shown in Figure 7.26.

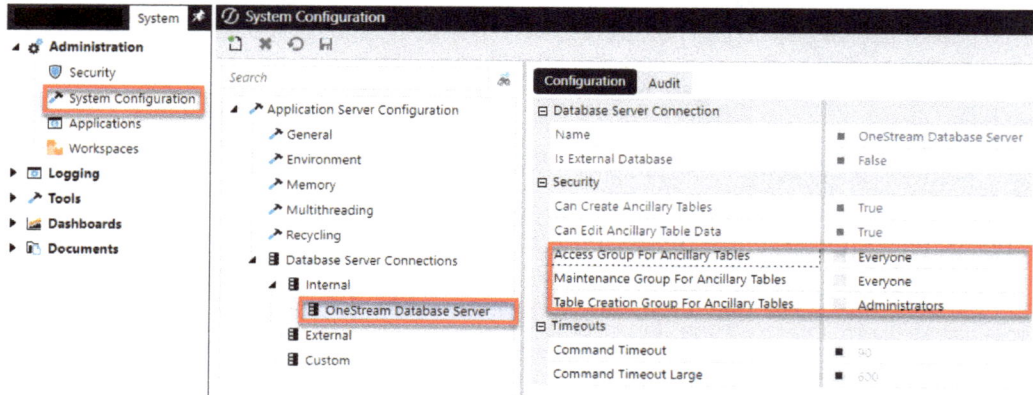

Figure 7.26

The second important item to point out with Solution Exchange tools is that most are launched from, or as, a dashboard. Therefore, to use these tools, a user will need access to either the Dashboard Profile or the Workflow Profile where the dashboard has been attached.

Below is an example for Account Reconciliation Manager, showing both the Dashboard Profile access for OnePlace (Figure 7.27), as well as Workflow Profile access (Figure 7.28).

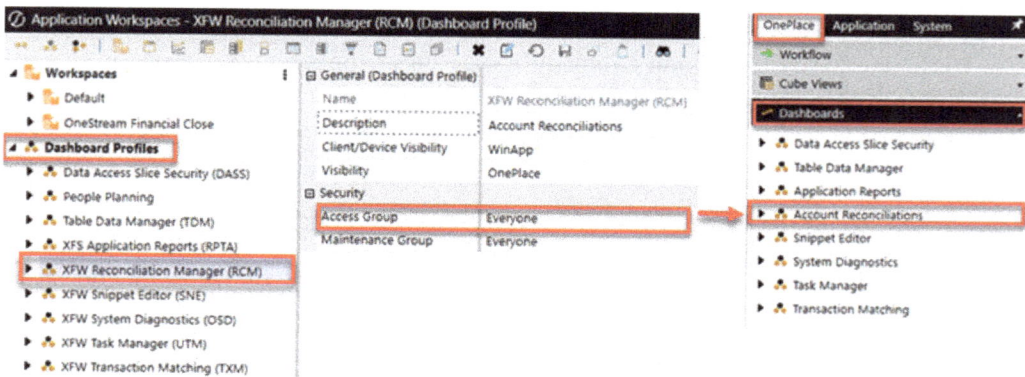

Figure 7.27

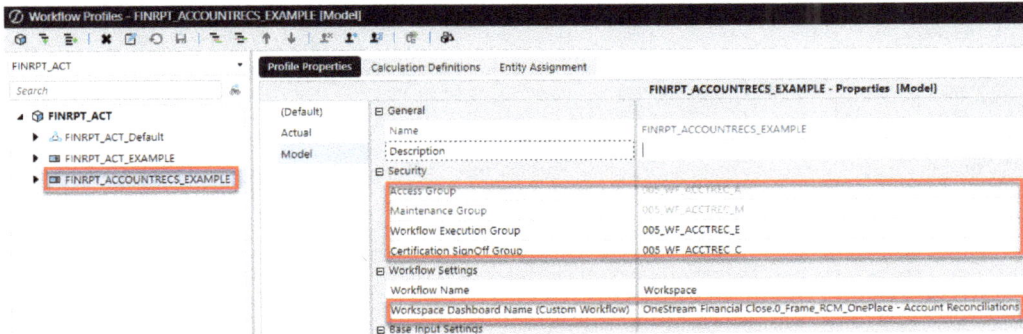

Figure 7.28

So, before a user can gain access to use the tools and proceed further, they will need both ancillary table access as well as Dashboard Profile and/or Workflow Profile access to launch these tools.

Now that we have covered basic access for Solution Exchange tools, let's dive a little deeper and look at three popular Solution Exchange tools, and the added security that resides *within* them.

## Account Reconciliations

The Account Reconciliation solution (aka RCM or OFC) allows customers to deliver a level of data quality and risk reporting around substantiating their balance sheet information. As mentioned, once you have downloaded, loaded, and granted appropriate workflow access, there are additional layers of security within this tool.

Many of the Solution Exchange tools will have a Global Setup page where additional security can be applied, related to working within that solution. For Account Reconciliations, there are three additional security roles that can be applied for users working inside this tool, as shown in Figure 7.29.

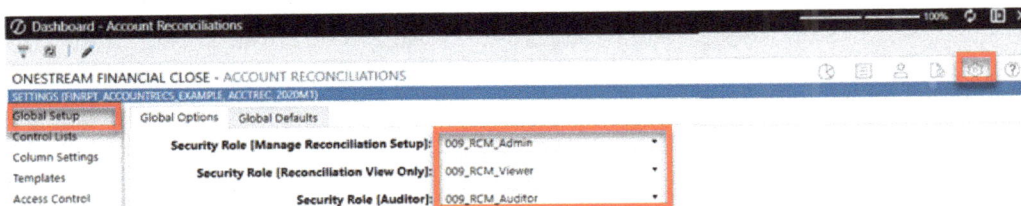

Figure 7.29

In addition to the Global Setup page, Account Reconciliations also has an Access Control page, which allows you to further expand how security works within this solution, as shown in Figure 7.30.

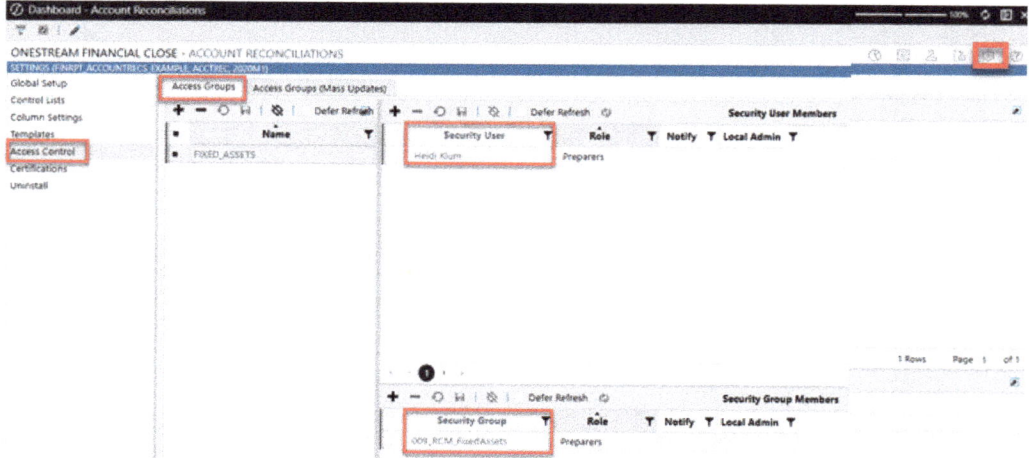

Figure 7.30

Lastly, within Account Reconciliations, you can even apply security to individual reconciliations within the **Account Reconciliation Inventory** by accessing the Show Administration Page, then selecting an individual reconciliation and clicking the Access icon, as shown in Figure 7.31.

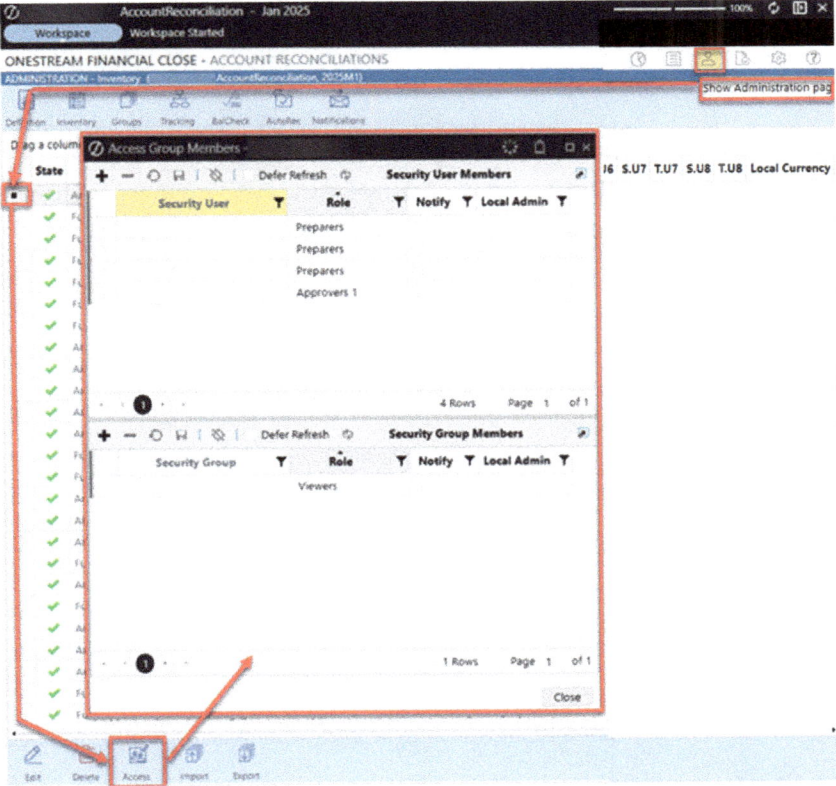

Figure 7.31

The point with the above figures is not to explain RCM security in detail (for that, I would suggest you read the OneStream Financial Close Handbook!) but instead to demonstrate that – with these Solution Exchange tools – some of them come with additional layers of security once you are within the tool.

Let's take a look at another common Solution Exchange tool, People Planning, for which security questions quite often arise.

## People Planning

The People Planning solution enables detailed, complex, driver-based workforce planning within OneStream. Information is planned in a table-based solution and then integrated with your other cube data at a more summary level.

Like Account Reconciliations, there is also a Global Setup page where additional security can be applied, related to working within People Planning. There are two groups that can be administered: View Employee Name and Manage Calculation Definition, as shown in Figure 7.32.

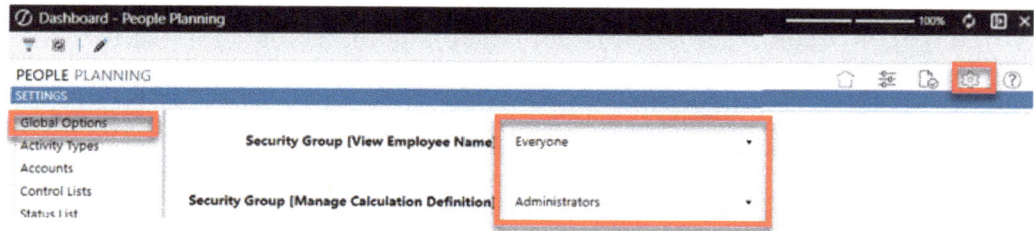

Figure 7.32

Another question that often comes up around the People Planning solution is the protection of sensitive employee salary data. Any individual in the native administrators group has full access to ancillary tables added to an application, which includes the tables and data for People Planning. Again, in Chapter 2, we talked about someone having the keys to the whole kingdom, and that is anyone in your native administrators group.

There are a few options if you do not want certain individuals to see salary, compensation, or employee data in the People Planning Register solution.

One option may be to use local admin groups other than the native administrators group. In this way, you could grant those individuals access to everything except the workflow where the People Planning dashboard is attached, and also restrict them from the database page on the System tab itself.

Another option is not to use employee names in your PLP register. Instead, you could use a unique identifier, such as employee IDs, for this data to maintain confidentiality.

A less preferred but possible option includes segregating the PLP data into its own OneStream application. Only grant people access to that app who can see salary data. You will still need one overall administrator, but you can greatly limit those who can get to the People Planning data.

## Task Manager

The last tool I will mention is Task Manager, which is a solution that provides a central place to monitor the collaboration and completion of processes by aggregating workflows, assigning tasks with dates, and communicating through emails and commentary. The tool can provide visibility into a Closing, Budget, or Forecast cycle, with charts and graphs to easily drill into and monitor process completion.

Like the other tools mentioned previously, users will need to have access to the Dashboard Profile to access this solution. From there, once inside the solution, further access can be granted by going to the Administration page.

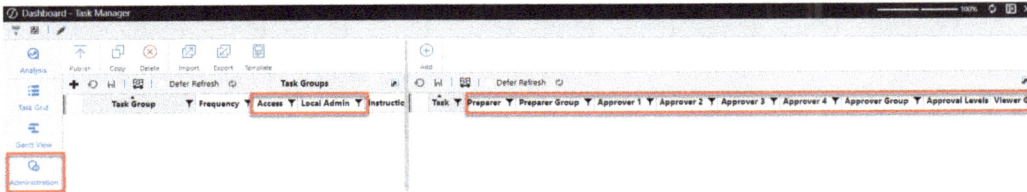

Figure 7.33

All Solution Exchange tools allow customers and partners to extend upon the core functionality within OneStream. Thus, you can extend your security model to include further restrictions inside these tools.

> Tips for Solution Exchange security:
>
> ✓ Be sure to grant appropriate access to ancillary tables.
>
> ✓ Be sure to grant access to the appropriate Dashboard Profile or Workflow Profile to launch the tools.
>
> ✓ Once inside each solution, additional access may be refined from Global Settings or Administration pages.

# BI Blend

BI Blend is a read-only aggregate storage model designed to support reporting on large volumes of data that are not appropriate to store in a traditional OneStream Cube. Because BI Blend involves data *not stored* within a cube, the security for BI Blend falls into a category of its own.

Like Solution Exchange tools, if BI Blend is employed within an application, it entails additional security above and beyond standard application security.

The security for BI Blend consists primarily of:

- Access to the BI Blend database and tables
- Access to Workflow(s)
- Access to Dashboard(s)

## BI Blend Database

For customers using OneStream BI Blend for reporting and analysis within their application(s), a separate database (e.g., not the framework nor application databases discussed in prior chapters) is established by OneStream support as an external connection set up on the System Configuration page. This is shown in Figure 7.34.

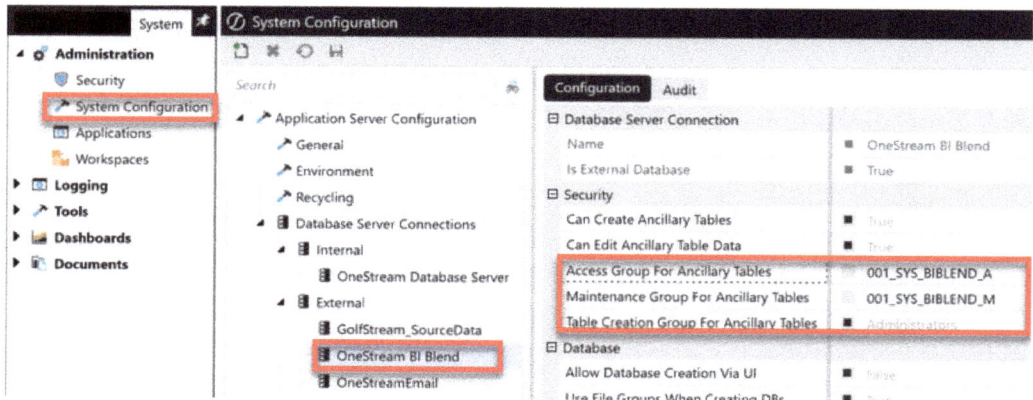

Figure 7.34

As we saw in Figure 7.26, you will want to grant your users access to Access Group for Ancillary Tables (001_SYS_BIBLEND_A) and Maintenance Group for Ancillary Tables (001_SYS_BIBLEND_M) accordingly. You will likely be able to keep the Table Creation Group for Ancillary Tables set to administrators in your BI Blend database, similar to what was done for the OneStream application database server.

Like the Solution Exchange tools that install and use custom tables within the **OneStream Database Server** connection, BI Blend has its own set of custom tables that reside in their own OneStream BI Blend external database connection on the System Configuration page.

Therefore, the first step to allow users to view or load BI Blend data is to grant access to these ancillary tables, as shown in Figure 7.34. Once that access has been granted, the remaining BI Blend security follows the workflow and dashboard security discussed in prior chapters. Let's review these pieces below.

## BI Blend Workflow(s)

The interface to the BI Blend model is through a traditional OneStream workflow. The workflow is how data is loaded into the BI Blend database and tables, using cube dimensions, metadata and attributes to derive the aggregation points that are stored in the BI Blend database.

For a user to be able to load data into the BI Blend database, they will need workflow access (005_WF_BIBLEND_A) and execution (005_WF_BIBLEND_E), as shown in Figure 7.35.

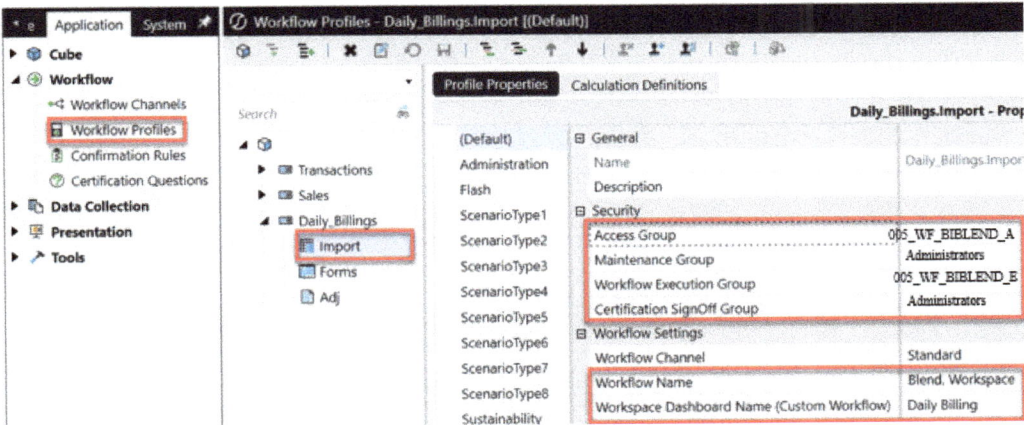

Figure 7.35

So, the second piece to establishing BI Blend security is, therefore, workflow access.

As we recall from Chapter 4, a typical person loading data to the cube needs the following access (recall Figure 4.8):

- application security role to open an app (001_APP_OPENPROD)

- application security role to modify data (001_APP_MODIFYDATA)

- a cube (002_CUBE_FINRPT) security group

- write access to the Actual scenario (003_SCN_ACTUAL_WRITE)

- write access to entities (004_ENT_ALLCOMPANY_WRITE)

- access to the import workflow where data is loaded (005_WF_CORP_A)

- execute to the import workflow where data is loaded (005_WF_CORP_E)

However, a person loading BI Blend data will need slightly different access since the BI Blend data does not load to the cube but to a separate database. The typical data load profile for a BI Blend load user may look something like:

- application security role to open an app (001_APP_OPENPROD)

- access to the ancillary tables (001_SYS_BIBLEND_A)

- modify to the ancillary tables (001_SYS_BIBLEND_M)

- access to the import workflow where data is loaded (005_WF_BIBLEND_A)

- execute to the import workflow where data is loaded (005_WF_BIBLEND_E)

This is shown in Figure 7.36.

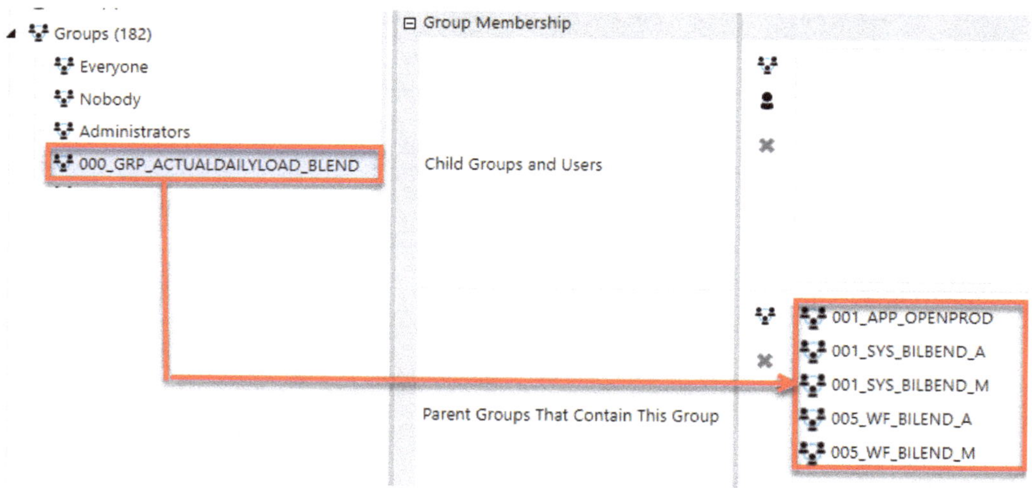

Figure 7.36

## BI Blend Dashboards

The final piece of access required for users who will be consuming (aka viewing since BI Blend is a read-only tool) reports is access to a dashboard profile, which can either be presented to the user via OnePlace or via a workflow Workspace. In either case, the user will need access (006_DB_BIBLEND_A) to the BI Blend dashboard, as shown in Figure 7.37.

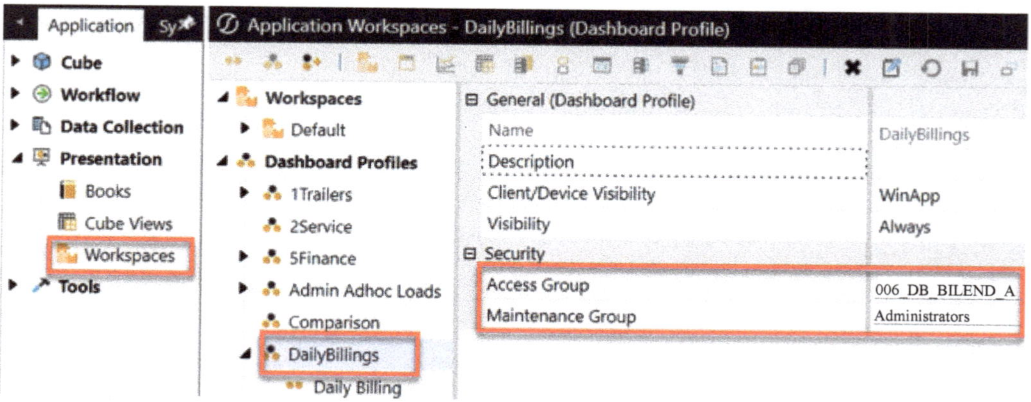

Figure 7.37

Once within a dashboard profile, additional parameters can be leveraged to further limit what data is presented to a user on the BI Blend reports. The parameters can be based on user security groups to limit what users can select in those parameters. Then, in the SQL on the data adapter, those parameters can be fed into the WHERE clause to again restrict what information is presented to a person viewing BI Blend data.

Tips for BI Blend security:

✓ Be sure to grant appropriate access to BI Blend ancillary tables.

✓ Be sure to grant access to the appropriate Dashboard Profile and Workflow Profile used for BI Blend loads and reporting.

✓ Additional parameters can be leveraged within the WHERE clause on the BI Blend data adapter to further limit what data can be viewed.

In the next chapter, we will talk about the important concepts of testing, migrating, and reporting on security changes. Now that you are well-versed in designing and setting up your security, let's talk about how to maintain it and report off it!

# 8
# Security Tools

We have gone around the block and back in learning about OneStream security. In this final chapter, we will look at how to test and report off the wonderful security framework you have implemented.

## Security Reports

The best way to report off your security framework is to download and install a handful of Solution Exchange tools, all of which have a wealth of reports around security. Why reinvent the wheel when you can download and extend your OneStream platform with existing tools?

The first solution is **Security Audit Reports**, shown in Figure 8.1. You can reach this tool and other tools by going to the OneStream website, logging into the Solution Exchange, and searching by name.

**Security Audit Reports**

by: OneStream

A series of user security reports that display user and group information for audit purposes.

Figure 8.1

Once you have downloaded and set up this tool within an application, a dashboard profile called **Security Audit Reports** will appear within your application's OnePlace pane. This dashboard contains approximately eight reports showing both user and security group activity.

Chapter 8

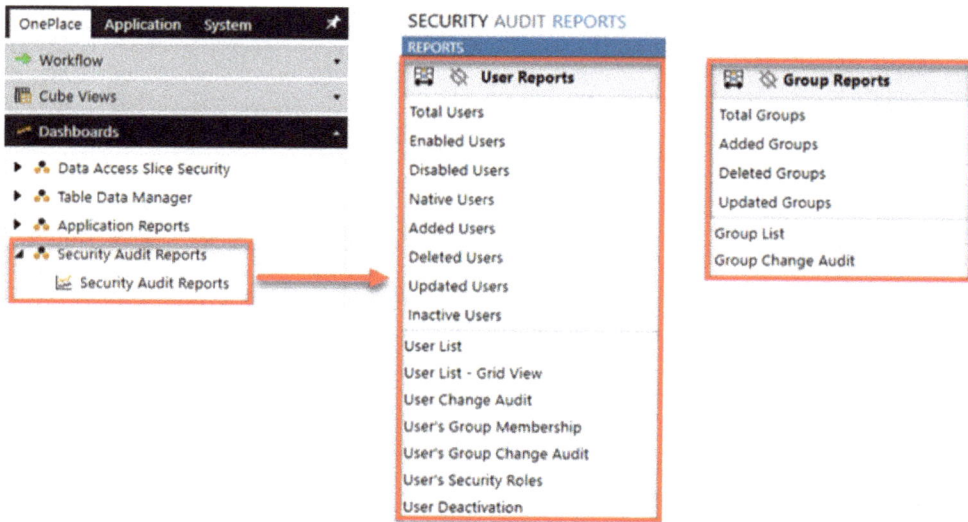

Figure 8.2

While this dashboard will only appear within the OnePlace pane for the application in which it was loaded, it is important to note that it works off the Framework database discussed in Chapter 2. So, no matter which application has this tool, you will be able to view security across your *entire* environment.

These reports show security as it relates to all users and security groups within the current environment's framework database. These reports do not show security as it relates to the application of groups *within* a specific application, as discussed in Chapter 5; that information relates to the application database and tables, which are separate from your framework database.

This dashboard and related reports show information such as:

- Changes to user IDs and security groups
- Users' group membership, including nested groups
- De-activated users

All the reports contained within this tool can be run with Start Date and End Dates, allowing you to monitor your security and compliance changes over time. For example, if you monitor your security on a quarterly basis, you could review each quarter's changes for the prior quarter using these date ranges.

The list of Enabled Users will allow you to monitor compliance with your OneStream license agreement. The Disabled Users and Deleted Users reports will allow you to monitor users (as discussed in Chapter 2) that have been disabled versus deleted. These reports are shown in Figure 8.3.

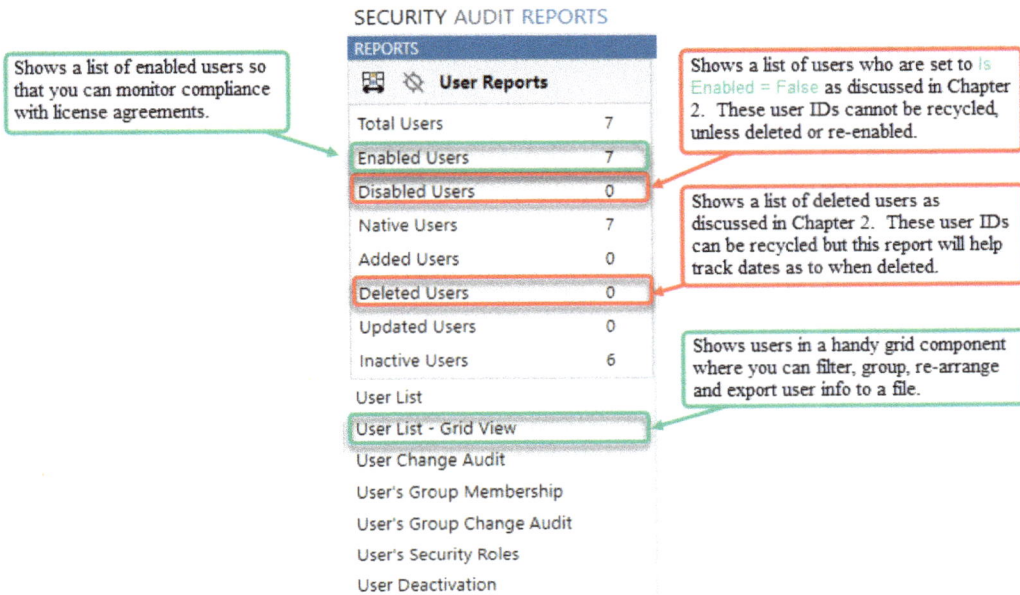

SECURITY AUDIT REPORTS

Shows a list of enabled users so that you can monitor compliance with license agreements.

Shows a list of users who are set to Is Enabled = False as discussed in Chapter 2. These user IDs cannot be recycled, unless deleted or re-enabled.

REPORTS

User Reports

| | |
|---|---|
| Total Users | 7 |
| Enabled Users | 7 |
| Disabled Users | 0 |
| Native Users | 7 |
| Added Users | 0 |
| Deleted Users | 0 |
| Updated Users | 0 |
| Inactive Users | 6 |

User List
User List - Grid View
User Change Audit
User's Group Membership
User's Group Change Audit
User's Security Roles
User Deactivation

Shows a list of deleted users as discussed in Chapter 2. These user IDs can be recycled but this report will help track dates as to when deleted.

Shows users in a handy grid component where you can filter, group, re-arrange and export user info to a file.

Figure 8.3

The most useful report in this tool is the User List – Grid View, which puts your users in a dashboard grid component that can be filtered, grouped, and exported to Excel for ease of use. The grid view will show your users and all user properties listed in Figure 8.4.

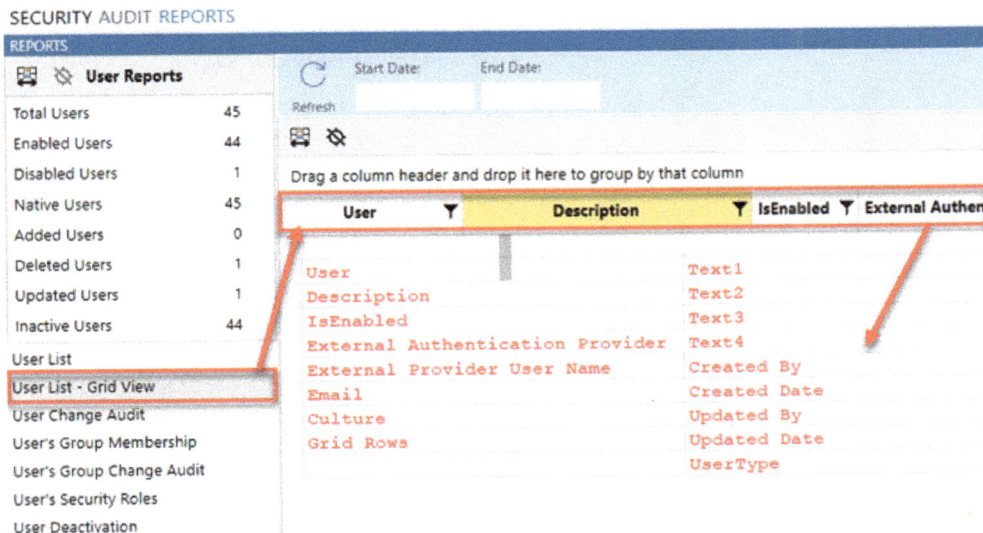

SECURITY AUDIT REPORTS

REPORTS

User Reports

| | |
|---|---|
| Total Users | 45 |
| Enabled Users | 44 |
| Disabled Users | 1 |
| Native Users | 45 |
| Added Users | 0 |
| Deleted Users | 1 |
| Updated Users | 1 |
| Inactive Users | 44 |

User List
User List - Grid View
User Change Audit
User's Group Membership
User's Group Change Audit
User's Security Roles
User Deactivation

Start Date:  End Date:

Refresh

Drag a column header and drop it here to group by that column

| User | Description | IsEnabled | External Authen |
|---|---|---|---|

| | |
|---|---|
| User | Text1 |
| Description | Text2 |
| IsEnabled | Text3 |
| External Authentication Provider | Text4 |
| External Provider User Name | Created By |
| Email | Created Date |
| Culture | Updated By |
| Grid Rows | Updated Date |
| | UserType |

Figure 8.4

Another useful tool within the Solution Exchange is called **Standard Application Reports,** and is shown in Figure 8.5. Within this dashboard tool, there are several useful audit reports relating to security.

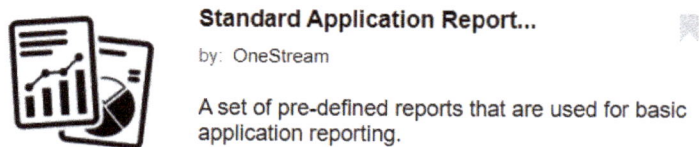

**Standard Application Report...**

by: OneStream

A set of pre-defined reports that are used for basic application reporting.

Figure 8.5

Once you have downloaded and set up this tool within an application, a dashboard profile called **Application Reports** will appear within the OnePlace pane (see Figure 8.6). This dashboard will appear within whichever application it was loaded and contains information from the **Application Database Tables**.

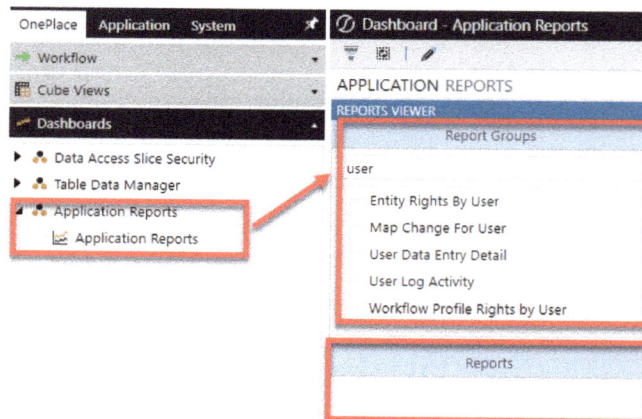

Figure 8.6

This dashboard shows information such as:

- Entity and workflow rights by user ID

- Mapping changes by user ID

- Data entry info by user ID

- User login activity

Both tools contain various bits of useful information for monitoring, auditing, and reporting off both framework and application security.

Within the Solution Exchange tool called **Cloud Administration Tools** (Figure 8.7) and available for customers on the OneStream cloud, is a tool called the **User Management Console**.

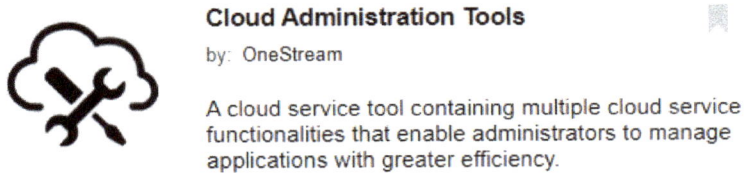

**Cloud Administration Tools**

by: OneStream

A cloud service tool containing multiple cloud service functionalities that enable administrators to manage applications with greater efficiency.

Figure 8.7

This tool helps manage the relationship between users hosted in Microsoft Azure Active Directory (Azure AD) and the OneStream framework database. With this dashboard, a system administrator can self-manage their Azure AD users in OneStream by inviting, creating, deleting (disabling) and importing users, and resetting passwords.

This User Management Console is only available to customers with Azure AD hosted by OneStream Cloud Services and to members of the native administrator's security group. If your company fits these criteria, you may want to consider leveraging this Solution Exchange tool.

Continuing with Solution Exchange tools, the next one helps display slice security, and is called **Data Access Slice Security**.

**Data Access Slice Security**

by: OneStream

Data Access Slice Security displays data access security for cubes in a cube view.

Productivity    Community

Figure 8.8

The Data Access Slice Security tool allows you to view the security discussed in Chapter 7 (aka slice) more easily. It allows you to view your slice security across all your cubes in a grid view component, which you can filter, group, and export to Excel for ease of use.

It takes the cube screen in the top half of Figure 8.9 and re-visualizes it in a dashboard grid, shown at the bottom of this same figure.

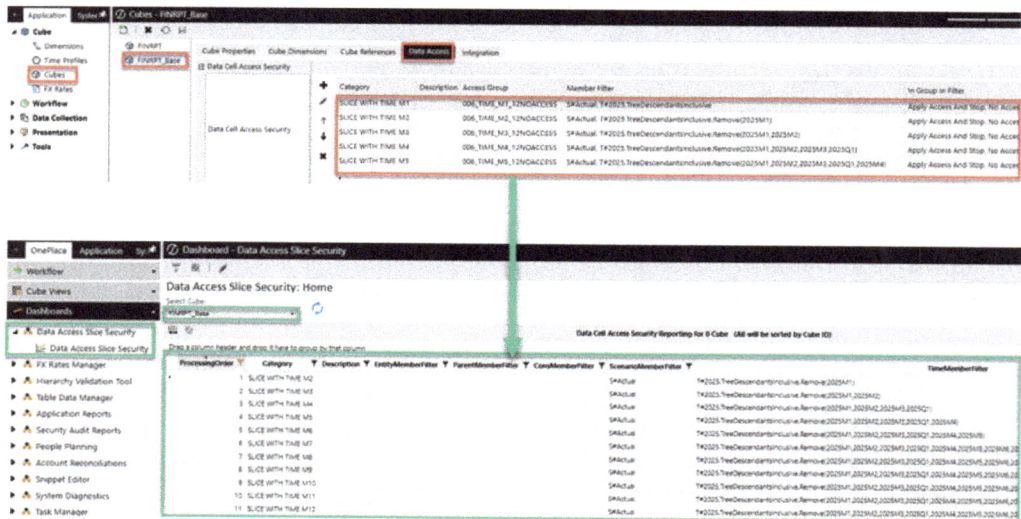

Figure 8.9

Lastly, the **XML Security Remover** Solution Exchange tool (Figure 8.10) allows consultants and administrators to modify all security references in an application extract .zip file. This is most useful when you extract an application without data and load that application into a different environment containing a different framework database.

**XML Security Remover**

by: OneStream

A quick and simple way to upload an XML file, modify all security references, and export an updated copy to deliver to users.

Productivity

Figure 8.10

For example, this tool is useful when you want to load an application extract from one environment to another. Be aware that you would *not* use this if you want to load an application extract to a new application *within the same environment*.

As discussed in Chapter 2, each environment has its own security framework. And each application within an environment has various security groups assigned to application and data objects. Those security groups from one environment may not exist in the secondary environment to which you are loading an application.

As such, to avoid seeing (Unassigned) or blank security groups in the secondary environment, you can use this tool to change (aka "cleanse") all security groups in the XML files to Everyone, Administrators, or Nobody security groups. As we learned previously, those three security groups exist in every customer environment. As such, they can be applied as default security groups via this tool.

The Solution Exchange offers an ever-improving set of tools, *some* with an additional partner fee, that can help you manage and report off your OneStream security. More information on all these solutions can be found by visiting the OneStream website and logging into the Solution Exchange. I encourage you to continually revisit the Solution Exchange as new tools are added regularly that may help you view and manage your security model.

In the next section, we will cover more ways you can migrate your security between environments, keeping security groups and users intact.

# Migrating Security

It is very common for customers to have multiple environments, most commonly a production (PRD1) environment and a development (DEV1) environment. Again, the security framework – which includes all users, groups, and exclusion groups – is specific to *each* environment. As a result, the need can arise to migrate security between environments so that you can also copy applications between environments with ease. So, how do you achieve this in OneStream?

There are two primary ways you can tackle migration and keep your security in sync between environments:

1. Extract and Import
2. Framework Database Copy

## Extract and Import

A best practice is to extract the security from the source environment (e.g., PRD1) into an XML file that you can then load to a target environment (e.g., DEV1). This is a best practice because it is a more efficient (fewer steps) and seamless (can be managed by your administrator) way to keep your security in sync.

Let's cover the steps to do this.

1. Go to the System tab > Load/Extract page > Extract tab
2. Choose Security under the File Type dropdown menu
3. Be sure to check the box in front of Extract Unique IDs
4. Put a check in front of all Items to Extract for which you want migration

These steps are shown in Figure 8.11. As mentioned, make sure to select the option to Extract Unique IDs, as this ensures that users and groups are created with the *same* Unique IDs in the target environment, which is crucial for maintaining security integrity during migration.

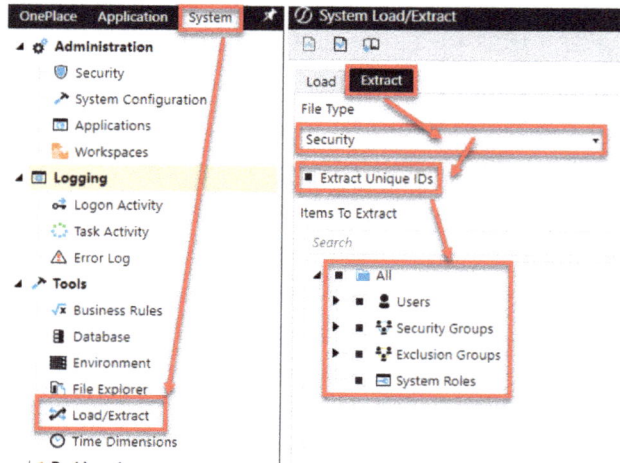

Figure 8.11

Now, you import that XML file into the target environment. To do so, navigate to the System tab > Load/Extract page > Load tab, then navigate to your saved file from the source environment and upload, as shown in Figure 8.12.

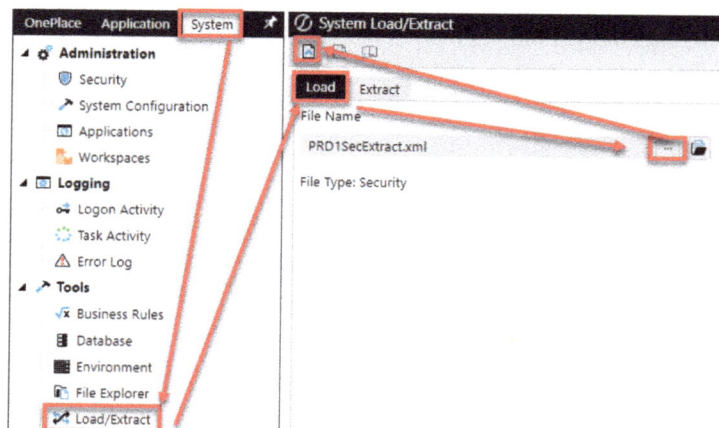

Figure 8.12

In this way, both environments will stay synchronized and – when applications are copied from source to target environment – they will not lose their security.

If both environments have existing users and groups with the same user or group name but with *different* unique IDs, the import will result in an error message, and it will stop. So, what can be done? You will need to run a **Framework Database Copy** to get things back in sync. Let's cover that process next.

## Framework Database Copy

If frequent security changes in a target environment make the traditional extract and import described above impractical, *or* if you run into an error message when employing the extract and import method, you can copy the entire framework database from the source to the target environment.

This method will synchronize all security records; however, it may result in losing security assignments for *existing* applications in the target environment. You can take steps to work around this situation, as described below.

Here are the steps involved in copying the entire framework database from the source environment (e.g., PRD1) into a target environment (e.g., DEV1):

1. Before copying the framework database between environments, extract users and groups from the *target* environment *without* unique IDs. This step will allow you to recreate users and groups that already existed in the *target* environment but might not exist in the *source* environment in a later step.

2. Then, again, in the *target* environment, extract all application components by going to the Application tab > Load/Extract > Extract tab.

3. Choose Application Zip File (All Except Data and FX) under the File Type dropdown menu (Figure 8.13). Do this for *each* application in the *target* environment. You will use these application zip extract files to recreate security for all target applications once the framework database has been copied in a subsequent step.

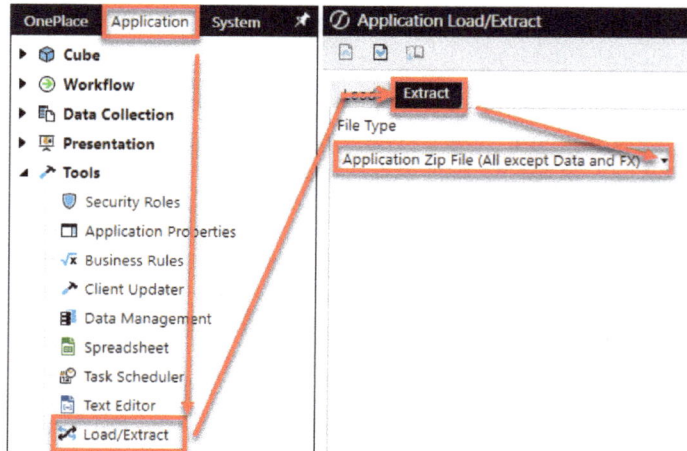

Figure 8.13

4. Copy the framework database from source to target. This is typically done by opening a support case with OneStream for cloud customers. This step may result in losing the security assignments within existing applications in the target environment (since the Unique IDs are now different).

5. Import the XML file generated in step 1 to re-create potential users or groups that previously existed in the target environment but not in the source environment (the framework that was copied over).

6. For each application, import the zip file generated in step 3 in order to restore security against the new users and groups by Unique IDs recreated in the prior step.

Once you have done this, your source and target environments are now synchronized (i.e., unique IDs of users and groups are matched), and every time application databases are copied from source to target, or you choose to use the extract and import method, you should be fine.

You can set up these processes to happen regularly or on a schedule by customizing and creating a scheduled task to extract from one environment and load to a target environment. For example, you may want a regular cadence to extract your security from the production environment and update your development environment, so long as anyone developing is aware of this process and can re-import their work.

Should you run into any issues or have questions when migrating your OneStream security, your OneStream Customer Support Portal can be a great resource for knowledge-based articles and self-service catalog options (Figure 8.14).

Figure 8.14

## Deleting Security Groups

Deleting security groups follows the same discussion points made in Chapter 2 about deleting versus disabling users. The details are different, but some of the same principles apply.

First, let me say I do not recommend deleting security groups unless you are certain that group is not attached to an application or system object. And, as we mentioned earlier in this chapter, there is currently no dashboard, report, or tool (other than one of the two partner Solution Exchange tools) that will allow you to see all the places a security group has been assigned to an application.

Because security groups can be applied to *any* application or system object within an environment, you would need to extract all your applications (and system security) for an environment to XML files, and search for a particular security group to confirm if the group has – or has not – been assigned to an application or system object.

For this reason, I do not recommend deleting security groups unless you are confident the group has not been used. Instead, my recommendation is simply to rename the security group with a prefix of z_ and a suffix of _OLD. In this way, you keep the integrity of the existing security group in case it has been assigned to an application or system object of which you are unaware. This is similar to the concept of disabling, but not fully deleting, users. The added bonus of this naming convention is that all obsolete security groups will sort to the bottom of the alphabetical list!

If you delete a security group and it was assigned to an application or system object of which you were unaware, the default group of administrators will be assigned. At least you can rest assured that if you accidentally delete a used security group, the default is for the strictest security to be applied, that of your native administrators group!

Speaking of making changes to security groups, let's move on to the last section of this book and cover best practices around testing and ensuring your security is behaving as designed.

# Testing

The easiest way I have found to evaluate security is to set up a native user ID, apply the security you want to evaluate to that user ID, and then log in as that user. Logged in as that native user, you will be able to navigate to various OneStream screens, confirming access as you go.

If you recall from Chapter 2, the ability to set up native user IDs is a toggle setting of True/False in the Application Server Configuration Settings, which can only be accessed by OneStream Support for cloud customers. Even if your company does not permit long-term native ID access, it is a great idea to have this set to True – during development – so security can be easily and thoroughly vetted before you go live.

After going live, and if this toggle is set to False, you can test security by shadowing or screen sharing with your user to review their access or (as a last resort) have your access temporarily changed to allow you to review access as an end-user. Do not forget that in testing security, administrators have full access to OneStream, so it is hard for a native administrator to confirm or evaluate the end-user experience unless they shadow or use a native ID.

Another clever way to evaluate security, especially data access security, is to set up a Quick View spreadsheet in Excel. In the columns and rows of that Quick View, set up various points of view to which a user should and should not have access. Logging in as a native user with specific access (or shadowing this user in Excel) will allow you – in a spreadsheet – to drill through various hierarchies denoting **No Access** versus green intersections (read-only access) versus white intersections (write access).

The final key to remember when setting up and testing security is that you will want to put users into security groups (recall the `000_GRP` naming convention from Chapter 3) and test group access. You do not want to individually provision a bunch of security groups to a particular user, as this will make it hard to diagnose what is or is not working. Instead, you want to create a group, evaluate the group's access collectively, and then place users into groups. In this way, you can more efficiently assess and grant access to groups of users with similar needs.

# Conclusion

We started the book broadly discussing OneStream's security framework and environment, and the settings and ways people can access your gated community. Once a user has access to the environment (aka gated community), we moved inside the neighborhood and learned how different sets of users may access houses (aka applications) within the environment.

With the keys to the front door of a particular house in hand, we then took a deep dive into all the elements inside a OneStream application and the myriad ways you can go about securing every corner of your house. We discussed how the simplicity or complexity of your security model will depend on factors, including your user base, your company's needs, and any regulatory and compliance requirements.

Following your home security, we then took a step back and talked about other tools and ways you can add on or extend your security framework. Much like adding a pool to the backyard of your home may require a new fence to be added, so too will adding additional Solution Exchange tools to your OneStream application. These tools, like a swimming pool, can be a great investment in your application, but they do raise additional security concerns.

Lastly, like with a home, we talked about how you will want to maintain, assess, and report off your investment in OneStream software. I hope that this book has taken you on a trip around your OneStream neighborhood and provided you with a much better understanding and level of confidence in OneStream security!

# Index

Index

Index

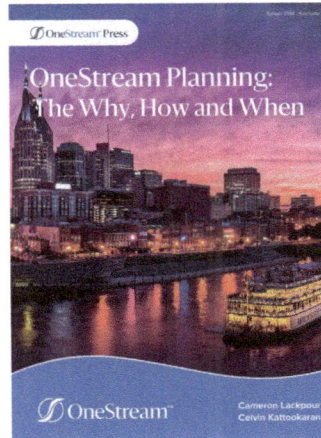

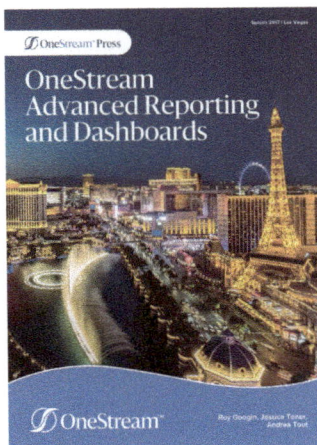

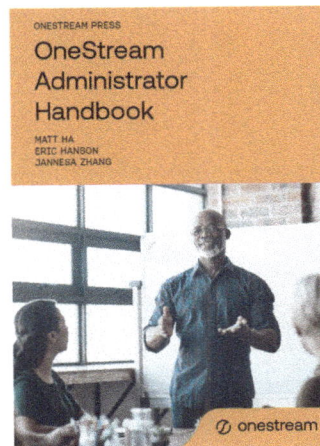

www.ingramcontent.com/pod-product-compliance
Lightning Source LLC
Chambersburg PA
CBHW050236220326
41598CB00044B/7417